ST/ESA/STAT/SER.W/34

Department of Economic and Social Affairs
Statistics Division

2018
Electricity Profiles

United Nations
New York, 2020

Department of Economic and Social Affairs

The Department of Economic and Social Affairs of the United Nations Secretariat is a vital interface between global policies in the economic, social and environmental spheres and national action. The Department works in three main interlinked areas: (i) it compiles, generates and analyses a wide range of economic, social and environmental data and information on which States Members of the United Nations draw to review common problems and to take stock of policy options; (ii) it facilitates the negotiations of Member States in many intergovernmental bodies on joint courses of action to address ongoing or emerging global challenges; and (iii) it advises interested Governments on the ways and means of translating policy frameworks developed in United Nations conferences and summits into programmes at the country level and, through technical assistance, helps build national capacities.

Note

Symbols of United Nations documents are composed of capital letters combined with figures.

General Disclaimer

The designations employed and the presentation of material in this publication do not imply the expression of any opinion whatsoever on the part of the Secretariat of the United Nations concerning the legal status of any country, territory, city or area, or of its authorities, or concerning the delimitation of its frontiers or boundaries.

Where the designation "country or area" appears in this publication, it covers countries, territories, cities or areas. In previous issues of this publication, where the designation "country" appears in the headings of tables, it should be interpreted to cover countries, territories, cities or areas.

The Electricity Profiles is published by United Nations Publications, 405 East 42nd Street, S-09FW001, New York, NY 10017 USA, Email: publications@un.org, Website: shop.un.org.

ST/ESA/STAT/SER.W/34

Sales number: E.21.XVII.4

ISBN 978-92-1-259161-2
eISBN 978-92-1-005523-9
ISSN 1014-465X
online ISSN 2412-1037

CONTENTS

CONTENTS

Electricity Profiles (2013 - 2018) (continued)

CONTENTS

Electricity Profiles (2013-2018) (continued)

Statistics compiled as of December 2020

INTRODUCTION

The *Electricity Profiles 2018* provides detailed information on production, trade and consumption of electricity, on net installed capacity and thermal power plant inputs and efficiency for 224 countries and areas on an internationally comparable basis, for the years 2013-2018. It is published by the United Nations Statistics Division with the aim of providing an overall picture of the electricity sector of such countries and areas.

This is the seventh issue of *Electricity Profiles* as a stand-alone publication, whereas until the 2011 edition it was part of the series *Energy Balances and Electricity Profiles*. The series was split in two and in addition to the *Electricity Profiles* a sister publication, the *Energy Balances*, is released.

This split followed the incorporation of the standards brought about by the *International Recommendations for Energy Statistics*[1] (IRES). IRES, in its draft form, was endorsed in 2011 by the United Nations Statistical Commission. Previously, energy statistics published by the Statistics Division followed the format described in detail in the technical report entitled *Concepts and Methods in Energy Statistics, with Special Reference to Energy Accounts and Balances*[2] and also discussed in the publication *Energy Statistics: A Manual for Developing Countries.*[3]

Electricity production and electric installed capacity are disaggregated by source, as coming from Combustible fuels, Hydro, Nuclear and Other sources; and by type of producer, whether from main activity producers or autoproducers. The latter is given implicitly as the difference between Total production/capacity and Main activity production/capacity.

Thermal power plant inputs are listed by energy product, together with the total output, which are used together to calculate the overall efficiency of electricity production from combustible fuels (displayed at the bottom). Up to ten main products (by input contribution in the latest year available) are displayed and then listed alphabetically, with the remaining ones, if any, aggregated in the category Others.

More detailed disaggregation of electricity capacity and production is published in the *Energy Statistics Yearbook,* where wind and solar are identified separately as electricity sources rather than in the category Other.

The information contained in this publication is also available in electronic format.[4] Requests for information should be directed to United Nations Publications at: order@un.org.

Acknowledgement is due to the following specialized and intergovernmental agencies whose publications have been utilized in supplementing our statistics: African Energy Commission (AFREC), Asia-Pacific Economic Cooperation (APEC), Food and Agriculture Organization of the United Nations (FAO), International Atomic Energy Agency (IAEA), International Energy Agency of the Organisation for Economic Cooperation and Development (IEA/OECD), International Renewable Energy Agency (IRENA), International Sugar Organization (ISO), Organization of Arab Petroleum Exporting Countries (OAPEC), Organization of the Petroleum Exporting Countries (OPEC), Organización Latinoamericana de Energía (OLADE), Statistical Office of the European Union (Eurostat), World Energy Council (WEC). Acknowledgement is also made to governmental, energy and statistical authorities of the Member States which have been cooperative in providing data.

The annual energy data are being collected and processed by the Energy Statistics Section of UNSD, headed by Mr. Leonardo Souza. The processing of the energy data and preparation for publication were carried out by Ms. Agnieszka Koscielniak, Ms. Costanza Giovannelli, Ms. Peng Guo, Mr. Man Soni and Mr. Graham Osborn.

Enquiries, comments and suggestions for improving this publication are welcome and should be addressed to: energy_stat@un.org.

---

[1] Available at unstats.un.org/unsd/energystats/methodology/ires/

[2] Statistical Papers, Series F, No. 29 (United Nations publication, Sales No.E.82.XVII.13).

[3] Statistical Papers, Series F, No. 56 (United Nations publication, Sales No.E.91.XVII.10).

[4] For details, see unstats.un.org/unsd/energystats/pubs/eprofiles/

CONCEPTS AND DEFINITIONS

ELECTRICITY PROFILES

The electricity profiles intend to provide an overall picture of the electricity sector in countries and areas on a comparable basis. As such, a simplified approach is taken, where for production and capacity the three main electricity sources (or production processes) are singled out; namely, combustible fuels, hydro and nuclear; while the remaining electricity production processes (mostly renewable) are aggregated in the category Other. Detailed information on each source for the same countries and areas is available from the United Nations Energy Statistics Database.[5]

Each electricity profile is divided into three blocks, which are listed below and described in detail next:

- The top block on electricity production, trade and consumption;
- The middle block on net installed capacity; and
- The bottom block on combustible fuel input, output and efficiency.

Top block – Electricity production, trade and consumption

Electricity is defined in energy statistics as the transfer of energy through the physical phenomena involving electric charges and their effects when at rest and in motion.

Electricity can be generated through different processes such as: the conversion of energy contained in falling or streaming water, wind or waves; the direct conversion of solar radiation through photovoltaic processes in semiconductor devices (solar cells); or by the combustion of fuels.

Electricity **production** (or electricity generation) in the electricity profiles refers to gross production, which is the sum of the electrical energy production by all the generating units/installations concerned (including pumped storage) measured at the output terminals of the main generators.

The different types of technology/processes for the generation of electricity are defined as follows.

Electricity from **combustible fuels** refers to the production of electricity from the combustion of fuels which are capable of igniting or burning, i.e. reacting with oxygen to produce a significant rise in temperature.

Hydro electricity refers to electricity produced from devices driven by fresh, flowing or falling water.

Nuclear electricity refers to electricity generated by nuclear plants.

Other electricity includes all other processes, which are described below.

- Solar Electricity refers to electricity produced from solar photovoltaics, i.e. by the direct conversion of solar radiation through photovoltaic processes in semiconductor devices (solar cells), including concentrating photovoltaic systems; as well as electricity produced from solar thermal heat (both concentrating and non-concentrating).

- Heat from concentrating solar thermal refers to high temperature heat produced from solar radiation captured by concentrating solar thermal systems. Heat from non-concentrating solar thermal refers to low temperature heat produced from solar radiation captured by non-concentrating solar thermal systems.

- Wind electricity refers to electricity produced from devices driven by wind.

- Wave electricity refers to electricity produced from devices driven by the motion of waves.

- Tidal electricity refers to electricity generated from devices driven by tidal currents or the differences of water level caused by tides.

- Other marine electricity refers to electricity generated from devices which exploit sources of marine energy not elsewhere specified. Examples of sources are non-tidal currents, temperature differences and salinity gradients in seas or salinity differences between sea and fresh water.

[5] http://data.un.org/Explorer.aspx?d=EDATA

CONCEPTS AND DEFINITIONS

• Geothermal electricity refers to the electricity generated from the heat from geothermal sources.

• Electricity generated from chemical heat, which refers to recovered heat generated in the chemical industry by exothermic reactions other than combustion.

• Electricity from other sources not elsewhere specified.

As regards the type of producer, both for electricity production and for net installed capacity, a distinction is made between main activity producers and autoproducers, as defined below:

Main activity producer are enterprises which produce electricity as their principal activity. Formerly known as public utilities, these enterprises may be privately or publicly owned companies.

Autoproducers are enterprises which produce electricity but for whom the production is not their principal activity.

In the *Electricity Profiles*, autoproducer figures are not provided explicitly, but can be easily derived as the difference between total producers and main activity producers.

Own use in electricity, CHP and heat plants refers to consumption of electricity for the direct support of electricity, CHP and heat plants. It includes consumption by station auxiliaries, and losses in transformers which are considered as integral parts of the electric energy, CHP or heat generating plants.

• **Electricity plants** refer to plants producing only electricity.

• **CHP plants** (Combined Heat and Power) refer to plants which produce both heat and electricity from at least one generating unit in the plant. They are sometimes referred to as "co-generation" plants.

• **Heat plants** refer to plants (including heat pumps and electric boilers) designed to produce heat only, for deliveries to third parties.

Net production is (gross) production minus own use in electricity, CHP and heat plants. It is equivalent to the electricity sent out from the plants that is available to the network or ready for use in the premises in the case of autoproducers.

Imports comprise all electricity entering the national territory.

Exports comprise all electricity leaving the national territory.

For electricity, as an exception to general energy statistics, trade data include electricity transmitted through the country from one neighbour to another, as there is no practical way of discerning which quantities are re-exported and which are consumed by the transit country.

Losses refer to losses during the transmission and distribution of electricity. Losses also include pilferage of electricity (sometimes referred to as non-technical losses).

Consumption in the *Electricity Profiles* refers to **Energy industries own use** and **Final consumption**.

Energy industries own use refers to consumption of electricity for the direct support of the production, and preparation for use of fuels and energy. Quantities which are used for transportation purposes in the energy industry are not included here, but in Consumption by transport. Quantities used for pumped storage are included here.

Note that pumped storage plants are plants where electricity is used during periods of lower demand to pump water into reservoirs for subsequent release and electricity generation during periods of higher demand. Less electricity is eventually produced than is consumed to pump the water into the higher reservoir.

In general energy statistics, Own use in electricity, CHP and heat plants is part of Energy industries own use, but it is displayed apart in this publication so that Net production can be derived.

CONCEPTS AND DEFINITIONS

Final consumption refers to the consumption of electricity by Manufacturing, construction and non-fuel mining, by Transport, and by households and other consumers (non-energy use being irrelevant for electricity).

By industry and construction refers to final electricity consumption by manufacturing, construction and non-fuel mining industries. The final consumption recorded under this category covers the use of electricity by economic units belonging to the industry groups listed below (excluding the use of energy products for transport, which is recorded under Transport in its respective row).

- Iron and steel
- Chemical and petrochemical
- Non-ferrous metals
- Non-metallic minerals
- Transport equipment
- Machinery
- Mining and quarrying
- Food and tobacco
- Paper, pulp and print
- Wood and wood products (other than pulp and paper)
- Textile and leather
- Construction
- Industries, not elsewhere specified

By transport refers to the consumption of electricity by any economic entity to transport goods or persons between points of departure and destination within the national territory.

By households and other consumers: This group consists of energy consumers not classified in Manufacturing, construction and non-fuel mining industries, and consists of the following subgroups:

- Agriculture, Forestry, Fishing
- Commerce and public services
- Households
- Not elsewhere specified

Middle block – Net installed capacity

Net installed capacity refers to the Net maximum electrical capacity, which is the maximum active power that can be supplied continuously, with all plants running, at the point of outlet (i.e., after taking the power supplies for the station auxiliaries and allowing for the losses in those transformers considered integral to the station).

This assumes no restriction of interconnection to the network, but does not include overload capacity that can only be sustained for a short period of time (e.g., internal combustion engines momentarily running above their rated capacity).

The net maximum electricity-generating capacity represents the sum of all individual plants' maximum capacities available to run continuously throughout a prolonged period of operation in a day.

As mentioned for electricity production, a distinction is made between main activity producers and autoproducers. In the *Electricity Profiles*, autoproducer figures are not provided explicitly, but can be easily derived as the difference between total producers and main activity producers.

Bottom block – Combustible fuel input, output and efficiency

As defined in the section about the top block, electricity from **combustible fuels** refers to the production of electricity from the combustion of fuels which are capable of igniting or burning, i.e. reacting with oxygen to produce a significant rise in temperature.

Therefore, for some countries and areas this block may be empty if such processes are not utilized in the country or area in question.

Combustible fuel input is the energy content (in Terajoules) of those fuels which are combusted to generate electricity. This input is broken down by fuel (as applicable) and is calculated from the fuel quantities expressed in their original units (e.g., thousand metric tons) through the application of conversion factors.

Up to 10 fuels (by input contribution in the latest year available) are displayed alphabetically, with the remaining ones, if any, aggregated in the category Others.

CONCEPTS AND DEFINITIONS

Total input is the total aggregate of combustible fuel input.

Total production is the total electricity production from combustible fuels (both main activity and autoproducers), expressed in Terajoules by using the equivalence: 1 GWh = 3.6 Terajoules.

The **estimated efficiency** (of total electricity generation from combustible fuels) is calculated by dividing the Total production by the Total input. It gives an idea of how much energy from the fuels is converted into electricity on average in the electricity and CHP plants in the country or area.

It is important to note that the formula considers all inputs to CHP plants but only the electricity output from these plants and not the heat generated, so the calculated efficiency should be used with caution to compare countries with differing levels of CHP generation (and these levels are not apparent from this publication).

For ease of reference, the table below displays typical efficiencies for electricity and CHP plants for the main types of fuel used as input.

Generation process	Typical plant efficiency
Electricity plants	
Coal	32-40%
Oil	35-40%
Natural gas	45-55%
Biomass	20-30%
CHP plants	
Coal	50-75%
Oil	50-75%
Natural gas	60-90%
Biomass	60-85%

ABBREVIATIONS AND SYMBOLS

The following abbreviations and symbols have been used in the publication:

CHP	Combined Heat and Power
GCV	Gross Calorific Value
GJ	gigajoule (10^9 joules)
GWh	gigawatt-hour (10^6 kWh)
IRES	International Recommendations for Energy Statistics
kcal	kilocalorie
kg	kilogramme
kJ	kilojoule (10^3 joules)
kWh	kilowatt-hour
NCV	Net Calorific Value
t	metric ton
TJ	terajoule (10^{12} joules)
UNSD	United Nations Statistics Division
*	estimate by the United Nations Statistics Division
..	data not applicable or not available

ELECTRICITY PROFILES

Afghanistan

Item	2013	2014	2015	2016	2017	2018
Production, trade and consumption			Million kilowatt-hours			
Total main activity and autoproducer	*1022	1356	1339	1394	1420	1266
Combustible fuels	*218	159	149	155	176	200
Hydro	*804	1197	1190	1239	1244	1066
Nuclear	..	..	..	..	..	..
Other	..	..	..	..	..	..
Main activity	*746	1049	1034	1076	1098	979
Combustible fuels	*213	154	144	150	168	193
Hydro	*533	895	890	927	930	786
Nuclear	..	..	..	..	..	..
Other	..	..	..	..	..	..
Own use in electricity, CHP and heat plants	*57	*365	*365	*398	*410	*287
Net production	*965	991	974	996	1010	979
Imports	3615	3711	3779	4333	4611	4986
Exports	..	..	..	..	..	..
Losses	*490	*500	*600	*660	*710	*790
Consumption	*3322	*3767	*3888	*4386	*4515	*4740
Energy industries own use	..	..	..	..	..	..
By industry and construction	*800	*800	*900	*920	*945	*992
By transport	..	..	..	..	..	..
By households and other cons.	*2522	*2967	*2988	*3466	*3570	*3748
Net installed capacity			Thousand kilowatts			
Total main activity and autoproducer	*431	*431	519	*519	*519	*519
Combustible fuels	*115	*115	*135	*135	*135	*135
Hydro	*316	*316	384	*384	*384	*384
Nuclear	..	..	..	..	..	..
Other	..	..	..	..	..	..
Main activity	*249	*249	324	*324	*324	*324
Combustible fuels	*60	*60	*70	*70	*70	*70
Hydro	*189	*189	254	*254	*254	*254
Nuclear	..	..	..	..	..	..
Other	..	..	..	..	..	..
Combustible fuel input			Terajoules			
Hard Coal	*1419	*1290	*1264	*1290	*1367	*1445
Gas-diesel oil	*1075	*645	*645	*860	*860	*1402
Fuel oil	*40	*40	*40	*40	40	*40
Total input	*2534	*1975	*1950	*2190	*2268	*2887
Total production	*786	572	537	557	635	720
Estimated efficiency (% of production to input)	31	29	28	25	28	25

Statistics on electricity

Albania

Item	2013	2014	2015	2016	2017	2018
Production, trade and consumption			**Million kilowatt-hours**			
Total main activity and autoproducer	6956	4724	5895	7136	4526	8552
Combustible fuels	..	..	..	..	..	..
Hydro	6956	4724	5895	7136	4526	8552
Nuclear	..	..	..	..	..	..
Other	..	..	..	..	..	..
Main activity	6956	4724	5895	7136	4526	8552
Combustible fuels	..	..	..	..	..	..
Hydro	6956	4724	5895	7136	4526	8552
Nuclear	..	..	..	..	..	..
Other	..	..	..	..	..	..
Own use in electricity, CHP and heat plants	0	0	29	0	28	45
Net production	6956	4724	5866	7136	4498	8507
Imports	2323	3250	2355	1827	2915	850
Exports	0	183	956	1869	0	1764
Losses	1953	1119	1250	1986	1276	1156
Consumption	7325	6672	6015	5237	6135	6199
Energy industries own use	433	149	118	141	179	115
By industry and construction	1388	1466	1245	1272	1255	1316
By transport	..	..	..	..	..	..
By households and other cons.	5505	5057	4652	3823	4701	4769
Net installed capacity			**Thousand kilowatts**			
Total main activity and autoproducer	1904	1849	1922	1925	2172	2229
Combustible fuels	123	123	123	*123	123	123
Hydro	1781	1726	1799	1801	2048	2105
Nuclear	..	..	..	..	..	..
Other	0	0	0	1	1	1
Main activity	1879	1824	1897	1900	2147	2204
Combustible fuels	98	98	98	*98	98	98
Hydro	1781	1726	1799	1801	2048	2105
Nuclear	..	..	..	..	..	..
Other	0	0	0	1	1	1
Combustible fuel input			**Terajoules**			
Refinery gas	0	0	0	0	0	0
Other oil products	0	0	0	0	0	..
Total input	0	0	0	0	0	0
Total production	..	..	..	..	..	..
Estimated efficiency (% of production to input)	..	..	..	..	..	..

Algeria

Item	2013	2014	2015	2016	2017	2018
Production, trade and consumption	Million kilowatt-hours					
Total main activity and autoproducer	59890	64242	68798	70839	76018	76664
Combustible fuels	59560	63988	68576	70661	75383	75880
Hydro	330	254	145	145	*517	*638
Nuclear	..	..	..	..	..	..
Other	..	..	77	33	*118	*146
Main activity	56148	60500	64663	66075	70898	71227
Combustible fuels	55818	60246	64441	65897	70263	70443
Hydro	330	254	145	145	*517	*638
Nuclear	..	..	..	..	..	..
Other	..	..	77	33	*118	*146
Own use in electricity, CHP and heat plants	4873	6549	6586	6807	7473	7702
Net production	55017	57693	62212	64032	68545	68962
Imports	295	686	610	257	537	506
Exports	384	877	641	507	880	597
Losses	11023	11003	11196	10682	10869	9904
Consumption	43908	46499	50985	53100	57333	58966
Energy industries own use	750	748	832	812	957	813
By industry and construction	15670	16020	17441	18574	20181	20669
By transport	796	867	974	1014	1069	1173
By households and other cons.	26692	28864	31738	32700	35126	36311
Net installed capacity	Thousand kilowatts					
Total main activity and autoproducer	15098	*16199	17239	19006	19474	20963
Combustible fuels	14870	*15971	16961	18549	18892	20480
Hydro	228	228	228	228	228	129
Nuclear	..	..	..	..	..	..
Other	..	..	50	229	354	354
Main activity	10784	*11885	12925	14692	15160	14884
Combustible fuels	10556	*11657	12647	14235	14578	14401
Hydro	228	228	228	228	228	129
Nuclear	..	..	..	..	..	..
Other	..	..	50	229	354	354
Combustible fuel input	Terajoules					
Gas-diesel oil	15265	15695	18103	17544	9761	9469
Natural gas	573653	623247	701791	680994	722981	740892
Total input	588918	638942	719894	698538	732742	750361
Total production	214416	230357	246874	254380	271379	273168
Estimated efficiency (% of production to input)	36	36	34	36	37	36

American Samoa

Item	2013	2014	2015	2016	2017	2018
Production, trade and consumption			**Million kilowatt-hours**			
Total main activity and autoproducer	156	156	161	170	167	*168
Combustible fuels	154	153	159	167	162	*163
Hydro	..	..	..	..	..	..
Nuclear	..	..	..	..	..	..
Other	2	2	2	3	5	5
Main activity	156	156	161	170	167	*168
Combustible fuels	154	153	159	167	162	*163
Hydro	..	..	..	..	..	..
Nuclear	..	..	..	..	..	..
Other	2	2	2	3	5	5
Own use in electricity, CHP and heat plants	7	7	7	8	8	*8
Net production	149	149	154	161	159	*161
Imports	..	..	..	..	..	..
Exports	..	..	..	..	..	..
Losses	14	13	13	14	11	*12
Consumption	136	136	141	147	*148	*149
Energy industries own use	..	..	..	..	..	..
By industry and construction	23	23	22	32	*30	*32
By transport	..	..	..	..	..	..
By households and other cons.	112	113	119	115	*118	*117
Net installed capacity			**Thousand kilowatts**			
Total main activity and autoproducer	*43	43	46	50	50	*51
Combustible fuels	*41	41	44	46	46	*46
Hydro	..	..	..	..	..	..
Nuclear	..	..	..	..	..	..
Other	2	2	2	4	4	5
Main activity	*43	43	46	50	50	*51
Combustible fuels	*41	41	44	46	46	*46
Hydro	..	..	..	..	..	..
Nuclear	..	..	..	..	..	..
Other	2	2	2	4	4	5
Combustible fuel input			**Terajoules**			
Gas-diesel oil	1544	1514	1574	1694	1602	*1634
Total input	1544	1514	1574	1694	1602	*1634
Total production	554	553	572	600	583	*588
Estimated efficiency (% of production to input)	36	37	36	35	36	36

Statistics on electricity

Andorra

Item	2013	2014	2015	2016	2017	2018
Production, trade and consumption	Million kilowatt-hours					
Total main activity and autoproducer	115	127	100	99	*106	*139
Combustible fuels	13	13	14	14	17	20
Hydro	102	113	86	84	*88	*118
Nuclear	..	..	..	..	..	..
Other	..	0	0	0	1	*1
Main activity	115	127	100	99	*106	*139
Combustible fuels	13	13	14	14	17	20
Hydro	102	113	86	84	*88	*118
Nuclear	..	..	..	..	..	..
Other	..	0	0	0	1	*1
Own use in electricity, CHP and heat plants	0	0	0	0	0	0
Net production	115	127	99	99	*106	*139
Imports	466	439	471	485	470	439
Exports	0	0	0	0	0	0
Losses	71	68	68	67	67	68
Consumption	482	475	484	491	490	492
Energy industries own use	..	..	..	..	..	..
By industry and construction	10	8	8	8	8	11
By transport	..	..	..	..	..	..
By households and other cons.	473	467	476	483	482	482
Net installed capacity	Thousand kilowatts					
Total main activity and autoproducer	51	51	51	51	52	53
Combustible fuels	5	5	5	5	5	5
Hydro	46	46	46	46	46	46
Nuclear	..	..	..	..	..	..
Other	..	0	0	0	1	2
Main activity	51	51	51	51	52	53
Combustible fuels	5	5	5	5	5	5
Hydro	46	46	46	46	46	46
Nuclear	..	..	..	..	..	..
Other	..	0	0	0	1	2
Combustible fuel input	Terajoules					
Municipal waste	*232	*241	*248	*255	*306	*366
Total input	*232	*241	*248	*255	*306	*366
Total production	46	48	50	51	61	73
Estimated efficiency (% of production to input)	20	20	20	20	20	20

Angola

Item	2013	2014	2015	2016	2017	2018
Production, trade and consumption	**Million kilowatt-hours**					
Total main activity and autoproducer	8231	9497	9783	10379	10737	11753
Combustible fuels	3449	4439	4572	4546	3066	3001
Hydro	4767	5041	5193	5815	7653	8734
Nuclear	..	..	..	..	..	..
Other	15	17	18	18	18	18
Main activity	7758	8951	9221	9783	10307	11332
Combustible fuels	2976	3893	4010	3950	2636	2580
Hydro	4767	5041	5193	5815	7653	8734
Nuclear	..	..	..	..	..	..
Other	15	17	18	18	18	18
Own use in electricity, CHP and heat plants	218	251	259	274	283	308
Net production	8013	9246	9524	10105	10454	11445
Imports	..	..	..	..	..	..
Exports	..	..	..	..	..	..
Losses	926	1068	1100	1167	1207	1322
Consumption	7087	8178	8424	8938	9247	10124
Energy industries own use	..	..	..	..	..	..
By industry and construction	2389	2757	2840	3013	3117	3413
By transport	..	..	..	..	..	..
By households and other cons.	4698	5421	5584	5925	6130	6711
Net installed capacity	**Thousand kilowatts**					
Total main activity and autoproducer	*1541	*2082	*2546	*2886	*4422	5010
Combustible fuels	*770	*770	*1091	*1284	*2067	*2298
Hydro	*760	*1300	*1442	*1589	*2342	2699
Nuclear	..	..	..	..	..	..
Other	11	12	13	13	13	13
Main activity	*1411	*1952	*2362	*2669	*4172	4760
Combustible fuels	*640	*640	*907	*1067	*1817	*2048
Hydro	*760	*1300	*1442	*1589	*2342	2699
Nuclear	..	..	..	..	..	..
Other	11	12	13	13	13	13
Combustible fuel input	**Terajoules**					
Gas-diesel oil	28294	*42226	*42398	*39345	*25499	*23951
Fuel oil	2788	3030	1697	2343	1535	3208
Bagasse	..	432	502	1861	2402	2402
Total input	31082	*45688	*44597	*43549	*29436	*29560
Total production	12416	15980	16459	16366	11038	10804
Estimated efficiency (% of production to input)	40	35	37	38	37	37

Anguilla

Item	2013	2014	2015	2016	2017	2018
Production, trade and consumption	Million kilowatt-hours					
Total main activity and autoproducer	89	90	95	104	80	87
Combustible fuels	89	90	94	103	80	87
Hydro	..	..	..	..	..	..
Nuclear	..	..	..	..	..	..
Other	..	..	0	*1	0	0
Main activity	89	90	95	104	80	87
Combustible fuels	89	90	94	103	80	87
Hydro	..	..	..	..	..	..
Nuclear	..	..	..	..	..	..
Other	..	..	0	*1	0	0
Own use in electricity, CHP and heat plants	3	3	3	3	3	3
Net production	86	87	92	100	77	84
Imports	..	..	..	..	..	..
Exports	..	..	..	..	..	..
Losses	9	9	10	9	*9	*10
Consumption	*77	*78	*81	*91	*68	74
Energy industries own use	..	..	..	..	..	..
By industry and construction	..	..	..	..	..	..
By transport	..	..	..	..	..	..
By households and other cons.	*77	*78	*81	*91	*68	74
Net installed capacity	Thousand kilowatts					
Total main activity and autoproducer	33	33	34	34	24	*25
Combustible fuels	33	33	33	33	24	*24
Hydro	..	..	..	..	..	..
Nuclear	..	..	..	..	..	..
Other	..	..	1	1	*1	*1
Main activity	33	33	34	34	24	*25
Combustible fuels	33	33	33	33	24	*24
Hydro	..	..	..	..	..	..
Nuclear	..	..	..	..	..	..
Other	..	..	1	1	*1	*1
Combustible fuel input	Terajoules					
Gas-diesel oil	796	821	860	*925	*808	*839
Total input	796	821	860	*925	*808	*839
Total production	319	322	339	371	287	312
Estimated efficiency (% of production to input)	40	39	39	40	35	37

Antigua and Barbuda

Item	2013	2014	2015	2016	2017	2018
Production, trade and consumption	**Million kilowatt-hours**					
Total main activity and autoproducer	*332	*338	*347	*353	*353	362
Combustible fuels	*330	*336	*340	*344	*344	349
Hydro	..	..	..	..	..	..
Nuclear	..	..	..	..	..	..
Other	2	2	7	9	9	13
Main activity	*331	*337	*346	*352	*352	361
Combustible fuels	*329	*335	*339	*343	*343	348
Hydro	..	..	..	..	..	..
Nuclear	..	..	..	..	..	..
Other	2	2	7	9	9	13
Own use in electricity, CHP and heat plants	*17	*9	*10	*13	*8	27
Net production	*315	*329	*337	*340	*345	335
Imports	..	..	..	..	..	..
Exports	..	..	..	..	..	..
Losses	76	*87	*87	*87	*90	*55
Consumption	*237	*242	*250	*253	*255	*287
Energy industries own use	..	..	..	..	..	..
By industry and construction	*8	*9	*10	*12	*12	*13
By transport	..	..	..	..	..	..
By households and other cons.	*229	*233	*240	*241	*243	*274
Net installed capacity	**Thousand kilowatts**					
Total main activity and autoproducer	*113	*116	*117	*117	*119	91
Combustible fuels	*111	*111	*111	*111	*113	82
Hydro	..	..	..	..	..	..
Nuclear	..	..	..	..	..	..
Other	2	5	6	6	6	9
Main activity	*112	*115	*116	*116	*118	90
Combustible fuels	*110	*110	*110	*110	*112	81
Hydro	..	..	..	..	..	..
Nuclear	..	..	..	..	..	..
Other	2	5	6	6	6	9
Combustible fuel input	**Terajoules**					
Gas-diesel oil	*2365	*2365	*2365	*2365	*2365	*2365
Fuel oil	*1414	*1414	*1454	*1495	*1495	*1535
Total input	*3779	*3779	*3819	*3860	*3860	*3900
Total production	*1188	*1210	*1224	*1238	*1238	1256
Estimated efficiency (% of production to input)	31	32	32	32	32	32

Argentina

Item	2013	2014	2015	2016	2017	2018
Production, trade and consumption	Million kilowatt-hours					
Total main activity and autoproducer	140868	138551	145363	146353	145618	152224
Combustible fuels	100763	90825	96159	99479	97257	102820
Hydro	33422	41335	41451	38028	41645	41430
Nuclear	6207	5756	7139	*8285	6088	6453
Other	476	635	614	561	628	1521
Main activity	126147	124338	131402	131526	130874	137480
Combustible fuels	86095	76649	82225	84698	82559	88122
Hydro	33369	41298	41424	37982	41599	41384
Nuclear	6207	5756	7139	*8285	6088	6453
Other	476	635	614	561	628	1521
Own use in electricity, CHP and heat plants	5216	3641	3869	3865	3696	3917
Net production	135652	134910	141494	142488	141922	148307
Imports	8303	10027	10320	11078	10529	10030
Exports	247	166	55	327	69	280
Losses	22289	17805	22061	23994	22981	23672
Consumption	121419	126966	129700	129246	129402	129145
Energy industries own use	497	723	578	465	401	401
By industry and construction	48919	51387	52281	50466	50374	50751
By transport	621	588	566	546	660	544
By households and other cons.	71382	74268	76275	77769	77967	77449
Net installed capacity	Thousand kilowatts					
Total main activity and autoproducer	39563	35945	37593	37430	39764	42128
Combustible fuels	28269	24651	25541	25314	26510	28122
Hydro	10074	10074	10063	10127	11262	11308
Nuclear	1018	1018	1763	1763	1755	1755
Other	202	202	226	226	237	943
Main activity	35500	31931	33947	33816	36150	38514
Combustible fuels	24228	20659	21917	21722	22918	24530
Hydro	10054	10054	10043	10107	11242	11288
Nuclear	1018	1018	1763	1763	1755	1755
Other	200	200	224	224	235	941
Combustible fuel input	Terajoules					
Hard Coal	25995	28963	27825	21219	19386	19658
Gas-diesel oil	95589	68499	84366	89225	53922	34873
Fuel oil	93082	114494	122493	113241	58216	29128
Liquefied petroleum gas	0	0	0	0	..	..
Refinery gas	3762	2475	3515	2376	2673	2624
Natural gas	582890	576765	585550	625835	699685	659367
Coke-oven gas	2428	435	435	427	460	462
Blast furnace gas	5568	5892	5398	4430	2143	2143
Fuelwood	9325	7484	7665	8168	8320	6900
Bagasse	5405	5483	5429	5328	5869	5892
Total input	824043	810489	842675	870249	850674	761047
Total production	362747	326970	346172	358124	350125	370152
Estimated efficiency (% of production to input)	44	40	41	41	41	49

Armenia

Item	2013	2014	2015	2016	2017	2018
Production, trade and consumption	**Million kilowatt-hours**					
Total main activity and autoproducer	7710	7750	7799	7315	7765	7791
Combustible fuels	3173	3289	2801	2581	2872	3376
Hydro	2173	1992	2206	2350	2269	2318
Nuclear	2360	2465	2788	2381	2620	2076
Other	4	4	4	3	5	21
Main activity	7710	7750	7799	7315	7763	7777
Combustible fuels	3173	3289	2801	2581	2872	3376
Hydro	2173	1992	2206	2350	2269	2318
Nuclear	2360	2465	2788	2381	2620	2076
Other	4	4	4	3	2	7
Own use in electricity, CHP and heat plants	329	361	369	327	354	354
Net production	7381	7389	7430	6988	7412	7437
Imports	148	206	174	275	319	204
Exports	1313	1314	1424	1229	1440	1627
Losses	949	929	812	706	668	611
Consumption	5403	5353	5372	5334	5623	5403
Energy industries own use	..	..	..	..	..	..
By industry and construction	1208	1479	1577	1631	1655	1491
By transport	124	115	105	106	102	96
By households and other cons.	4071	3759	3690	3597	3867	3815
Net installed capacity	**Thousand kilowatts**					
Total main activity and autoproducer	4095	4091	3538	3564	3582	3591
Combustible fuels	2394	2390	1840	1840	1840	1827
Hydro	1289	1289	1286	1312	1327	1336
Nuclear	408	408	408	408	408	408
Other	4	4	4	4	7	21
Main activity	4095	4091	3538	3564	3580	3581
Combustible fuels	2394	2390	1840	1840	1840	1827
Hydro	1289	1289	1286	1312	1327	1336
Nuclear	408	408	408	408	408	408
Other	4	4	4	4	5	11
Combustible fuel input	**Terajoules**					
Natural gas	*28760	22398	25191	23231	24537	29391
Total input	*28760	22398	25191	23231	24537	29391
Total production	11423	11840	10084	9292	10338	12152
Estimated efficiency (% of production to input)	40	53	40	40	42	41

Statistics on electricity

Aruba

Item	2013	2014	2015	2016	2017	2018
Production, trade and consumption			**Million kilowatt-hours**			
Total main activity and autoproducer	*928	*917	*932	*947	*978	*983
Combustible fuels	*790	*778	*793	*802	*835	*808
Hydro	..	..	..	..	..	..
Nuclear	..	..	..	..	..	..
Other	*138	*138	*138	*145	*144	*175
Main activity	*928	*917	*932	*947	*978	*983
Combustible fuels	*790	*778	*793	*802	*835	*808
Hydro	..	..	..	..	..	..
Nuclear	..	..	..	..	..	..
Other	*138	*138	*138	*145	*144	*175
Own use in electricity, CHP and heat plants	0	0	0	0	0	0
Net production	*928	*917	*932	*947	*978	*983
Imports	..	..	..	..	..	..
Exports	..	..	..	..	..	..
Losses	149	138	153	*158	*165	*166
Consumption	*779	*779	*778	*789	*813	*817
Energy industries own use	..	..	..	..	..	..
By industry and construction	..	..	..	..	..	..
By transport	..	..	..	..	..	..
By households and other cons.	*779	*779	*778	*789	*813	*817
Net installed capacity			**Thousand kilowatts**			
Total main activity and autoproducer	288	288	288	288	288	288
Combustible fuels	258	258	258	258	258	258
Hydro	..	..	..	..	..	..
Nuclear	..	..	..	..	..	..
Other	30	30	30	30	30	30
Main activity	288	288	288	288	288	288
Combustible fuels	258	258	258	258	258	258
Hydro	..	..	..	..	..	..
Nuclear	..	..	..	..	..	..
Other	30	30	30	30	30	30
Combustible fuel input			**Terajoules**			
Gas-diesel oil	*559	*568	*581	*581	*602	*606
Fuel oil	*7595	*7716	*7918	*7716	*7676	*7393
Total input	*8154	*8284	*8499	*8297	*8278	*8000
Total production	*2843	*2802	*2856	*2887	*3005	*2908
Estimated efficiency (% of production to input)	35	34	34	35	36	36

Statistics on electricity

Australia

Item	2013	2014	2015	2016	2017	2018
Production, trade and consumption	Million kilowatt-hours					
Total main activity and autoproducer	249369	247451	251415	256563	258019	260998
Combustible fuels	219663	214767	221479	222837	221065	219884
Hydro	18270	18421	13445	15318	16285	16021
Nuclear	..	..	..	..	..	..
Other	11436	14263	16491	18408	20669	25093
Main activity	226356	223990	226896	232479	229078	229024
Combustible fuels	200120	195263	201872	204501	199558	196915
Hydro	18270	18421	13445	15318	16285	16021
Nuclear	..	..	..	..	..	..
Other	7966	10306	11579	12660	13235	16088
Own use in electricity, CHP and heat plants	13847	14830	12882	13301	14502	13706
Net production	235522	232621	238533	243262	243517	247292
Imports	..	..	..	..	..	..
Exports	..	..	..	..	..	..
Losses	13429	11149	13009	16373	13221	13416
Consumption	222093	221472	225524	226889	230296	233876
Energy industries own use	12248	13627	14207	15225	19217	20533
By industry and construction	79645	79483	76624	77291	74948	75874
By transport	4439	4560	5741	6097	5883	5962
By households and other cons.	125761	123802	128952	128276	130248	131507
Net installed capacity	Thousand kilowatts					
Total main activity and autoproducer	66232	68060	68435	67265	66761	69274
Combustible fuels	50171	50704	49983	47977	46319	46445
Hydro	8271	8271	8271	8271	8271	8523
Nuclear	..	..	..	..	..	..
Other	7790	9085	10181	11017	12171	14306
Main activity	56757	57928	57362	55929	54976	56841
Combustible fuels	45261	45806	44762	42994	41436	41254
Hydro	8271	8271	8271	8271	8271	8523
Nuclear	..	..	..	..	..	..
Other	3225	3851	4329	4664	5269	7064
Combustible fuel input	Terajoules					
Hard Coal	696294	648712	636963	659756	672798	699594
Brown Coal	1024432	955774	1028036	1057550	1012516	920982
Lignite briquettes	1029	861	672	461	168	..
Biogas	11743	14005	14520	14247	13723	14633
Gas-diesel oil	51987	37195	46569	46612	45967	44290
Fuel oil	7030	6262	7070	1818	1414	1495
Other oil products	3658	2894	3538	3095	3739	2211
Natural gas	517482	530826	553022	559114	558516	572280
Fuelwood	*1182	*1731	*3669	*4193	*6857	*6776
Bagasse	*10233	*14980	*16886	*19298	*27336	*27014
Others	0	0	0	0	..	..
Total input	2325070	2213240	2310945	2366145	2343033	2289275
Total production	790787	773161	797324	802213	795834	791582
Estimated efficiency (% of production to input)	34	35	35	34	34	35

Statistics on electricity

Austria

Item	2013	2014	2015	2016	2017	2018
Production, trade and consumption	**Million kilowatt-hours**					
Total main activity and autoproducer	68351	65436	65299	68308	71325	68597
Combustible fuels	18781	15959	18916	18953	21296	19900
Hydro	45778	44833	40591	43009	42175	41216
Nuclear	..	..	..	..	..	..
Other	3792	4644	5792	6346	7854	7481
Main activity	60235	57740	57455	60432	63114	60610
Combustible fuels	11231	8839	11576	11619	13576	12400
Hydro	45226	44270	40102	42482	41697	40742
Nuclear	..	..	..	..	..	..
Other	3778	4631	5777	6331	7841	7468
Own use in electricity, CHP and heat plants	3051	3198	3342	3447	3413	3477
Net production	65300	62238	61957	64861	67912	65120
Imports	24960	26712	29389	26366	29362	28076
Exports	17689	17437	19328	19207	22817	19129
Losses	3541	3410	3467	3339	3459	3459
Consumption	69028	68104	68552	68680	71002	70607
Energy industries own use	7840	7911	7367	6642	8110	7533
By industry and construction	27262	27069	27355	28226	28249	28670
By transport	3108	3064	3155	3206	3261	3273
By households and other cons.	30818	30060	30675	30606	31382	31131
Net installed capacity	**Thousand kilowatts**					
Total main activity and autoproducer	23855	24287	24742	25217	24920	25620
Combustible fuels	8170	7859	7665	7273	6613	6532
Hydro	13383	13532	13650	14117	14150	14516
Nuclear	..	..	..	..	..	..
Other	2302	2896	3427	3827	4157	4572
Main activity	21476	22029	22504	22959	23147	23904
Combustible fuels	6326	6136	5964	5561	5272	5244
Hydro	12848	12997	13113	13571	13718	14088
Nuclear	..	..	..	..	..	..
Other	2302	2896	3427	3827	4157	4572
Combustible fuel input	**Terajoules**					
Hard Coal	38085	27024	27341	19019	16559	17657
Biogas	6445	10276	10594	10683	11024	8140
Fuel oil	8484	6262	8646	6626	6100	4727
Refinery gas	941	1436	1535	6188	7524	8564
Natural gas	63326	54077	70170	78009	100203	90760
Coke-oven gas	2017	2771	4328	3352	3367	3166
Blast furnace gas	13501	13507	12825	12040	14177	12173
Fuelwood	*43308	*39740	*39747	*37414	*38306	*37890
Municipal waste	13552	15903	17283	19084	17640	17316
Black liquor	*4526	*4418	*4615	*3281	*3021	*3286
Others	8498	7320	6966	6321	6652	5583
Total input	202683	182734	204049	202016	224574	209261
Total production	67612	57452	68098	68231	76666	71640
Estimated efficiency (% of production to input)	33	31	33	34	34	34

Azerbaijan

Item	2013	2014	2015	2016	2017	2018
Production, trade and consumption	**Million kilowatt-hours**					
Total main activity and autoproducer	23354	24728	24688	24953	24320	25229
Combustible fuels	21863	23423	23041	22936	22515	23339
Hydro	1489	1300	1637	1959	1746	1768
Nuclear	..	..	..	..	..	..
Other	2	5	10	58	59	122
Main activity	21556	22706	22551	22699	22231	23133
Combustible fuels	20065	21401	20904	20699	20445	21243
Hydro	1489	1300	1637	1959	1746	1768
Nuclear	..	..	..	..	..	..
Other	2	5	10	41	40	122
Own use in electricity, CHP and heat plants	961	998	982	918	877	869
Net production	22393	23730	23706	24035	23444	24361
Imports	127	124	108	114	108	131
Exports	495	489	265	1096	1283	1445
Losses	3281	3363	2869	2350	2251	2220
Consumption	18661	19914	20573	20660	19987	20804
Energy industries own use	2679	3007	2954	3042	2902	2993
By industry and construction	2996	3161	3163	3517	3611	3724
By transport	531	536	482	428	397	384
By households and other cons.	12455	13210	13974	13673	13077	13704
Net installed capacity	**Thousand kilowatts**					
Total main activity and autoproducer	7353	7353	7808	7911	7942	7829
Combustible fuels	6267	6270	6692	6766	6791	6597
Hydro	1083	1078	1103	1105	1106	1131
Nuclear	..	..	..	..	..	..
Other	4	5	13	41	44	101
Main activity	7114	7111	7145	7167	7172	6977
Combustible fuels	6028	6028	6029	6029	6029	5746
Hydro	1083	1078	1103	1105	1106	1131
Nuclear	..	..	..	..	..	..
Other	4	5	13	33	36	101
Combustible fuel input	**Terajoules**					
Gas-diesel oil	172	215	215	430	430	546
Fuel oil	0	162	15716	24846	12605	-12
Natural gas	206854	214193	212772	196866	213287	232430
Municipal waste	2104	2628	3037	2772	2782	2966
Total input	209130	217198	231739	224914	229104	235930
Total production	78707	84323	82948	82570	81055	84021
Estimated efficiency (% of production to input)	38	39	36	37	35	36

Bahamas

Item	2013	2014	2015	2016	2017	2018
Production, trade and consumption	Million kilowatt-hours					
Total main activity and autoproducer	1885	1922	1998	1966	*1987	*2280
Combustible fuels	1885	1922	1998	1966	*1987	*2280
Hydro	..	..	..	..	..	..
Nuclear	..	..	..	..	..	..
Other	..	..	..	..	..	..
Main activity	1811	1848	1922	1890	*1912	*2200
Combustible fuels	1811	1848	1922	1890	*1912	*2200
Hydro	..	..	..	..	..	..
Nuclear	..	..	..	..	..	..
Other	..	..	..	..	..	..
Own use in electricity, CHP and heat plants	74	*74	*76	*76	*87	*80
Net production	1811	1848	1922	1890	*1900	*2200
Imports	..	..	..	..	..	..
Exports	..	..	..	..	..	..
Losses	*43	*34	*11	*10	*9	*9
Consumption	1768	1814	1930	1965	*1841	*2209
Energy industries own use	..	..	..	..	..	..
By industry and construction	1049	1108	1167	1075	*1092	*1310
By transport	..	..	..	..	..	..
By households and other cons.	719	706	763	890	*749	*899
Net installed capacity	Thousand kilowatts					
Total main activity and autoproducer	591	576	576	576	576	576
Combustible fuels	591	576	576	576	576	576
Hydro	..	..	..	..	..	..
Nuclear	..	..	..	..	..	..
Other	..	..	..	..	..	..
Main activity	536	537	537	537	537	537
Combustible fuels	536	537	537	537	537	537
Hydro	..	..	..	..	..	..
Nuclear	..	..	..	..	..	..
Other	..	..	..	..	..	..
Combustible fuel input	Terajoules					
Gas-diesel oil	*15394	*16598	*17243	*16942	*17114	*18920
Total input	*15394	*16598	*17243	*16942	*17114	*18920
Total production	6786	6919	7193	7078	*7153	*8208
Estimated efficiency (% of production to input)	44	42	42	42	42	43

Bahrain

Item	2013	2014	2015	2016	2017	2018
Production, trade and consumption	**Million kilowatt-hours**					
Total main activity and autoproducer	25867	27203	28461	28479	29193	29517
Combustible fuels	25867	27203	28452	28469	29183	29507
Hydro	..	..	..	..	..	..
Nuclear	..	..	..	..	..	..
Other	..	..	9	10	*10	*10
Main activity	14701	16214	17192	17056	17949	17834
Combustible fuels	14701	16214	17183	17046	17939	17824
Hydro	..	..	..	..	..	..
Nuclear	..	..	..	..	..	..
Other	..	..	9	10	*10	*10
Own use in electricity, CHP and heat plants	42	43	43	39	40	0
Net production	25825	27160	28418	28440	29153	29517
Imports	86	109	109	137	263	448
Exports	72	95	95	151	260	182
Losses	517	569	604	597	632	540
Consumption	24432	26186	27815	27749	27765	28987
Energy industries own use	..	..	..	..	..	..
By industry and construction	13180	13633	13990	14013	13889	14511
By transport	..	..	..	..	..	..
By households and other cons.	11252	12553	13825	13736	13876	14476
Net installed capacity	**Thousand kilowatts**					
Total main activity and autoproducer	6927	6975	6978	6977	6977	6977
Combustible fuels	6927	6975	6972	6971	6971	6971
Hydro	..	..	..	..	..	..
Nuclear	..	..	..	..	..	..
Other	..	..	6	6	*6	*6
Main activity	3927	3925	3928	3927	3927	3927
Combustible fuels	3927	3925	3922	3921	3921	3921
Hydro	..	..	..	..	..	..
Nuclear	..	..	..	..	..	..
Other	..	..	6	6	*6	*6
Combustible fuel input	**Terajoules**					
Natural gas	389899	365581	362096	343040	368948	365591
Total input	389899	365581	362096	343040	368948	365591
Total production	93121	97931	102427	102488	105059	106225
Estimated efficiency (% of production to input)	24	27	28	30	28	29

Bangladesh

Item	2013	2014	2015	2016	2017	2018
Production, trade and consumption			Million kilowatt-hours			
Total main activity and autoproducer	53174	55908	59103	68909	73249	78612
Combustible fuels	52086	55108	58287	67650	71934	77229
Hydro	948	623	600	1020	1041	1086
Nuclear	..	..	..	..	..	..
Other	140	177	216	239	274	297
Main activity	38811	40490	42994	51645	56012	61368
Combustible fuels	37723	39690	42178	50386	54697	59985
Hydro	948	623	600	1020	1041	1086
Nuclear	..	..	..	..	..	..
Other	140	177	216	239	274	297
Own use in electricity, CHP and heat plants	3038	3141	3321	3872	4115	4417
Net production	50136	52767	55782	65037	69134	74195
Imports	..	2401	3583	4051	4935	5070
Exports	..	..	..	..	..	..
Losses	7032	6819	7120	7187	7717	8447
Consumption	42881	47946	51757	59180	65861	70409
Energy industries own use	..	..	..	..	..	..
By industry and construction	24056	26244	29832	33380	35861	37545
By transport	..	..	..	..	..	..
By households and other cons.	18825	21702	21925	25800	30000	32864
Net installed capacity			Thousand kilowatts			
Total main activity and autoproducer	8633	9443	11150	11866	12213	*15293
Combustible fuels	8307	9091	10784	11495	11817	*14927
Hydro	*230	*230	*230	230	230	230
Nuclear	..	..	..	..	..	..
Other	96	122	136	141	166	136
Main activity	6311	7141	8773	9587	9809	*12657
Combustible fuels	5985	6789	8407	9216	9413	*12291
Hydro	*230	*230	*230	230	230	230
Nuclear	..	..	..	..	..	..
Other	96	122	136	141	166	136
Combustible fuel input			Terajoules			
Hard Coal	12388	11300	10944	11321	11321	16471
Gas-diesel oil	8901	15781	20210	21457	25843	41981
Fuel oil	42582	48036	36118	28361	31108	36097
Natural gas	509963	530247	557675	546014	660829	652782
Total input	573834	605364	624947	607153	729101	747331
Total production	187510	198389	209833	243540	258963	278024
Estimated efficiency (% of production to input)	33	33	34	40	36	37

Barbados

Item	2013	2014	2015	2016	2017	2018
Production, trade and consumption			**Million kilowatt-hours**			
Total main activity and autoproducer	1020	1031	1043	1064	1047	1055
Combustible fuels	1016	1021	1029	1037	1009	1011
Hydro	..	..	..	..	..	..
Nuclear	..	..	..	..	..	..
Other	4	10	14	27	38	44
Main activity	1017	1017	1026	1046	1030	1038
Combustible fuels	1013	1007	1012	1020	992	994
Hydro	..	..	..	..	..	..
Nuclear	..	..	..	..	..	..
Other	4	10	14	27	38	44
Own use in electricity, CHP and heat plants	58	58	76	65	54	17
Net production	962	972	968	999	993	1038
Imports	..	..	..	..	..	..
Exports	..	..	..	..	..	..
Losses	43	48	20	21	21	20
Consumption	*919	*924	*947	978	974	943
Energy industries own use	..	..	..	..	..	..
By industry and construction	73	79	80	81	117	117
By transport	..	..	..	..	..	..
By households and other cons.	*846	*846	*867	897	857	825
Net installed capacity			**Thousand kilowatts**			
Total main activity and autoproducer	244	256	258	268	281	259
Combustible fuels	241	249	249	249	262	234
Hydro	..	..	..	..	..	..
Nuclear	..	..	..	..	..	..
Other	3	7	9	19	19	25
Main activity	242	246	248	258	271	249
Combustible fuels	239	239	239	239	252	224
Hydro	..	..	..	..	..	..
Nuclear	..	..	..	..	..	..
Other	3	7	9	19	19	25
Combustible fuel input			**Terajoules**			
Gas-diesel oil	1689	773	248	252	253	233
Fuel oil	8632	7413	8060	8191	6369	7479
Other kerosene	*327	*274	*306	*340	*374	..
Natural gas	255	0	179	181	175	261
Bagasse	29	23	23	23	25	28
Total input	10932	8482	8815	8987	7197	8001
Total production	3657	3674	3705	3734	3633	3641
Estimated efficiency (% of production to input)	33	43	42	42	50	46

Statistics on electricity

Belarus

Item	2013	2014	2015	2016	2017	2018
Production, trade and consumption	**Million kilowatt-hours**					
Total main activity and autoproducer	31507	34735	34082	33566	34515	38927
Combustible fuels	31361	34602	33941	33321	33924	38386
Hydro	138	121	107	142	405	324
Nuclear	..	..	..	..	..	..
Other	8	12	34	103	186	217
Main activity	28531	31663	30676	30132	30742	34967
Combustible fuels	28394	31541	30554	29912	30207	34510
Hydro	131	114	101	128	396	316
Nuclear	..	..	..	..	..	..
Other	6	8	21	92	139	141
Own use in electricity, CHP and heat plants	2189	2217	2100	2082	2106	2220
Net production	29318	32518	31982	31484	32409	36707
Imports	9382	7806	6104	6319	5992	3257
Exports	3012	4488	3482	3298	3407	4248
Losses	3342	3187	2916	2876	2872	2835
Consumption	32346	32649	31688	31629	32122	32881
Energy industries own use	2411	2429	2400	2253	2170	2220
By industry and construction	12719	12899	12093	11956	12558	14084
By transport	1304	1280	1227	1181	1223	1225
By households and other cons.	15912	16041	15968	16239	16171	15351
Net installed capacity	**Thousand kilowatts**					
Total main activity and autoproducer	9214	10221	9798	10009	10151	*10269
Combustible fuels	9178	10181	9750	9826	9884	*9907
Hydro	34	34	34	74	103	*105
Nuclear	..	..	..	..	..	..
Other	2	6	14	109	164	258
Main activity	8508	9431	8989	9153	9297	*9369
Combustible fuels	8479	9398	8953	8985	9078	*9097
Hydro	28	28	28	68	97	*98
Nuclear	..	..	..	..	..	..
Other	1	5	8	100	122	175
Combustible fuel input	**Terajoules**					
Hard Coal	0	0	0	0	0	0
Peat	1081	1291	1222	1210	835	816
Biogas	337	363	390	370	441	439
Gas-diesel oil	0	0	0	0	0	0
Fuel oil	1293	2868	3394	5737	3232	3963
Refinery gas	2030	2228	2030	1436	1881	1539
Natural gas	441450	451493	427730	420232	438360	479261
Fuelwood	4832	5399	5965	6943	7080	5432
Industrial waste	686	880	993	617	675	674
Peat products	371	332	371	400	400	367
Others	0	0	0	0	0	0
Total input	452079	464853	442094	436944	452903	492492
Total production	112900	124567	122188	119956	122126	138190
Estimated efficiency (% of production to input)	25	27	28	27	27	28

Belgium

Item	2013	2014	2015	2016	2017	2018
Production, trade and consumption			**Million kilowatt-hours**			
Total main activity and autoproducer	83488	72645	69829	85813	86775	75095
Combustible fuels	32408	29549	33208	31744	32781	33315
Hydro	1704	1465	1418	1489	1397	1329
Nuclear	42644	33703	26103	43523	42227	28597
Other	6732	7928	9100	9057	10370	11854
Main activity	74363	62864	59791	75334	75301	62931
Combustible fuels	26359	23077	26697	24885	25166	25567
Hydro	1704	1465	1418	1489	1397	1329
Nuclear	42644	33703	26103	43523	42227	28597
Other	3656	4619	5573	5437	6511	7438
Own use in electricity, CHP and heat plants	3208	2827	2449	3356	3658	3114
Net production	80280	69818	67380	82457	83117	71981
Imports	17243	21791	23714	14648	14189	21636
Exports	7603	4188	2715	8465	8168	4308
Losses	4007	3785	3816	3881	3849	3798
Consumption	86211	84239	84623	85156	85350	85732
Energy industries own use	3182	3075	2955	2910	3072	2977
By industry and construction	37787	37820	37976	38266	38711	38898
By transport	1686	1569	1589	1625	1632	1657
By households and other cons.	43556	41775	42103	42355	41935	42200
Net installed capacity			**Thousand kilowatts**			
Total main activity and autoproducer	20952	20922	21167	21668	22236	22793
Combustible fuels	8910	8601	8520	8629	8483	8205
Hydro	1429	1431	1422	1425	1417	1418
Nuclear	5927	5927	5913	5913	5918	5918
Other	4686	4963	5312	5701	6418	7252
Main activity	16690	16497	16697	16851	17121	17229
Combustible fuels	7559	7202	7199	7162	7017	6660
Hydro	1429	1431	1422	1425	1417	1418
Nuclear	5927	5927	5913	5913	5918	5918
Other	1775	1937	2163	2351	2769	3233
Combustible fuel input			**Terajoules**			
Hard Coal	28423	21606	21708	3561	412	441
Biogas	4593	5240	5610	5657	5449	5430
Refinery gas	446	1139	1139	1188	1139	941
Natural gas	163294	148591	169641	168177	167350	176047
Blast furnace gas	16560	16739	16233	17756	18513	17943
Fuelwood	*30737	*23284	*31484	*30995	*32992	*30252
Municipal waste	28188	29725	30218	30579	30696	30249
Industrial waste	5581	6031	6152	6135	6248	6063
Other recovered gases	1238	1479	1224	1258	1213	1218
Other liquid biofuels	658	438	685	82	137	521
Others	1112	777	586	516	442	456
Total input	280828	255048	284679	265904	264591	269560
Total production	116669	106376	119549	114278	118012	119934
Estimated efficiency (% of production to input)	42	42	42	43	45	44

Belize

Item	2013	2014	2015	2016	2017	2018
Production, trade and consumption	Million kilowatt-hours					
Total main activity and autoproducer	371	404	417	414	*636	*651
Combustible fuels	*112	*148	*181	*153	*365	*401
Hydro	259	256	236	261	271	250
Nuclear	..	..	..	..	..	..
Other	..	..	..	..	..	..
Main activity	282	279	260	284	309	308
Combustible fuels	*23	*23	*24	*23	*39	*58
Hydro	259	256	236	261	271	250
Nuclear	..	..	..	..	..	..
Other	..	..	..	..	..	..
Own use in electricity, CHP and heat plants	17	16	17	17	26	27
Net production	354	388	400	397	*610	*624
Imports	234	233	255	243	230	235
Exports	..	..	..	..	..	..
Losses	50	49	51	51	78	80
Consumption	539	572	603	589	761	779
Energy industries own use	..	..	..	..	..	..
By industry and construction	122	137	137	133	172	176
By transport	..	..	..	..	..	..
By households and other cons.	417	436	467	456	589	603
Net installed capacity	Thousand kilowatts					
Total main activity and autoproducer	143	154	154	146	165	165
Combustible fuels	88	99	99	94	113	113
Hydro	55	55	55	51	51	51
Nuclear	..	..	..	..	..	..
Other	0	0	0	0	0	0
Main activity	121	121	121	112	120	120
Combustible fuels	66	66	66	60	68	68
Hydro	55	55	55	51	51	51
Nuclear	..	..	..	..	..	..
Other	0	0	0	0	0	0
Combustible fuel input	Terajoules					
Crude oil	17	14	14	14	40	49
Gas-diesel oil	*55	*59	*64	*54	*103	*113
Fuel oil	*174	*174	*176	163	256	358
Natural gas	38	44	60	60	*51	*32
Bagasse	1927	1927	2153	1742	1841	2350
Total input	2211	2219	2467	2033	2291	2903
Total production	*404	*532	*652	*552	*1315	*1445
Estimated efficiency (% of production to input)	18	24	26	27	57	50

Benin

Item	2013	2014	2015	2016	2017	2018
Production, trade and consumption	**Million kilowatt-hours**					
Total main activity and autoproducer	130	348	330	276	331	202
Combustible fuels	130	348	324	266	325	197
Hydro	..	..	1	5	1	..
Nuclear	..	..	..	..	..	..
Other	..	..	5	5	5	5
Main activity	111	236	218	180	233	88
Combustible fuels	111	236	212	170	227	83
Hydro	..	..	1	5	1	..
Nuclear	..	..	..	..	..	..
Other	..	..	5	5	5	5
Own use in electricity, CHP and heat plants	0	0	0	0	0	0
Net production	130	348	330	276	331	202
Imports	1085	1074	1048	1089	1111	1293
Exports	..	..	..	..	..	..
Losses	235	272	277	288	297	295
Consumption	931	974	1099	1071	1139	1181
Energy industries own use	..	..	..	..	..	..
By industry and construction	155	198	277	232	256	286
By transport	..	..	..	..	..	..
By households and other cons.	776	776	822	839	883	895
Net installed capacity	**Thousand kilowatts**					
Total main activity and autoproducer	209	*246	*383	*383	*383	*383
Combustible fuels	207	*244	*312	*312	*312	*312
Hydro	*1	*1	*66	*66	*66	*66
Nuclear	..	..	..	..	..	..
Other	*1	*1	*5	*5	5	5
Main activity	201	*201	*338	*338	*338	*338
Combustible fuels	199	*199	*267	*267	*267	*267
Hydro	*1	*1	*66	*66	*66	*66
Nuclear	..	..	..	..	..	..
Other	*1	*1	*5	*5	5	5
Combustible fuel input	**Terajoules**					
Gas-diesel oil	946	2279	1376	1806	1032	860
Fuel oil	0	0	566	646	646	808
Natural gas	415	1136	1211	76	1526	750
Kerosene-type jet fuel	..	132	176	..	..	..
Total input	1361	3547	3329	2528	3204	2418
Total production	468	1253	1166	958	1170	709
Estimated efficiency (% of production to input)	34	35	35	38	37	29

Bermuda

Item	2013	2014	2015	2016	2017	2018
Production, trade and consumption	Million kilowatt-hours					
Total main activity and autoproducer	677	661	674	665	675	642
Combustible fuels	677	661	674	665	675	642
Hydro	..	..	..	..	..	..
Nuclear	..	..	..	..	..	..
Other	..	..	..	..	..	..
Main activity	665	649	662	653	662	629
Combustible fuels	665	649	662	653	662	629
Hydro	..	..	..	..	..	..
Nuclear	..	..	..	..	..	..
Other	..	..	..	..	..	..
Own use in electricity, CHP and heat plants	45	38	40	35	46	37
Net production	632	623	634	630	629	605
Imports	..	..	..	..	..	..
Exports	..	..	..	..	..	..
Losses	*45	*44	*44	*44	*45	*38
Consumption	586	577	591	586	585	568
Energy industries own use	..	..	..	..	..	..
By industry and construction	..	..	..	..	..	..
By transport	..	..	..	..	..	..
By households and other cons.	586	577	591	586	585	568
Net installed capacity	Thousand kilowatts					
Total main activity and autoproducer	*171	*171	*171	*171	*171	*176
Combustible fuels	*171	*171	*171	*171	*171	*172
Hydro	..	..	..	..	..	..
Nuclear	..	..	..	..	..	..
Other	..	..	..	..	..	4
Main activity	*167	*167	*167	*167	*167	*167
Combustible fuels	*167	*167	*167	*167	*167	*167
Hydro	..	..	..	..	..	..
Nuclear	..	..	..	..	..	..
Other	..	..	..	..	..	..
Combustible fuel input	Terajoules					
Gas-diesel oil	*820	*1511	*769	*860	*903	*912
Fuel oil	*4977	*3838	*3838	*3628	*4464	*4949
Municipal waste	*565	*605	*605	*605	*590	*600
Total input	*6363	*5954	*5212	*5093	*5957	*6461
Total production	2438	2379	2427	2395	2431	2313
Estimated efficiency (% of production to input)	38	40	47	47	41	36

Bhutan

Item	2013	2014	2015	2016	2017	2018
Production, trade and consumption	**Million kilowatt-hours**					
Total main activity and autoproducer	7551	7165	7748	7954	7730	6960
Combustible fuels	1	0	0	0	0	0
Hydro	7550	7164	7747	7953	7728	6959
Nuclear	..	..	..	..	..	..
Other	1	1	1	1	2	2
Main activity	7551	7165	7748	7954	7730	6960
Combustible fuels	1	0	0	0	0	0
Hydro	7550	7164	7747	7953	7728	6959
Nuclear	..	..	..	..	..	..
Other	1	1	1	1	2	2
Own use in electricity, CHP and heat plants	1	1	1	1	1	0
Net production	7550	7164	7747	7954	7730	6960
Imports	37	159	125	84	92	134
Exports	5625	5147	5721	5763	5701	4581
Losses	83	81	67	*266	58	277
Consumption	1841	2004	2057	2009	2186	2186
Energy industries own use	..	..	..	..	..	..
By industry and construction	1519	1661	1636	1548	1599	1815
By transport	..	..	..	..	..	..
By households and other cons.	322	343	421	460	587	371
Net installed capacity	**Thousand kilowatts**					
Total main activity and autoproducer	1499	1499	1622	1624	1623	1623
Combustible fuels	11	11	8	9	8	8
Hydro	1488	1488	1614	1614	1614	1614
Nuclear	..	..	..	..	..	..
Other	0	0	0	1	1	1
Main activity	1499	1499	1622	1624	1623	1623
Combustible fuels	11	11	8	9	8	8
Hydro	1488	1488	1614	1614	1614	1614
Nuclear	..	..	..	..	..	..
Other	0	0	0	1	1	1
Combustible fuel input	**Terajoules**					
Gas-diesel oil	*6	0	0	0	*3	0
Total input	*6	0	0	0	*3	0
Total production	2	0	0	0	1	0
Estimated efficiency (% of production to input)	32	32	32	42	32	33

Bolivia (Plur. State of)

Item	2013	2014	2015	2016	2017	2018
Production, trade and consumption	Million kilowatt-hours					
Total main activity and autoproducer	7763	8225	9034	9313	9627	9883
Combustible fuels	5224	5960	6554	7552	7327	7084
Hydro	2535	2251	2463	1720	2234	2613
Nuclear	..	..	..	..	..	..
Other	4	14	17	41	66	186
Main activity	7670	8132	8733	9028	9275	9521
Combustible fuels	5134	5873	6255	7271	6979	6729
Hydro	2535	2251	2461	1716	2230	2606
Nuclear	..	..	..	..	..	..
Other	1	8	17	41	66	186
Own use in electricity, CHP and heat plants	161	157	158	168	184	377
Net production	7602	8068	8876	9145	9443	9506
Imports	..	..	..	..	..	..
Exports	..	..	..	..	..	..
Losses	728	805	815	934	1039	1095
Consumption	6962	7392	7875	8201	8375	8450
Energy industries own use	..	..	..	..	..	..
By industry and construction	1882	2016	2112	2134	2152	2071
By transport	..	..	..	..	..	..
By households and other cons.	5080	5376	5763	6067	6223	6379
Net installed capacity	Thousand kilowatts					
Total main activity and autoproducer	*1913	*2212	*2417	*2447	*2611	*2772
Combustible fuels	*1417	*1713	*1913	*1919	*1953	*1983
Hydro	493	494	496	496	620	692
Nuclear	..	..	..	..	..	..
Other	*3	5	8	32	38	98
Main activity	*1820	*2100	*2243	*2259	*2415	*2588
Combustible fuels	*1326	*1603	*1740	*1732	*1758	*1800
Hydro	493	494	495	495	619	690
Nuclear	..	..	..	..	..	..
Other	*1	3	8	32	38	98
Combustible fuel input	Terajoules					
Gas-diesel oil	1935	2322	2537	2537	2666	2838
Natural gas	58603	67929	68114	83361	78768	71951
Bagasse	*4569	*4470	*4553	*6904	*6197	*6209
Vegetal waste	..	*31	*58	*146	*242	*670
Total input	65107	74752	75262	92948	87873	81668
Total production	18806	21456	23594	27187	26377	25502
Estimated efficiency (% of production to input)	29	29	31	29	30	31

Bonaire, St Eustatius, Saba

Item	2013	2014	2015	2016	2017	2018
Production, trade and consumption			**Million kilowatt-hours**			
Total main activity and autoproducer	116	120	127	137	142	*143
Combustible fuels	80	79	87	95	101	*95
Hydro	..	..	..	..	..	..
Nuclear	..	..	..	..	..	..
Other	37	41	40	43	40	*48
Main activity	116	120	127	137	142	*143
Combustible fuels	80	79	87	95	101	*95
Hydro	..	..	..	..	..	..
Nuclear	..	..	..	..	..	..
Other	37	41	40	43	40	*48
Own use in electricity, CHP and heat plants	12	11	11	16	17	*18
Net production	105	109	116	121	125	*125
Imports	..	..	..	..	..	..
Exports	..	..	..	..	..	..
Losses	*20	*21	*20	*20	*21	*20
Consumption	*85	*88	*96	*101	*104	*105
Energy industries own use	..	..	..	..	..	..
By industry and construction	*50	*50	*51	*53	*53	*54
By transport	..	..	..	..	..	..
By households and other cons.	*36	*38	*45	*48	*51	*51
Net installed capacity			**Thousand kilowatts**			
Total main activity and autoproducer	*27	*27	*27	33	*33	*34
Combustible fuels	*16	*16	*16	20	*20	*20
Hydro	..	..	..	..	..	..
Nuclear	..	..	..	..	..	..
Other	11	11	*11	13	*13	*14
Main activity	*27	*27	*27	33	*33	*34
Combustible fuels	*16	*16	*16	20	*20	*20
Hydro	..	..	..	..	..	..
Nuclear	..	..	..	..	..	..
Other	11	11	*11	13	*13	*14
Combustible fuel input			**Terajoules**			
Fuel oil	*1042	*1042	*1050	*1147	*1228	*1151
Total input	*1042	*1042	*1050	*1147	*1228	*1151
Total production	287	284	312	340	365	*342
Estimated efficiency (% of production to input)	27	27	30	30	30	30

Bosnia and Herzegovina

Item	2013	2014	2015	2016	2017	2018
Production, trade and consumption	Million kilowatt-hours					
Total main activity and autoproducer	17451	16160	15629	17767	16439	19160
Combustible fuels	10215	10225	10078	12102	12431	12517
Hydro	7236	5935	5551	5641	3987	6519
Nuclear	..	..	..	..	..	..
Other	..	..	..	24	21	124
Main activity	17082	15803	15204	17373	15998	18722
Combustible fuels	9846	9868	9653	11708	11990	12079
Hydro	7236	5935	5551	5641	3987	6519
Nuclear	..	..	..	..	..	..
Other	..	..	..	24	21	124
Own use in electricity, CHP and heat plants	998	988	985	1158	1200	1248
Net production	16453	15172	14644	16609	15239	17912
Imports	3167	3162	3872	3084	3346	3092
Exports	6862	5998	6007	6841	5187	7698
Losses	1448	1322	1394	1358	1347	1349
Consumption	11310	11014	11115	11494	12038	11957
Energy industries own use	377	427	440	406	640	501
By industry and construction	4149	3910	3999	4079	4344	4367
By transport	84	80	91	73	76	59
By households and other cons.	6700	6597	6585	6936	6978	7030
Net installed capacity	Thousand kilowatts					
Total main activity and autoproducer	*4304	4135	*4304	4364	4522	4440
Combustible fuels	*2187	2086	*2187	2200	2295	2135
Hydro	*2117	2049	*2117	2155	2211	2236
Nuclear	..	..	..	..	..	..
Other	..	..	..	9	16	69
Main activity	*4074	3905	*4074	4134	4292	4370
Combustible fuels	*1957	1856	*1957	1970	2065	2065
Hydro	*2117	2049	*2117	2155	2211	2236
Nuclear	..	..	..	..	..	..
Other	..	..	..	9	16	69
Combustible fuel input	Terajoules					
Brown Coal	139422	116603	106377	137220	140569	139352
Fuel oil	485	485	566	606	646	444
Natural gas	530	416	460	307	297	289
Fuelwood	..	0	0	0	196	198
Total input	140437	117503	107403	138133	141708	140284
Total production	36774	36810	36281	43567	44752	45061
Estimated efficiency (% of production to input)	26	31	34	32	32	32

Botswana

Item	2013	2014	2015	2016	2017	2018
Production, trade and consumption	Million kilowatt-hours					
Total main activity and autoproducer	925	2315	*2967	2688	3022	3105
Combustible fuels	924	2314	*2966	2686	3020	3100
Hydro	..	..	..	..	..	..
Nuclear	..	..	..	..	..	..
Other	1	1	1	2	2	5
Main activity	925	2315	*2967	2688	3022	3105
Combustible fuels	924	2314	*2966	2686	3020	3100
Hydro	..	..	..	..	..	..
Nuclear	..	..	..	..	..	..
Other	1	1	1	2	2	5
Own use in electricity, CHP and heat plants	91	242	*410	307	440	375
Net production	834	2073	*2557	2381	2582	2730
Imports	2981	1684	1468	1650	1288	277
Exports	..	..	..	..	..	..
Losses	340	255	535	564	576	410
Consumption	3310	3449	3495	3479	3280	3209
Energy industries own use	..	..	..	..	..	..
By industry and construction	1128	1463	1462	1382	1090	933
By transport	..	..	..	..	..	..
By households and other cons.	2183	1986	2033	2097	2190	2276
Net installed capacity	Thousand kilowatts					
Total main activity and autoproducer	753	621	621	621	753	796
Combustible fuels	752	620	620	620	752	795
Hydro	..	..	..	..	..	..
Nuclear	..	..	..	..	..	..
Other	1	1	1	1	1	1
Main activity	733	601	601	601	733	796
Combustible fuels	732	600	600	600	732	795
Hydro	..	..	..	..	..	..
Nuclear	..	..	..	..	..	..
Other	1	1	1	1	1	1
Combustible fuel input	Terajoules					
Hard Coal	12152	38534	27800	38227	45212	33673
Gas-diesel oil	1591	1419	1548	86	129	129
Total input	13743	39953	29348	38313	45341	33802
Total production	3326	8330	*10677	9670	10872	11159
Estimated efficiency (% of production to input)	24	21	36	25	24	33

Brazil

Item	2013	2014	2015	2016	2017	2018
Production, trade and consumption	**Million kilowatt-hours**					
Total main activity and autoproducer	570838	590542	581228	578897	589326	601396
Combustible fuels	157810	189498	185066	148549	159476	144815
Hydro	390992	373439	359743	380911	370906	388971
Nuclear	15450	15378	14734	15864	15739	15674
Other	6586	12227	21685	33573	43205	51936
Main activity	484675	496510	484922	480360	491147	500232
Combustible fuels	93705	117565	109876	71486	80093	63542
Hydro	368939	351351	338673	359499	352313	369641
Nuclear	15450	15378	14734	15864	15739	15674
Other	6581	12216	21639	33511	43002	51375
Own use in electricity, CHP and heat plants	7666	8688	8435	7523	7765	7820
Net production	563172	581854	572793	571374	581561	593576
Imports	40334	33778	34642	41313	36511	34980
Exports	0	3	219	518	156	1
Losses	94995	89157	91067	98317	97619	97973
Consumption	508510	526473	516148	513854	520295	530581
Energy industries own use	22056	22472	23461	22249	21875	23642
By industry and construction	210159	207046	197931	196213	199682	200760
By transport	1884	1979	2055	2007	2055	1968
By households and other cons.	274411	294976	292701	293385	296683	304211
Net installed capacity	**Thousand kilowatts**					
Total main activity and autoproducer	126743	133913	140857	150422	157579	163509
Combustible fuels	36528	37827	39563	41286	41881	40561
Hydro	86018	89193	91650	96931	100319	104198
Nuclear	1990	1990	1990	1990	1990	1990
Other	2207	4903	7654	10215	13389	16760
Main activity	106831	113012	118006	126223	132638	138011
Combustible fuels	21426	21800	21607	22101	22130	20636
Hydro	81213	84330	86766	91982	95300	99137
Nuclear	1990	1990	1990	1990	1990	1990
Other	2202	4892	7643	10150	13218	16248
Combustible fuel input	**Terajoules**					
Hard Coal	213523	236154	237028	229610	205225	182108
Gas-diesel oil	116788	145039	107113	53105	44634	52288
Fuel oil	91748	145400	132835	54500	64882	39026
Refinery gas	30210	22459	22295	18332	19153	20316
Other oil products	8643	9447	9970	9246	8683	8603
Natural gas	611516	739443	722325	501923	577284	481645
Coke-oven gas	11153	14839	10749	11417	16320	15411
Fuelwood	12570	14141	15785	14178	15466	17037
Bagasse	190829	207176	216072	221516	222813	220118
Vegetal waste	103244	194488	236450	286638	327563	368888
Others	7257	11019	10119	8157	10127	12046
Total input	1397481	1739604	1720742	1408621	1512150	1417486
Total production	568116	682193	666238	534776	574114	521334
Estimated efficiency (% of production to input)	41	39	39	38	38	37

British Virgin Islands

Item	2013	2014	2015	2016	2017	2018
Production, trade and consumption	**Million kilowatt-hours**					
Total main activity and autoproducer	198	199	*210	*212	*149	*146
Combustible fuels	197	197	*208	*211	*148	*145
Hydro	..	..	..	..	..	..
Nuclear	..	..	..	..	..	..
Other	*1	*2	*2	*2	*1	*1
Main activity	198	199	*210	*212	*149	*146
Combustible fuels	197	197	*208	*211	*148	*145
Hydro	..	..	..	..	..	..
Nuclear	..	..	..	..	..	..
Other	*1	*2	*2	*2	*1	*1
Own use in electricity, CHP and heat plants	7	9	*7	*7	*5	*6
Net production	191	190	*203	*205	*143	*140
Imports	..	..	..	..	..	..
Exports	..	..	..	..	..	..
Losses	18	12	*23	*22	*19	*23
Consumption	*173	*179	*181	*183	*124	*117
Energy industries own use	..	..	..	..	..	..
By industry and construction	*10	*10	*10	*10	*7	*7
By transport	..	..	..	..	..	..
By households and other cons.	*163	*169	*171	*173	*117	*110
Net installed capacity	**Thousand kilowatts**					
Total main activity and autoproducer	45	45	45	45	*32	*33
Combustible fuels	44	44	44	44	*31	*32
Hydro	..	..	..	..	..	..
Nuclear	..	..	..	..	..	..
Other	1	1	1	1	*1	*1
Main activity	45	45	45	45	*32	*33
Combustible fuels	44	44	44	44	*31	*32
Hydro	..	..	..	..	..	..
Nuclear	..	..	..	..	..	..
Other	1	1	1	1	*1	*1
Combustible fuel input	**Terajoules**					
Gas-diesel oil	*1720	*1763	*1763	*1763	*1518	*1462
Total input	*1720	*1763	*1763	*1763	*1518	*1462
Total production	708	710	*751	*758	*531	*522
Estimated efficiency (% of production to input)	41	40	43	43	35	36

Brunei Darussalam

Item	2013	2014	2015	2016	2017	2018
Production, trade and consumption			Million kilowatt-hours			
Total main activity and autoproducer	4402	4506	4200	4270	4157	4294
Combustible fuels	4400	4504	4198	4269	4155	4292
Hydro	..	..	..	..	..	..
Nuclear	..	..	..	..	..	..
Other	2	2	2	1	2	2
Main activity	3942	4010	3738	3843	3724	3854
Combustible fuels	3940	4008	3736	3842	3722	3852
Hydro	..	..	..	..	..	..
Nuclear	..	..	..	..	..	..
Other	2	2	2	1	2	2
Own use in electricity, CHP and heat plants	440	451	420	379	136	611
Net production	3962	4055	3780	3891	4021	3683
Imports	..	..	..	..	..	..
Exports	..	..	..	..	..	..
Losses	409	289	269	243	481	..
Consumption	3553	3765	3737	3648	3538	3683
Energy industries own use	398	408	346	421	426	433
By industry and construction	189	203	189	132	134	156
By transport	..	..	..	..	..	..
By households and other cons.	2966	3154	3202	3095	2978	3094
Net installed capacity			Thousand kilowatts			
Total main activity and autoproducer	*811	*811	*819	*820	993	993
Combustible fuels	*810	*810	*818	*819	992	992
Hydro	..	..	..	..	..	..
Nuclear	..	..	..	..	..	..
Other	*1	*1	*1	*1	1	1
Main activity	*701	*701	*709	*709	876	876
Combustible fuels	*700	*700	*708	*708	875	875
Hydro	..	..	..	..	..	..
Nuclear	..	..	..	..	..	..
Other	*1	*1	*1	*1	1	1
Combustible fuel input			Terajoules			
Gas-diesel oil	430	473	473	473	559	559
Natural gas	53434	55145	46433	50501	51660	54943
Total input	53864	55618	46906	50974	52219	55502
Total production	15840	16214	15113	15368	14958	15451
Estimated efficiency (% of production to input)	29	29	32	30	29	28

Bulgaria

Item	2013	2014	2015	2016	2017	2018
Production, trade and consumption			**Million kilowatt-hours**			
Total main activity and autoproducer	43784	47485	49228	45277	45612	46837
Combustible fuels	22067	23858	24840	22088	23633	22606
Hydro	4795	5163	6147	4568	3493	5423
Nuclear	14171	15867	15383	15776	15545	16125
Other	2751	2597	2858	2845	2941	2683
Main activity	43516	47232	48840	44786	44925	46130
Combustible fuels	21815	23619	24475	21631	22980	21921
Hydro	4795	5163	6147	4568	3493	5423
Nuclear	14171	15867	15383	15776	15545	16125
Other	2735	2583	2835	2811	2907	2661
Own use in electricity, CHP and heat plants	3966	4254	4501	4056	4260	4122
Net production	39818	43231	44727	41221	41352	42715
Imports	3351	4319	4251	4568	3705	2223
Exports	9532	13774	14826	10940	9186	10030
Losses	3895	4013	3785	3577	3476	3102
Consumption	29809	29710	30353	31328	32348	31721
Energy industries own use	2277	2036	2027	2430	2441	1826
By industry and construction	8511	8706	9033	9083	9736	9872
By transport	277	306	352	354	377	324
By households and other cons.	18744	18662	18941	19461	19794	19699
Net installed capacity			**Thousand kilowatts**			
Total main activity and autoproducer	11651	11425	11016	10904	11069	11286
Combustible fuels	4701	4470	3991	3822	3785	4017
Hydro	3202	3219	3219	3223	3372	3379
Nuclear	1982	1975	1975	1967	*1967	*1967
Other	1766	1761	1831	1892	1945	1923
Main activity	11539	11330	10776	10552	10624	10861
Combustible fuels	4636	4410	3854	3635	3551	3783
Hydro	3202	3219	3219	3223	3372	3379
Nuclear	1982	1975	1975	1967	*1967	*1967
Other	1719	1726	1728	1727	1734	1732
Combustible fuel input			**Terajoules**			
Hard Coal	33215	39086	17788	13147	9346	12012
Brown Coal	181217	194391	227468	194380	216372	192446
Lignite briquettes	15517	16641	12610	14836	13256	9535
Biogas	81	412	661	1569	1630	1876
Fuel oil	646	525	485	606	808	687
Refinery gas	743	347	99	495	1089	594
Petroleum coke	6110	7150	6695	8418	5168	1658
Natural gas	36528	33056	28851	28808	27601	28684
Fuelwood	*757	*1279	1281	*1556	*1668	16298
Industrial waste	..	..	..	..	0	1107
Others	129	86	86	86	86	86
Total input	274942	292972	296024	263901	277024	264983
Total production	79441	85889	89424	79517	85079	81382
Estimated efficiency (% of production to input)	29	29	30	30	31	31

Burkina Faso

Item	2013	2014	2015	2016	2017	2018
Production, trade and consumption			Million kilowatt-hours			
Total main activity and autoproducer	731	870	999	973	1095	1021
Combustible fuels	625	780	906	834	958	875
Hydro	106	90	93	140	128	91
Nuclear	..	..	..	..	..	..
Other	..	..	..	..	9	54
Main activity	731	870	999	973	1095	1021
Combustible fuels	625	780	906	834	958	875
Hydro	106	90	93	140	128	91
Nuclear	..	..	..	..	..	..
Other	..	..	..	..	9	54
Own use in electricity, CHP and heat plants	53	59	59	59	65	55
Net production	678	811	941	915	1030	966
Imports	532	488	443	630	645	837
Exports	..	..	..	..	..	..
Losses	158	175	183	*183	*224	*219
Consumption	*1052	*1125	*1200	*1361	*1452	*1568
Energy industries own use	..	..	..	..	..	..
By industry and construction	400	414	456	*517	*535	*578
By transport	..	..	..	..	..	..
By households and other cons.	*652	*711	*744	*844	*917	*990
Net installed capacity			Thousand kilowatts			
Total main activity and autoproducer	248	285	325	325	329	349
Combustible fuels	216	253	293	293	293	293
Hydro	32	32	32	32	32	32
Nuclear	..	..	..	..	..	..
Other	..	..	..	..	*4	*24
Main activity	248	285	325	325	329	349
Combustible fuels	216	253	293	293	293	293
Hydro	32	32	32	32	32	32
Nuclear	..	..	..	..	..	..
Other	..	..	..	..	*4	*24
Combustible fuel input			Terajoules			
Biogas	..	..	..	*36	*36	*36
Gas-diesel oil	3307	3006	2455	*2455	*2821	*2580
Fuel oil	2424	3919	5446	*5446	*5737	*5777
Total input	5731	6925	7901	*7937	*8594	*8393
Total production	2251	2807	3261	3001	3448	3151
Estimated efficiency (% of production to input)	39	41	41	38	40	38

Burundi

Item	2013	2014	2015	2016	2017	2018
Production, trade and consumption	**Million kilowatt-hours**					
Total main activity and autoproducer	170	184	177	181	192	246
Combustible fuels	28	40	35	31	84	105
Hydro	138	140	137	143	100	133
Nuclear	..	..	..	..	..	..
Other	4	4	5	6	8	8
Main activity	163	178	171	174	182	240
Combustible fuels	21	34	29	24	74	99
Hydro	138	140	137	143	100	133
Nuclear	..	..	..	..	..	..
Other	4	4	5	6	8	8
Own use in electricity, CHP and heat plants	19	18	19	21	27	30
Net production	151	166	158	159	165	216
Imports	103	91	*96	*128	*94	*100
Exports	..	..	..	..	..	..
Losses	40	40	*40	*40	*40	*40
Consumption	*214	*217	*214	*216	*225	*276
Energy industries own use	..	..	..	..	..	..
By industry and construction	*86	*89	*86	*87	*91	*120
By transport	..	..	..	..	..	..
By households and other cons.	*128	*128	*128	*130	*134	*156
Net installed capacity	**Thousand kilowatts**					
Total main activity and autoproducer	44	46	65	64	70	70
Combustible fuels	*9	*11	*11	*9	*17	*17
Hydro	32	32	51	51	48	48
Nuclear	..	..	..	..	..	..
Other	3	3	3	4	5	5
Main activity	42	44	63	62	67	67
Combustible fuels	*7	*9	*9	*7	*14	*14
Hydro	32	32	51	51	48	48
Nuclear	..	..	..	..	..	..
Other	3	3	3	4	5	5
Combustible fuel input	**Terajoules**					
Fuel oil	*242	*404	*368	*307	*921	*1212
Bagasse	*126	*108	*108	*126	*180	*160
Total input	*368	*512	*476	*433	*1101	*1372
Total production	100	142	125	112	302	378
Estimated efficiency (% of production to input)	27	28	26	26	27	28

Cabo Verde

Item	2013	2014	2015	2016	2017	2018
Production, trade and consumption			Million kilowatt-hours			
Total main activity and autoproducer	404	409	421	444	492	*497
Combustible fuels	321	338	336	361	409	*394
Hydro	..	..	..	..	..	..
Nuclear	..	..	..	..	..	..
Other	83	71	85	83	83	*103
Main activity	404	408	420	443	491	*496
Combustible fuels	321	338	336	361	408	*393
Hydro	..	..	..	..	..	..
Nuclear	..	..	..	..	..	..
Other	83	71	85	83	83	*103
Own use in electricity, CHP and heat plants	10	11	12	11	12	*15
Net production	394	398	409	433	480	*482
Imports	..	..	..	..	..	..
Exports	..	..	..	..	..	..
Losses	102	103	104	*118	*131	*126
Consumption	291	295	*305	*316	*343	*356
Energy industries own use	..	..	..	..	..	..
By industry and construction	37	33	*34	*36	*36	*37
By transport	..	..	..	..	..	..
By households and other cons.	255	262	*270	*280	*307	*319
Net installed capacity			Thousand kilowatts			
Total main activity and autoproducer	142	154	162	*169	*200	*209
Combustible fuels	109	121	129	*136	*166	*169
Hydro	..	..	..	..	..	..
Nuclear	..	..	..	..	..	..
Other	33	33	33	33	35	*40
Main activity	142	154	162	*168	*200	*209
Combustible fuels	108	121	129	*135	*165	*168
Hydro	..	..	..	..	..	..
Nuclear	..	..	..	..	..	..
Other	33	33	33	33	35	*40
Combustible fuel input			Terajoules			
Gas-diesel oil	602	615	*602	*688	*753	*830
Fuel oil	2275	2339	2445	2631	*2881	*2998
Total input	2877	2954	3047	3319	*3633	*3828
Total production	1156	1217	1210	1301	1472	*1417
Estimated efficiency (% of production to input)	40	41	40	39	41	37

Cambodia

Item	2013	2014	2015	2016	2017	2018
Production, trade and consumption			Million kilowatt-hours			
Total main activity and autoproducer	1778	3062	4397	5594	6998	8173
Combustible fuels	759	1207	2394	2972	4260	3420
Hydro	1016	1852	2000	2619	2733	4737
Nuclear	..	..	..	..	..	..
Other	3	3	3	3	5	16
Main activity	1778	3062	4397	5594	6998	8173
Combustible fuels	759	1207	2394	2972	4260	3420
Hydro	1016	1852	2000	2619	2733	4737
Nuclear	..	..	..	..	..	..
Other	3	3	3	3	5	16
Own use in electricity, CHP and heat plants	52	90	129	186	372	435
Net production	1726	2972	4268	5408	6626	7738
Imports	2282	1803	1526	1583	1480	1567
Exports	..	..	..	..	..	..
Losses	499	717	810	936	1332	1090
Consumption	3509	4058	4984	6053	6774	8215
Energy industries own use	..	..	..	..	..	..
By industry and construction	635	734	901	1511	1545	1874
By transport	..	..	..	..	..	..
By households and other cons.	2874	3324	4083	4542	5229	6341
Net installed capacity			Thousand kilowatts			
Total main activity and autoproducer	1157	1513	1659	1683	1878	2187
Combustible fuels	472	582	728	751	888	847
Hydro	683	929	930	930	980	1330
Nuclear	..	..	..	..	..	..
Other	*2	*2	*2	*2	10	10
Main activity	1157	1513	1659	1683	1878	2187
Combustible fuels	472	582	728	751	888	847
Hydro	683	929	930	930	980	1330
Nuclear	..	..	..	..	..	..
Other	*2	*2	*2	*2	10	10
Combustible fuel input			Terajoules			
Brown Coal	1909	9745	24023	27722	40112	31342
Gas-diesel oil	1591	903	645	1075	1462	1462
Fuel oil	4646	2626	1818	3030	2182	2182
Vegetal waste	158	201	545	1118	1132	*1385
Total input	8304	13475	27031	32945	44888	36371
Total production	2732	4345	8618	10699	15336	12312
Estimated efficiency (% of production to input)	33	32	32	32	34	34

Cameroon

Item	2013	2014	2015	2016	2017	2018
Production, trade and consumption	Million kilowatt-hours					
Total main activity and autoproducer	6095	7115	7985	7167	8099	8626
Combustible fuels	2007	2546	3616	2782	2993	3584
Hydro	4083	4562	4359	4373	5090	5023
Nuclear	..	..	..	..	..	..
Other	5	7	10	12	16	19
Main activity	4458	4982	4748	4663	5392	5335
Combustible fuels	370	413	379	278	286	293
Hydro	4083	4562	4359	4373	5090	5023
Nuclear	..	..	..	..	..	..
Other	5	7	10	12	16	19
Own use in electricity, CHP and heat plants	52	60	233	209	236	252
Net production	6043	7055	7752	6958	7863	8374
Imports	1044	540	18	16	18	19
Exports	..	..	..	..	..	..
Losses	1879	2114	1663	1290	1536	1639
Consumption	5208	5482	6107	5482	6195	6598
Energy industries own use	..	..	..	..	..	..
By industry and construction	2836	3005	3408	3059	3456	3682
By transport	..	..	..	..	..	..
By households and other cons.	2372	2477	2699	2423	2739	2916
Net installed capacity	Thousand kilowatts					
Total main activity and autoproducer	1676	*1848	*1909	*1944	*2054	*1669
Combustible fuels	939	*1109	*1167	*1200	*1265	*918
Hydro	732	*732	*732	*732	777	732
Nuclear	..	..	..	..	..	..
Other	*5	*7	*10	*12	*12	*19
Main activity	1276	*1256	*1259	*1294	1404	1019
Combustible fuels	539	517	*517	*550	615	268
Hydro	732	*732	*732	*732	777	732
Nuclear	..	..	..	..	..	..
Other	*5	*7	*10	*12	*12	*19
Combustible fuel input	Terajoules					
Gas-diesel oil	7568	8471	10019	10277	10535	10836
Fuel oil	2626	2788	3272	3353	3434	3555
Natural gas	11759	17069	18966	20483	22759	29872
Fuelwood	*637	*675	*327	*342	*354	*369
Total input	22590	29003	32584	34455	37082	44632
Total production	7225	9166	13018	10015	10775	12902
Estimated efficiency (% of production to input)	32	32	40	29	29	29

Canada

Item	2013	2014	2015	2016	2017	2018
Production, trade and consumption	Million kilowatt-hours					
Total main activity and autoproducer	657695	658762	657944	663808	662972	654399
Combustible fuels	140323	141973	143856	141715	131719	130508
Hydro	391861	382574	382266	385505	394659	385951
Nuclear	103439	107280	101809	101429	101299	100731
Other	22072	26935	30013	35159	35295	37209
Main activity	599505	599310	591300	602562	599707	595294
Combustible fuels	113526	113695	111269	110323	100447	103022
Hydro	360615	351528	348595	357230	364520	356398
Nuclear	103439	107280	101809	101429	101299	100731
Other	21925	26807	29627	33580	33441	35143
Own use in electricity, CHP and heat plants	19133	19414	19450	19371	18831	18587
Net production	638562	639348	638494	644437	644141	635812
Imports	10694	12808	8726	9303	9904	13195
Exports	62739	58421	68287	73103	72040	61401
Losses	26030	29295	33263	32537	35407	34101
Consumption	530983	538149	536135	532166	552113	562977
Energy industries own use	37901	37203	37810	38037	38387	38607
By industry and construction	174516	175985	174463	174309	182145	183858
By transport	5520	5985	6717	7533	7865	7960
By households and other cons.	313046	318976	317145	312287	323716	332552
Net installed capacity	Thousand kilowatts					
Total main activity and autoproducer	134933	137859	144846	146601	147449	148762
Combustible fuels	35204	35447	36871	37557	37307	37322
Hydro	75512	75474	79405	80304	80831	81396
Nuclear	14033	14033	14033	14033	14033	14033
Other	10184	12905	14537	14707	15278	16011
Main activity	123625	126172	132975	134654	135378	136350
Combustible fuels	29520	29616	31133	31873	31748	31648
Hydro	70225	70232	74135	75181	75699	76221
Nuclear	14033	14033	14033	14033	14033	14033
Other	9847	12291	13674	13567	13898	14448
Combustible fuel input	Terajoules					
Hard Coal	96900	54086	46701	48580	48616	52547
Brown Coal	540679	574279	535440	530956	524953	396763
Biogas	9893	10206	10206	10206	10206	10206
Gas-diesel oil	9546	11094	12814	13158	12728	15265
Fuel oil	18140	27391	30785	27957	26220	23109
Refinery gas	21285	12029	11831	11534	11039	13167
Petroleum coke	32695	30063	31655	28438	27755	28633
Natural gas	625574	658718	691392	667746	624031	718572
Fuelwood	*84614	*73238	*76944	*81859	*98620	*91363
Municipal waste	3162	3421	3421	3421	3421	3421
Others	1108	1211	3134	3053	3282	2711
Total input	1443596	1455734	1454323	1426907	1390871	1355756
Total production	505163	511103	517882	510174	474188	469829
Estimated efficiency (% of production to input)	35	35	36	36	34	35

Cayman Islands

Item	2013	2014	2015	2016	2017	2018
Production, trade and consumption			Million kilowatt-hours			
Total main activity and autoproducer	615	621	640	666	671	658
Combustible fuels	615	621	640	666	671	658
Hydro	..	..	..	..	..	..
Nuclear	..	..	..	..	..	..
Other	..	..	..	..	..	..
Main activity	615	621	640	666	671	658
Combustible fuels	615	621	640	666	671	658
Hydro	..	..	..	..	..	..
Nuclear	..	..	..	..	..	..
Other	..	..	..	..	..	..
Own use in electricity, CHP and heat plants	0	0	0	0	0	0
Net production	615	621	640	666	671	658
Imports	..	..	..	..	..	..
Exports	..	..	..	..	..	..
Losses	40	37	38	40	29	9
Consumption	575	584	601	627	642	649
Energy industries own use	..	..	..	..	..	..
By industry and construction	298	301	308	311	312	318
By transport	..	..	..	..	..	..
By households and other cons.	277	283	293	316	330	331
Net installed capacity			Thousand kilowatts			
Total main activity and autoproducer	150	132	132	161	161	161
Combustible fuels	150	132	132	161	161	161
Hydro	..	..	..	..	..	..
Nuclear	..	..	..	..	..	..
Other	..	..	..	..	..	..
Main activity	150	132	132	161	161	161
Combustible fuels	150	132	132	161	161	161
Hydro	..	..	..	..	..	..
Nuclear	..	..	..	..	..	..
Other	..	..	..	..	..	..
Combustible fuel input			Terajoules			
Gas-diesel oil	5074	5246	5332	5246	5547	5586
Total input	5074	5246	5332	5246	5547	5586
Total production	2214	2236	2304	2398	2414	2368
Estimated efficiency (% of production to input)	44	43	43	46	44	42

Central African Rep.

Item	2013	2014	2015	2016	2017	2018
Production, trade and consumption	**Million kilowatt-hours**					
Total main activity and autoproducer	139	140	142	143	145	147
Combustible fuels	1	1	*1	*1	*1	*1
Hydro	138	139	141	142	144	146
Nuclear	..	..	..	..	..	..
Other	0	0	0	0	0	0
Main activity	139	140	142	143	145	147
Combustible fuels	1	1	*1	*1	*1	*1
Hydro	138	139	141	142	144	146
Nuclear	..	..	..	..	..	..
Other	0	0	0	0	0	0
Own use in electricity, CHP and heat plants	0	0	0	0	0	0
Net production	139	140	142	143	145	147
Imports	..	..	..	..	..	..
Exports	..	..	..	..	..	..
Losses	*10	*10	*10	*10	*10	*10
Consumption	*129	*130	*132	*133	*135	*137
Energy industries own use	..	..	..	..	..	..
By industry and construction	*65	*65	*65	*65	*65	*65
By transport	..	..	..	..	..	..
By households and other cons.	*64	*65	*67	*68	*70	*72
Net installed capacity	**Thousand kilowatts**					
Total main activity and autoproducer	*44	*44	*44	*44	*44	*44
Combustible fuels	*19	*19	*19	*19	*19	*19
Hydro	*25	*25	*25	*25	*25	*25
Nuclear	..	..	..	..	..	..
Other	0	0	0	0	0	0
Main activity	*44	*44	*44	*44	*44	*44
Combustible fuels	*19	*19	*19	*19	*19	*19
Hydro	*25	*25	*25	*25	*25	*25
Nuclear	..	..	..	..	..	..
Other	0	0	0	0	0	0
Combustible fuel input	**Terajoules**					
Gas-diesel oil	*15	*15	*15	*15	*15	*15
Total input	*15	*15	*15	*15	*15	*15
Total production	4	4	*4	*4	*4	*4
Estimated efficiency (% of production to input)	24	24	24	24	24	24

Chad

Item	2013	2014	2015	2016	2017	2018
Production, trade and consumption	Million kilowatt-hours					
Total main activity and autoproducer	*225	*225	*228	*230	*230	*234
Combustible fuels	*225	*225	*228	*230	*230	*234
Hydro	..	..	..	..	..	..
Nuclear	..	..	..	..	..	..
Other	..	..	..	..	..	..
Main activity	*225	*225	*228	*230	*230	*234
Combustible fuels	*225	*225	*228	*230	*230	*234
Hydro	..	..	..	..	..	..
Nuclear	..	..	..	..	..	..
Other	..	..	..	..	..	..
Own use in electricity, CHP and heat plants	*19	*19	*13	*12	*12	*13
Net production	*206	*206	*215	*218	*218	*221
Imports	..	..	..	..	..	..
Exports	..	..	..	..	..	..
Losses	..	..	..	..	..	..
Consumption	*206	*206	*215	*218	*218	*221
Energy industries own use	..	..	..	..	..	..
By industry and construction	*73	*73	*75	*77	*78	*79
By transport	..	..	..	..	..	..
By households and other cons.	*133	*133	*140	*141	*140	*142
Net installed capacity	Thousand kilowatts					
Total main activity and autoproducer	*86	*86	*86	*86	*86	*86
Combustible fuels	*86	*86	*86	*86	*86	*86
Hydro	..	..	..	..	..	..
Nuclear	..	..	..	..	..	..
Other	..	..	..	..	..	..
Main activity	*86	*86	*86	*86	*86	*86
Combustible fuels	*86	*86	*86	*86	*86	*86
Hydro	..	..	..	..	..	..
Nuclear	..	..	..	..	..	..
Other	..	..	..	..	..	..
Combustible fuel input	Terajoules					
Gas-diesel oil	*2460	*2460	*2537	*2537	*2537	*2580
Total input	*2460	*2460	*2537	*2537	*2537	*2580
Total production	*810	*810	*821	*828	*828	*842
Estimated efficiency (% of production to input)	33	33	32	33	33	33

Chile

Item	2013	2014	2015	2016	2017	2018
Production, trade and consumption	Million kilowatt-hours					
Total main activity and autoproducer	73065	70753	75387	79308	79416	82313
Combustible fuels	52602	45440	48130	50946	50602	49927
Hydro	19737	23099	23881	23274	21315	23367
Nuclear	..	..	..	..	..	..
Other	726	2214	3376	5088	7499	9019
Main activity	66643	64841	69166	72332	72032	75338
Combustible fuels	46374	39706	41956	44131	43264	43017
Hydro	19562	22940	23837	23113	21271	23307
Nuclear	..	..	..	..	..	..
Other	707	2195	3373	5088	7497	9014
Own use in electricity, CHP and heat plants	3321	1301	3358	2854	2387	2430
Net production	69744	69452	72029	76454	77029	79883
Imports	0	0	0	0	0	0
Exports	..	..	..	2	39	..
Losses	4890	4364	3707	2873	4175	3511
Consumption	66065	67836	67650	70830	70349	73716
Energy industries own use	864	688	643	659	727	682
By industry and construction	42742	43333	42267	43611	41431	44091
By transport	536	944	1088	986	963	1151
By households and other cons.	21923	22871	23652	25574	27228	27792
Net installed capacity	Thousand kilowatts					
Total main activity and autoproducer	18515	20513	21436	24530	26309	27514
Combustible fuels	12105	13111	13451	15695	16500	16877
Hydro	6094	6445	6499	6671	6656	6630
Nuclear	..	..	..	..	..	..
Other	316	957	1486	2164	3153	4007
Main activity	17305	19203	20108	22044	22530	23174
Combustible fuels	10988	11829	12132	13247	12842	12652
Hydro	6012	6417	6491	6635	6648	6619
Nuclear	..	..	..	..	..	..
Other	305	957	1485	2162	3040	3903
Combustible fuel input	Terajoules					
Hard Coal	285220	240980	278760	270099	280905	264613
Biogas	340	2241	2794	2855	2905	3659
Gas-diesel oil	26230	27348	21586	21242	11438	7396
Fuel oil	7474	6908	3596	2868	3394	2101
Liquefied petroleum gas	..	..	47	..	95	47
Refinery gas	2624	0	0	0	0	..
Petroleum coke	14203	6273	6533	7800	6663	7215
Natural gas	96694	79254	90267	99283	105835	100813
Fuelwood	176837	141213	*146365	*140409	*157602	*147965
Black liquor	..	..	*3083	*32244	*33359	*38481
Total input	609621	504217	553030	576800	602195	572290
Total production	189367	163584	173268	183406	182167	179737
Estimated efficiency (% of production to input)	31	32	31	32	30	31

Statistics on electricity

China

Item	2013	2014	2015	2016	2017	2018
Production, trade and consumption	Million kilowatt-hours					
Total main activity and autoproducer	5431637	5649583	5814573	6145886	6530689	7166133
Combustible fuels	4247009	4268649	4284188	4437068	4662739	5096318
Hydro	920291	1064337	1130270	1193374	1194700	1231787
Nuclear	111613	132538	170789	213287	248100	294359
Other	152724	184059	229326	302157	425150	543669
Main activity	5087205	5303396	5467125	5786040	6152541	6752822
Combustible fuels	3902577	3922462	3936740	4077222	4284591	4683007
Hydro	920291	1064337	1130270	1193374	1194700	1231787
Nuclear	111613	132538	170789	213287	248100	294359
Other	152724	184059	229326	302157	425150	543669
Own use in electricity, CHP and heat plants	404279	419079	444674	494849	545179	553523
Net production	5027358	5230504	5369899	5651037	5985510	6612610
Imports	7438	6750	6210	6185	6423	5688
Exports	18669	18158	18654	18907	19470	20906
Losses	314071	309988	298786	306293	319583	335171
Consumption	4701991	4909301	5058537	5331967	5652882	6262126
Energy industries own use	217886	222925	227133	230306	246475	261166
By industry and construction	3054959	3200445	3254272	3353403	3499216	3848414
By transport	100092	105924	112561	125149	141798	160850
By households and other cons.	1329054	1380007	1464571	1623109	1765392	1991696
Net installed capacity	Thousand kilowatts					
Total main activity and autoproducer	1342467	1473101	1628711	1763172	1839700	1959450
Combustible fuels	945120	1014410	1095840	1160274	1149480	1194860
Hydro	288777	313981	331671	344371	356980	361130
Nuclear	14660	20080	27170	33642	35820	44660
Other	93910	124630	174030	224885	297420	358800
Main activity	1259100	1381890	1526280	1651542	1782300	1899720
Combustible fuels	870090	932320	1005540	1060944	1104950	1143670
Hydro	280440	304860	319540	332071	344110	352590
Nuclear	14660	20080	27170	33642	35820	44660
Other	93910	124630	174030	224885	297420	358800
Combustible fuel input	Terajoules					
Hard Coal	38346504	36892143	36349633	37620001	39127978	42227542
Gas-diesel oil	16426	11107	9615	12552	10268	11331
Refinery gas	0	0	24958	27938	33180	29928
Petroleum coke	34983	37161	44288	49280	47405	59387
Natural gas	1061128	1137996	1405429	1647023	1779527	1576693
Gasworks gas	82138	85229	91643	119217	145944	220865
Coke-oven gas	274931	299059	305213	347514	342284	326295
Blast furnace gas	468351	539699	552103	641506	713820	920280
Vegetal waste	189996	229758	310173	356699	412563	420814
Industrial waste	177157	186570	158824	164335	212014	193337
Others	91090	34479	24810	20794	18355	17761
Total input	40742704	39453201	39276687	41006857	42843337	46004232
Total production	15289234	15367138	15423075	15973446	16785860	18346745
Estimated efficiency (% of production to input)	38	39	39	39	39	40

China, Hong Kong SAR

Item	2013	2014	2015	2016	2017	2018
Production, trade and consumption	**Million kilowatt-hours**					
Total main activity and autoproducer	39063	39803	37924	38154	36970	36565
Combustible fuels	39063	39803	37924	38154	36970	36565
Hydro	..	..	..	..	..	..
Nuclear	..	..	..	..	..	..
Other	..	..	..	..	..	..
Main activity	39063	39803	37924	38154	36970	36565
Combustible fuels	39063	39803	37924	38154	36970	36565
Hydro	..	..	..	..	..	..
Nuclear	..	..	..	..	..	..
Other	..	..	..	..	..	..
Own use in electricity, CHP and heat plants	0	0	0	0	0	0
Net production	39063	39803	37924	38154	36970	36565
Imports	9969	10288	11742	11621	12576	12599
Exports	1650	1226	1187	1205	1341	556
Losses	4826	4986	4567	4542	4373	4303
Consumption	42556	43880	43912	44028	43832	44305
Energy industries own use	..	..	..	..	..	..
By industry and construction	3108	3134	3177	3126	3110	3078
By transport	..	..	..	..	..	..
By households and other cons.	39448	40746	40735	40902	40722	41227
Net installed capacity	**Thousand kilowatts**					
Total main activity and autoproducer	12625	12625	12625	12625	12492	12282
Combustible fuels	12625	12625	12625	12625	12492	12282
Hydro	..	..	..	..	..	..
Nuclear	..	..	..	..	..	..
Other	..	..	..	..	..	..
Main activity	12625	12625	12625	12625	12492	12282
Combustible fuels	12625	12625	12625	12625	12492	12282
Hydro	..	..	..	..	..	..
Nuclear	..	..	..	..	..	..
Other	..	..	..	..	..	..
Combustible fuel input	**Terajoules**					
Hard Coal	325274	340806	280287	280313	262592	269686
Gas-diesel oil	602	2064	2623	3827	4257	3182
Fuel oil	1212	40	0	0	0	..
Natural gas	79589	73829	103478	106574	106754	103006
Total input	406677	416739	386388	390714	373603	375874
Total production	140627	143291	136526	137354	133092	131634
Estimated efficiency (% of production to input)	35	34	35	35	36	35

Statistics on electricity

China, Macao SAR

Item	2013	2014	2015	2016	2017	2018
Production, trade and consumption	Million kilowatt-hours					
Total main activity and autoproducer	413	641	962	988	1465	656
Combustible fuels	413	641	962	988	1465	656
Hydro	..	..	..	..	..	..
Nuclear	..	..	..	..	..	..
Other	..	..	..	..	..	..
Main activity	227	435	753	787	1260	474
Combustible fuels	227	435	753	787	1260	474
Hydro	..	..	..	..	..	..
Nuclear	..	..	..	..	..	..
Other	..	..	..	..	..	..
Own use in electricity, CHP and heat plants	35	42	59	58	66	57
Net production	378	599	903	930	1399	599
Imports	4059	4099	4054	4306	3952	4911
Exports	..	..	..	..	..	..
Losses	146	166	124	158	139	150
Consumption	4290	4532	4833	5078	5211	5569
Energy industries own use	2	2	2	2	2	2
By industry and construction	221	251	253	218	204	248
By transport	..	..	..	..	..	..
By households and other cons.	4067	4279	4578	4858	5005	5319
Net installed capacity	Thousand kilowatts					
Total main activity and autoproducer	507	511	512	512	512	448
Combustible fuels	507	511	512	512	512	448
Hydro	..	..	..	..	..	..
Nuclear	..	..	..	..	..	..
Other	..	..	..	..	..	..
Main activity	472	472	472	472	472	408
Combustible fuels	472	472	472	472	472	408
Hydro	..	..	..	..	..	..
Nuclear	..	..	..	..	..	..
Other	..	..	..	..	..	..
Combustible fuel input	Terajoules					
Gas-diesel oil	0	0	430	86	43	0
Fuel oil	1778	1737	5616	6100	4727	1697
Natural gas	0	2210	0	0	6344	2902
Municipal waste	*4374	*4698	*4968	*5292	*5616	*5897
Total input	*6152	*8645	11014	11478	16730	*10496
Total production	1487	2308	3463	3557	5274	2362
Estimated efficiency (% of production to input)	24	27	31	31	32	23

Colombia

Item	2013	2014	2015	2016	2017	2018
Production, trade and consumption	**Million kilowatt-hours**					
Total main activity and autoproducer	74001	71072	78596	76800	79279	79964
Combustible fuels	23675	23123	29951	27644	17828	19967
Hydro	50260	47870	48568	49096	61434	59933
Nuclear	..	..	..	..	..	..
Other	66	79	77	60	17	64
Main activity	67338	63465	69695	67510	69939	69709
Combustible fuels	17141	15664	21176	18493	8645	9882
Hydro	50139	47731	48451	48966	61286	59772
Nuclear	..	..	..	..	..	..
Other	58	70	68	51	8	55
Own use in electricity, CHP and heat plants	1912	1977	2046	2027	2045	2120
Net production	72089	69095	76550	74773	77234	77844
Imports	29	47	45	378	78	122
Exports	1377	849	460	45	9	16
Losses	5262	5850	7118	7000	5560	8155
Consumption	61295	64115	65447	65751	67434	68094
Energy industries own use	5369	5488	5589	5602	5859	6252
By industry and construction	18219	18964	18855	18932	19633	19958
By transport	82	85	91	96	97	104
By households and other cons.	37625	39578	40912	41121	41845	41780
Net installed capacity	**Thousand kilowatts**					
Total main activity and autoproducer	16202	15848	17686	17622	17864	*17939
Combustible fuels	6131	6043	6093	5972	6084	*6084
Hydro	9967	9696	11484	11606	11726	*11726
Nuclear	..	..	..	..	..	..
Other	104	109	109	*43	*54	129
Main activity	14557	14203	16041	15973	16215	*16290
Combustible fuels	4603	4515	4565	4442	4554	*4554
Hydro	9875	9604	11392	11512	11632	*11632
Nuclear	..	..	..	..	..	..
Other	79	84	84	18	29	104
Combustible fuel input	**Terajoules**					
Hard Coal	55544	60415	65803	65504	32521	45583
Biogas	..	..	..	36	99	69
Crude oil	9560	9771	9856	10702	11379	11548
Gas-diesel oil	12599	12599	24080	28982	13373	13674
Fuel oil	2101	1576	7393	8040	768	1818
Other kerosene	88	44	482	745	..	..
Natural gas	139705	156119	155290	138920	109496	126013
Blast furnace gas	525	400	410	384	346	350
Total input	220121	240924	263314	253312	167981	199055
Total production	85230	83243	107824	99518	64181	71881
Estimated efficiency (% of production to input)	39	35	41	39	38	36

Comoros

Item	2013	2014	2015	2016	2017	2018
Production, trade and consumption	**Million kilowatt-hours**					
Total main activity and autoproducer	*56	*53	*53	*58	*91	*98
Combustible fuels	*56	*53	*53	*58	*91	*98
Hydro	..	..	..	..	..	..
Nuclear	..	..	..	..	..	..
Other	..	..	..	..	..	..
Main activity	*56	*53	*53	*58	*91	*98
Combustible fuels	*56	*53	*53	*58	*91	*98
Hydro	..	..	..	..	..	..
Nuclear	..	..	..	..	..	..
Other	..	..	..	..	..	..
Own use in electricity, CHP and heat plants	*7	*6	*6	*7	*11	*12
Net production	*49	*46	*47	*51	*80	*87
Imports	..	..	..	..	..	..
Exports	..	..	..	..	..	..
Losses	*16	*15	*15	*16	*25	*27
Consumption	*34	*32	*32	*35	*55	*59
Energy industries own use	..	..	..	..	..	..
By industry and construction	..	..	..	..	..	..
By transport	..	..	..	..	..	..
By households and other cons.	*34	*32	*32	*35	*55	*59
Net installed capacity	**Thousand kilowatts**					
Total main activity and autoproducer	*24	*25	*26	*26	*34	*34
Combustible fuels	*24	*25	*26	*26	*34	*34
Hydro	..	..	..	..	..	..
Nuclear	..	..	..	..	..	..
Other	..	..	..	..	..	..
Main activity	*24	*25	*26	*26	*34	*34
Combustible fuels	*24	*25	*26	*26	*34	*34
Hydro	..	..	..	..	..	..
Nuclear	..	..	..	..	..	..
Other	..	..	..	..	..	..
Combustible fuel input	**Terajoules**					
Gas-diesel oil	*709	*663	*668	*738	*1147	*1243
Total input	*709	*663	*668	*738	*1147	*1243
Total production	*202	*189	*190	*210	*327	*354
Estimated efficiency (% of production to input)	28	29	28	29	29	28

Congo

Item	2013	2014	2015	2016	2017	2018
Production, trade and consumption			**Million kilowatt-hours**			
Total main activity and autoproducer	1709	1740	2770	2953	3473	3509
Combustible fuels	738	788	1671	1825	2269	2269
Hydro	971	952	1098	1127	1203	1239
Nuclear	..	..	..	..	..	..
Other	..	..	1	1	1	1
Main activity	971	952	1099	1128	1204	1240
Combustible fuels	..	..	..	..	..	..
Hydro	971	952	1098	1127	1203	1239
Nuclear	..	..	..	..	..	..
Other	..	..	1	1	1	1
Own use in electricity, CHP and heat plants	192	195	310	330	388	392
Net production	1517	1545	2460	2623	3085	3117
Imports	56	18	13	21	22	19
Exports	19	22	33	22	22	26
Losses	761	775	1234	1362	1324	1335
Consumption	802	798	1318	1439	1555	1582
Energy industries own use	..	..	..	..	..	..
By industry and construction	375	373	75	84	103	105
By transport	..	..	..	..	..	..
By households and other cons.	427	425	1243	1355	1452	1477
Net installed capacity			**Thousand kilowatts**			
Total main activity and autoproducer	*530	*590	600	*600	*606	*606
Combustible fuels	*310	*370	391	*391	*391	*391
Hydro	*220	*220	209	*209	214	214
Nuclear	..	..	..	..	..	..
Other	0	0	0	0	1	1
Main activity	*230	*240	250	*250	256	256
Combustible fuels	*10	*20	41	*41	*41	*41
Hydro	*220	*220	209	*209	214	214
Nuclear	..	..	..	..	..	..
Other	0	0	0	0	1	1
Combustible fuel input			**Terajoules**			
Gas-diesel oil	..	..	2709	2107	1247	1247
Fuel oil	..	..	687	485	364	364
Natural gas	8584	9166	19968	22868	24045	24045
Total input	8584	9166	23364	25460	25656	25656
Total production	2657	2837	6016	6570	8168	8168
Estimated efficiency (% of production to input)	31	31	26	26	32	32

Cook Islands

Item	2013	2014	2015	2016	2017	2018
Production, trade and consumption	Million kilowatt-hours					
Total main activity and autoproducer	33	33	33	34	37	41
Combustible fuels	33	31	29	30	31	31
Hydro	..	..	..	..	..	..
Nuclear	..	..	..	..	..	..
Other	1	1	3	5	6	11
Main activity	33	33	33	34	37	41
Combustible fuels	33	31	29	30	31	31
Hydro	..	..	..	..	..	..
Nuclear	..	..	..	..	..	..
Other	1	1	3	5	6	11
Own use in electricity, CHP and heat plants	0	0	0	0	0	0
Net production	33	33	33	34	37	41
Imports	..	..	..	..	..	..
Exports	..	..	..	..	..	..
Losses	..	..	..	..	..	..
Consumption	33	33	33	34	37	41
Energy industries own use	..	..	..	..	..	..
By industry and construction	..	..	..	..	..	..
By transport	..	..	..	..	..	..
By households and other cons.	33	33	33	34	37	41
Net installed capacity	Thousand kilowatts					
Total main activity and autoproducer	*12	*10	*14	*15	*15	*17
Combustible fuels	*11	*8	*11	*11	*11	*11
Hydro	..	..	..	..	..	..
Nuclear	..	..	..	..	..	..
Other	1	2	3	4	4	6
Main activity	*12	*10	*14	*15	*15	*17
Combustible fuels	*11	*8	*11	*11	*11	*11
Hydro	..	..	..	..	..	..
Nuclear	..	..	..	..	..	..
Other	1	2	3	4	4	6
Combustible fuel input	Terajoules					
Gas-diesel oil	*335	*327	*301	*314	*344	*348
Total input	*335	*327	*301	*314	*344	*348
Total production	117	112	105	107	111	111
Estimated efficiency (% of production to input)	35	34	35	34	32	32

Costa Rica

Item	2013	2014	2015	2016	2017	2018
Production, trade and consumption			Million kilowatt-hours			
Total main activity and autoproducer	10234	10216	10812	10880	11332	11498
Combustible fuels	1379	1224	287	365	222	332
Hydro	6851	6717	8067	8026	8677	8343
Nuclear	..	..	..	..	..	..
Other	2004	2275	2458	2489	2433	2823
Main activity	8077	7858	7797	8028	11123	11279
Combustible fuels	1196	1043	108	193	37	159
Hydro	5490	5379	6256	6416	8677	8343
Nuclear	..	..	..	..	..	..
Other	1391	1436	1433	1420	2408	2777
Own use in electricity, CHP and heat plants	109	117	124	124	129	121
Net production	10125	10099	10688	10756	11203	11376
Imports	531	759	537	807	551	572
Exports	484	555	643	657	741	813
Losses	1083	1106	1161	1130	1096	1102
Consumption	9102	9207	9428	9785	9901	9989
Energy industries own use	..	..	..	..	..	..
By industry and construction	1897	1858	1873	1956	2026	1933
By transport	..	..	..	..	..	..
By households and other cons.	7205	7349	7556	7829	7875	8056
Net installed capacity			Thousand kilowatts			
Total main activity and autoproducer	2814	3274	3626	3824	3557	3676
Combustible fuels	638	622	661	597	617	629
Hydro	1729	2045	2152	2328	2328	2388
Nuclear	..	..	..	..	..	..
Other	*448	607	*813	*899	612	659
Main activity	2440	2845	3061	3217	3490	3579
Combustible fuels	613	597	636	572	572	572
Hydro	1519	1835	1942	2118	2328	2387
Nuclear	..	..	..	..	..	..
Other	309	413	483	527	590	620
Combustible fuel input			Terajoules			
Biogas	1	1	1	1	1	1
Gas-diesel oil	2690	2609	56	163	29	131
Fuel oil	8093	7102	892	1520	334	1285
Bagasse	1196	1129	1196	1196	1209	1209
Vegetal waste	118	118	118	118	118	118
Total input	12099	10959	2264	2998	1692	2746
Total production	4965	4406	1035	1312	799	1196
Estimated efficiency (% of production to input)	41	40	46	44	47	44

Côte d'Ivoire

Item	2013	2014	2015	2016	2017	2018
Production, trade and consumption	Million kilowatt-hours					
Total main activity and autoproducer	7650	8286	8711	10253	10121	10059
Combustible fuels	6044	6373	7359	8724	8074	7097
Hydro	1606	1913	1352	1529	2047	2962
Nuclear	..	..	..	..	..	..
Other	..	..	..	..	..	..
Main activity	7580	8214	8606	10080	9948	9998
Combustible fuels	5974	6301	7254	8551	7901	7036
Hydro	1606	1913	1352	1529	2047	2962
Nuclear	..	..	..	..	..	..
Other	..	..	..	..	..	..
Own use in electricity, CHP and heat plants	383	414	436	513	1420	193
Net production	7267	7872	8275	9740	8701	9866
Imports	0	0	23	19	37	102
Exports	820	877	872	1877	1247	1156
Losses	1680	1187	1744	1627	1197	1874
Consumption	5046	5561	6023	6615	6318	6927
Energy industries own use	..	..	..	..	..	1
By industry and construction	1900	1881	2011	2177	2177	1989
By transport	..	..	..	..	..	..
By households and other cons.	3146	3680	4012	4438	4141	4937
Net installed capacity	Thousand kilowatts					
Total main activity and autoproducer	*1525	*1655	1909	1909	2195	2184
Combustible fuels	*1154	*1223	1305	1305	1316	1305
Hydro	*371	*432	604	604	879	879
Nuclear	..	..	..	..	..	..
Other	..	..	..	..	..	..
Main activity	*1502	*1632	1886	1886	2172	2161
Combustible fuels	*1131	*1200	1282	1282	1293	1282
Hydro	*371	*432	604	604	879	879
Nuclear	..	..	..	..	..	..
Other	..	..	..	..	..	..
Combustible fuel input	Terajoules					
Gas-diesel oil	129	129	129	99	86	86
Fuel oil	2303	6141	4848	893	889	40
Natural gas	64384	64991	67526	81287	73437	64897
Vegetal waste	1439	1478	1885	1941	1941	2087
Total input	68255	72739	74388	84219	76353	67110
Total production	21758	22943	26492	31405	29066	25549
Estimated efficiency (% of production to input)	32	32	36	37	38	38

Croatia

Item	2013	2014	2015	2016	2017	2018
Production, trade and consumption	Million kilowatt-hours					
Total main activity and autoproducer	14052	13554	11403	12820	11986	13632
Combustible fuels	4797	3664	3994	4682	5195	4435
Hydro	8727	9125	6556	7058	5508	7785
Nuclear	..	..	..	..	..	..
Other	528	765	853	1080	1283	1412
Main activity	13720	13209	11087	12482	11566	13259
Combustible fuels	4470	3326	3684	4351	4781	4068
Hydro	8722	9118	6550	7051	5502	7779
Nuclear	..	..	..	..	..	..
Other	528	765	853	1080	1283	1412
Own use in electricity, CHP and heat plants	392	395	420	536	463	450
Net production	13660	13159	10983	12284	11523	13182
Imports	11260	10898	13158	12398	12158	12693
Exports	7391	6945	6369	6867	5204	7306
Losses	1944	1764	1802	1806	1765	1824
Consumption	15585	15348	15970	16009	16715	16744
Energy industries own use	513	515	627	709	733	570
By industry and construction	3148	3291	3429	3426	3609	3682
By transport	238	231	245	251	268	282
By households and other cons.	11686	11311	11669	11623	12105	12210
Net installed capacity	Thousand kilowatts					
Total main activity and autoproducer	4312	4428	4764	4794	4982	4999
Combustible fuels	1849	1933	2124	2082	2141	2142
Hydro	2190	2114	2207	2175	2205	2202
Nuclear	..	..	..	..	..	..
Other	273	381	*433	537	636	655
Main activity	4155	4271	4597	4627	4822	4834
Combustible fuels	1694	1778	1959	1917	1984	1980
Hydro	2188	2112	2205	2173	2202	2199
Nuclear	..	..	..	..	..	..
Other	273	381	*433	537	636	655
Combustible fuel input	Terajoules					
Hard Coal	23519	22796	21951	24409	13222	12357
Brown Coal	123	143	128	152	137	103
Biogas	655	974	1438	1881	2644	3062
Gas-diesel oil	43	43	86	43	86	43
Fuel oil	2222	1535	2303	404	1697	323
Liquefied petroleum gas	0	..	..	..	..	..
Refinery gas	99	99	149	149	248	248
Petroleum coke	0	..	..	..	..	..
Natural gas	24563	15770	17107	20405	31889	24894
Fuelwood	1146	1190	2189	3730	4245	7004
Total input	52370	42550	45350	51173	54167	48033
Total production	17269	13190	14378	16855	18702	15966
Estimated efficiency (% of production to input)	33	31	32	33	35	33

Cuba

Item	2013	2014	2015	2016	2017	2018
Production, trade and consumption	Million kilowatt-hours					
Total main activity and autoproducer	19156	19366	20288	20459	20558	20837
Combustible fuels	19004	19225	20190	20334	20394	20524
Hydro	127	104	48	64	83	146
Nuclear	..	..	..	..	..	..
Other	*26	*37	*50	*60	*81	*168
Main activity	18263	18529	19390	19509	19595	20074
Combustible fuels	18110	18387	19292	19385	19431	19761
Hydro	127	104	48	64	83	146
Nuclear	..	..	..	..	..	..
Other	*26	*37	*50	*60	*81	*168
Own use in electricity, CHP and heat plants	1042	1013	993	1058	1891	1958
Net production	18115	18354	19295	19400	18667	18879
Imports	..	..	..	..	..	..
Exports	..	..	..	..	..	..
Losses	2927	2961	3135	3117	3177	3290
Consumption	15188	15392	16160	16283	15490	15589
Energy industries own use	..	..	..	..	..	..
By industry and construction	3924	3679	3793	3772	3067	3060
By transport	296	302	312	287	293	290
By households and other cons.	10969	11411	12056	12224	12130	12239
Net installed capacity	Thousand kilowatts					
Total main activity and autoproducer	5927	6191	6314	6454	6476	6661
Combustible fuels	5842	6106	6217	6341	6325	6458
Hydro	63	63	63	66	66	64
Nuclear	..	..	..	..	..	..
Other	*22	*23	*34	*47	*85	*139
Main activity	5457	5694	5785	5960	5945	6108
Combustible fuels	5372	5608	5688	5847	5794	5905
Hydro	63	63	63	66	66	64
Nuclear	..	..	..	..	..	..
Other	*22	*23	*34	*47	*85	*139
Combustible fuel input	Terajoules					
Gas-diesel oil	*19780	*18877	*19823	*13721	*22545	*27825
Fuel oil	161224	166347	168440	171203	143973	148147
Natural gas	*14559	*14996	*16705	*15913	16045	*16143
Bagasse	10927	12657	13251	*13128	*12996	*10298
Total input	206490	212876	218219	213965	195560	202413
Total production	68413	69209	72683	73203	73418	73885
Estimated efficiency (% of production to input)	33	33	33	34	38	37

Curaçao

Item	2013	2014	2015	2016	2017	2018
Production, trade and consumption			**Million kilowatt-hours**			
Total main activity and autoproducer	894	872	878	884	891	866
Combustible fuels	769	726	737	735	703	613
Hydro	..	..	..	..	..	..
Nuclear	..	..	..	..	..	..
Other	125	146	141	149	188	253
Main activity	665	617	675	724	817	752
Combustible fuels	540	471	534	575	629	499
Hydro	..	..	..	..	..	..
Nuclear	..	..	..	..	..	..
Other	125	146	141	149	188	253
Own use in electricity, CHP and heat plants	18	17	18	18	18	17
Net production	876	855	860	866	873	849
Imports	..	..	..	..	..	..
Exports	..	..	..	..	..	..
Losses	120	95	96	97	98	95
Consumption	756	760	764	769	776	753
Energy industries own use	78	71	73	54	40	37
By industry and construction	209	213	209	209	203	183
By transport	..	..	..	..	..	..
By households and other cons.	469	476	482	506	533	533
Net installed capacity			**Thousand kilowatts**			
Total main activity and autoproducer	*268	*272	301	*307	*257	*258
Combustible fuels	*235	*235	262	*262	*200	*200
Hydro	..	..	..	..	..	..
Nuclear	..	..	..	..	..	..
Other	*33	*37	39	45	57	58
Main activity	*135	*139	155	*161	*173	*174
Combustible fuels	*102	*102	116	*116	*116	*116
Hydro	..	..	..	..	..	..
Nuclear	..	..	..	..	..	..
Other	*33	*37	39	45	57	58
Combustible fuel input			**Terajoules**			
Gas-diesel oil	2623	2580	1462	2322	2021	2795
Fuel oil	8040	7555	6222	6262	5373	3636
Total input	10663	10135	7684	8584	7394	6431
Total production	2768	2614	2653	2646	2531	2207
Estimated efficiency (% of production to input)	26	26	35	31	34	34

Cyprus

Item	2013	2014	2015	2016	2017	2018
Production, trade and consumption	Million kilowatt-hours					
Total main activity and autoproducer	4290	4350	4533	4887	5004	5061
Combustible fuels	4012	4084	4186	4515	4621	4640
Hydro	..	..	..	..	..	..
Nuclear	..	..	..	..	..	..
Other	278	266	347	372	383	421
Main activity	4230	4272	4447	4789	4896	4939
Combustible fuels	3954	4026	4142	4469	4574	4589
Hydro	..	..	..	..	..	..
Nuclear	..	..	..	..	..	..
Other	276	246	305	320	322	350
Own use in electricity, CHP and heat plants	171	205	221	219	226	233
Net production	4119	4145	4312	4668	4778	4828
Imports	..	..	..	..	..	..
Exports	..	..	..	..	..	..
Losses	186	173	215	263	228	158
Consumption	3935	3972	4098	4404	4546	4670
Energy industries own use	14	7	7	5	5	6
By industry and construction	462	463	459	486	518	529
By transport	..	..	..	..	..	..
By households and other cons.	3459	3502	3632	3913	4023	4135
Net installed capacity	Thousand kilowatts					
Total main activity and autoproducer	1696	1721	1752	1756	1782	1794
Combustible fuels	1514	1510	1519	1515	1515	1517
Hydro	..	..	..	..	..	..
Nuclear	..	..	..	..	..	..
Other	182	211	234	242	268	276
Main activity	1656	1671	1685	1689	1710	1716
Combustible fuels	1478	1478	1478	1478	1478	1481
Hydro	..	..	..	..	..	..
Nuclear	..	..	..	..	..	..
Other	178	193	208	212	233	236
Combustible fuel input	Terajoules					
Biogas	289	292	309	312	323	347
Gas-diesel oil	10234	5375	3913	6536	11051	10664
Fuel oil	26381	32199	34663	35673	31472	32482
Total input	36904	37866	38885	42521	42846	43493
Total production	14443	14702	15070	16254	16636	16704
Estimated efficiency (% of production to input)	39	39	39	38	39	38

Czechia

Item	2013	2014	2015	2016	2017	2018
Production, trade and consumption	Million kilowatt-hours					
Total main activity and autoproducer	86913	86148	83892	83309	87049	88032
Combustible fuels	49940	50174	51063	53279	52782	52339
Hydro	3639	2961	3071	3202	3040	2679
Nuclear	30745	30325	26841	24104	28340	29921
Other	2589	2688	2917	2724	2887	3093
Main activity	78254	77025	74637	73864	77939	79247
Combustible fuels	41952	41676	42427	44503	44361	44147
Hydro	3018	2397	2505	2604	2429	2185
Nuclear	30745	30325	26841	24104	28340	29921
Other	2539	2627	2864	2653	2809	2994
Own use in electricity, CHP and heat plants	7136	7032	6976	6911	7163	7171
Net production	79777	79116	76916	76398	79886	80861
Imports	10571	11842	16146	13817	15072	11573
Exports	27458	28142	28661	24791	28109	25481
Losses	4098	3847	4067	4080	4375	4269
Consumption	56340	56449	58045	59200	60632	61108
Energy industries own use	3123	3233	3568	3348	3255	3104
By industry and construction	21286	22130	22645	23006	23874	24203
By transport	1592	1559	1609	1636	1697	1753
By households and other cons.	30339	29527	30223	31210	31806	32048
Net installed capacity	Thousand kilowatts					
Total main activity and autoproducer	21079	21920	21866	21989	22267	22276
Combustible fuels	12211	13032	12960	13087	13334	13331
Hydro	2252	2252	2260	2262	2265	2264
Nuclear	4290	4290	4290	4290	4290	4290
Other	2326	2346	2356	2350	2378	2391
Main activity	19178	20040	19990	20096	20331	20348
Combustible fuels	10498	11342	11275	11385	11582	11586
Hydro	2064	2062	2069	2071	2081	2081
Nuclear	4290	4290	4290	4290	4290	4290
Other	2326	2346	2356	2350	2378	2391
Combustible fuel input	Terajoules					
Hard Coal	90684	85794	95799	96998	81236	63585
Brown Coal	426641	411944	417365	416741	417688	424953
Biogas	18284	19693	19813	18272	18808	18899
Natural gas	28457	24489	28224	38346	36325	36524
Gasworks gas	16126	16999	16474	16658	14892	13502
Coke-oven gas	6372	6328	5278	4717	6613	6199
Blast furnace gas	8575	8716	7840	8150	6694	7565
Fuelwood	*19610	*22605	*24479	*25123	*27123	*25858
Municipal waste	4201	4251	3953	4440	4869	4524
Other recovered gases	1222	1433	1108	1139	1126	1257
Others	2026	2309	2417	1963	2422	2108
Total input	622199	604560	622751	632547	617795	604975
Total production	179784	180626	183827	191804	190015	188420
Estimated efficiency (% of production to input)	29	30	30	30	31	31

Dem. Rep. of the Congo

Item	2013	2014	2015	2016	2017	2018
Production, trade and consumption			Million kilowatt-hours			
Total main activity and autoproducer	8256	8850	8953	9135	9510	12067
Combustible fuels	27	30	37	36	28	976
Hydro	8229	8820	8916	9099	9482	11064
Nuclear	..	..	..	..	..	..
Other	..	..	..	..	..	27
Main activity	8238	8824	8928	9111	9330	10756
Combustible fuels	9	4	12	12	6	5
Hydro	8229	8820	8916	9099	9324	10724
Nuclear	..	..	..	..	..	..
Other	..	..	..	..	..	27
Own use in electricity, CHP and heat plants	521	640	647	660	687	1519
Net production	7735	8210	8306	8475	8823	10548
Imports	626	1138	20	20	668	799
Exports	48	69	422	420	62	70
Losses	466	1895	1260	1216	1443	1291
Consumption	7269	7899	7266	7001	7240	9986
Energy industries own use	..	..	..	..	17	21
By industry and construction	3261	4342	3994	3848	4643	7385
By transport	0	0	0	0	10	10
By households and other cons.	4008	3557	3272	3153	2570	2570
Net installed capacity			Thousand kilowatts			
Total main activity and autoproducer	*2508	*2522	*2549	*2677	3120	3179
Combustible fuels	*92	*106	*120	*135	122	155
Hydro	*2416	*2416	*2429	*2542	2998	3005
Nuclear	..	..	..	..	..	..
Other	..	..	..	..	..	19
Main activity	*2079	*2089	*2100	*2110	2539	2578
Combustible fuels	*80	*90	*100	*110	29	32
Hydro	*1999	*1999	*2000	*2000	2510	2527
Nuclear	..	..	..	..	..	..
Other	..	..	..	..	..	19
Combustible fuel input			Terajoules			
Gas-diesel oil	43	43	129	129	86	43
Natural gas	0	80	46	14	12	15
Fuelwood	*270	*278	*301	*311	*301	..
Vegetal waste	..	..	..	..	..	4654
Total input	*313	*401	*476	*454	*399	4712
Total production	97	108	133	130	101	3514
Estimated efficiency (% of production to input)	31	27	28	29	25	75

Denmark

Item	2013	2014	2015	2016	2017	2018
Production, trade and consumption	Million kilowatt-hours					
Total main activity and autoproducer	34743	32185	28942	30541	31042	30377
Combustible fuels	23089	18495	14187	16996	15493	15510
Hydro	13	15	18	19	18	15
Nuclear	..	..	..	..	..	..
Other	11641	13675	14737	13526	15531	14852
Main activity	32315	29582	26148	27762	28203	27276
Combustible fuels	21179	16488	11997	14961	13405	13362
Hydro	13	15	18	19	18	15
Nuclear	..	..	..	..	..	..
Other	11123	13079	14133	12782	14780	13899
Own use in electricity, CHP and heat plants	1605	1370	1020	1460	1386	1054
Net production	33138	30815	27922	29081	29656	29323
Imports	11459	12702	15645	14976	15218	15634
Exports	10377	9847	9733	9919	10655	10409
Losses	1914	1974	1765	1873	1678	2203
Consumption	32152	31569	31749	32045	32237	32033
Energy industries own use	1046	794	940	950	949	949
By industry and construction	8359	8214	8364	8422	8573	8574
By transport	386	385	397	417	407	403
By households and other cons.	22361	22176	22048	22256	22308	22107
Net installed capacity	Thousand kilowatts					
Total main activity and autoproducer	13809	13624	14002	14226	14321	15073
Combustible fuels	8410	8122	8136	8120	7916	7945
Hydro	9	9	7	9	9	9
Nuclear	..	..	..	..	..	..
Other	5390	5493	5859	6097	6396	7119
Main activity	12664	12401	12605	12756	12785	13436
Combustible fuels	7836	7506	7521	7501	7286	7306
Hydro	9	9	7	9	9	9
Nuclear	..	..	..	..	..	..
Other	4819	4886	5077	5246	5490	6121
Combustible fuel input	Terajoules					
Hard Coal	130091	102110	71432	83315	60557	68310
Biogas	3697	4243	4280	4554	5171	5451
Gas-diesel oil	946	387	301	301	473	344
Fuel oil	2384	1495	1576	1495	1212	1050
Refinery gas	1337	1584	1485	1535	1337	1485
Natural gas	39517	23256	20326	24090	21735	21441
Fuelwood	*42200	*41155	*39833	*45796	*61149	*62635
Vegetal waste	0	0	0	0	0	0
Municipal waste	32301	33475	34362	34457	34723	33524
Other liquid biofuels	27	0	82	27	0	0
Others	47	47	47	47	..	..
Total input	252547	207752	173725	195617	186357	194240
Total production	83120	66582	51073	61186	55775	55836
Estimated efficiency (% of production to input)	33	32	29	31	30	29

Djibouti

Item	2013	2014	2015	2016	2017	2018
Production, trade and consumption	Million kilowatt-hours					
Total main activity and autoproducer	433	100	178	88	*59	*58
Combustible fuels	433	100	178	88	*59	*58
Hydro	..	..	..	..	..	..
Nuclear	..	..	..	..	..	..
Other	..	..	..	..	..	..
Main activity	433	100	178	88	*59	*58
Combustible fuels	433	100	178	88	*59	*58
Hydro	..	..	..	..	..	..
Nuclear	..	..	..	..	..	..
Other	..	..	..	..	..	..
Own use in electricity, CHP and heat plants	0	0	0	0	0	0
Net production	433	100	178	88	*59	*58
Imports	..	345	314	450	508	526
Exports	..	..	..	..	..	..
Losses	*86	*88	*98	*107	*113	*115
Consumption	*347	*357	*397	*423	*461	*469
Energy industries own use	..	..	..	..	..	..
By industry and construction	..	..	..	..	..	..
By transport	..	..	..	..	..	..
By households and other cons.	*347	*357	*397	*423	*461	*469
Net installed capacity	Thousand kilowatts					
Total main activity and autoproducer	130	130	130	130	130	*130
Combustible fuels	130	130	130	130	130	*130
Hydro	..	..	..	..	..	..
Nuclear	..	..	..	..	..	..
Other	..	..	..	..	..	..
Main activity	130	130	130	130	130	*130
Combustible fuels	130	130	130	130	130	*130
Hydro	..	..	..	..	..	..
Nuclear	..	..	..	..	..	..
Other	..	..	..	..	..	..
Combustible fuel input	Terajoules					
Gas-diesel oil	*1548	*1032	*1849	*903	*602	*645
Fuel oil	*2424	..	..	..	..	..
Total input	*3972	*1032	*1849	*903	*602	*645
Total production	1558	361	640	316	*211	*209
Estimated efficiency (% of production to input)	39	35	35	35	35	32

Dominica

Item	2013	2014	2015	2016	2017	2018
Production, trade and consumption	Million kilowatt-hours					
Total main activity and autoproducer	144	147	151	156	130	*110
Combustible fuels	107	117	127	120	103	*85
Hydro	37	31	24	36	27	24
Nuclear	..	..	..	..	..	..
Other	..	..	..	..	..	..
Main activity	101	102	107	112	86	65
Combustible fuels	64	72	83	75	58	41
Hydro	37	31	24	36	27	24
Nuclear	..	..	..	..	..	..
Other	..	..	..	..	..	..
Own use in electricity, CHP and heat plants	3	3	4	4	4	3
Net production	140	144	147	152	126	*106
Imports	..	..	..	..	..	..
Exports	..	..	..	..	..	..
Losses	8	8	8	9	5	6
Consumption	*132	*136	*139	*143	*121	*100
Energy industries own use	..	..	..	..	..	..
By industry and construction	*22	*22	*21	*22	*21	*22
By transport	..	..	..	..	..	..
By households and other cons.	*111	*114	*118	*121	*100	*79
Net installed capacity	Thousand kilowatts					
Total main activity and autoproducer	45	45	45	45	45	45
Combustible fuels	35	35	35	35	35	35
Hydro	10	10	10	10	10	10
Nuclear	..	..	..	..	..	..
Other	..	..	..	..	..	..
Main activity	27	27	27	27	27	27
Combustible fuels	20	20	20	20	20	20
Hydro	7	7	7	7	7	7
Nuclear	..	..	..	..	..	..
Other	..	..	..	..	..	..
Combustible fuel input	Terajoules					
Gas-diesel oil	*791	*824	*809	*831	*691	*464
Fuel oil	*481	*525	*570	*543	*489	*500
Total input	*1272	*1349	*1379	*1374	*1180	*964
Total production	385	420	456	430	369	*307
Estimated efficiency (% of production to input)	30	31	33	31	31	32

Dominican Republic

Item	2013	2014	2015	2016	2017	2018
Production, trade and consumption	Million kilowatt-hours					
Total main activity and autoproducer	17648	17167	17922	18690	19036	19651
Combustible fuels	15521	15634	16654	16773	16309	17144
Hydro	1875	1271	945	1519	2196	1780
Nuclear	..	..	..	..	..	..
Other	252	262	322	398	530	728
Main activity	15454	15164	15948	16728	17117	17640
Combustible fuels	13339	13654	14718	14869	14489	15288
Hydro	1872	1267	940	1513	2190	1773
Nuclear	..	..	..	..	..	..
Other	243	243	290	347	438	580
Own use in electricity, CHP and heat plants	546	665	673	687	665	693
Net production	17103	16502	17249	18003	18371	18958
Imports	..	..	..	..	..	..
Exports	..	..	..	..	..	..
Losses	2241	2181	2297	2412	2473	2549
Consumption	14862	14321	14952	15591	15887	16409
Energy industries own use	..	..	..	..	..	..
By industry and construction	5487	4518	5029	5294	5612	5789
By transport	46	52	54	54	51	57
By households and other cons.	9329	9750	9870	10244	10224	10563
Net installed capacity	Thousand kilowatts					
Total main activity and autoproducer	5352	5419	5230	5205	5134	5278
Combustible fuels	4646	4702	4503	4382	4276	4271
Hydro	614	617	617	617	617	617
Nuclear	..	..	..	..	..	..
Other	92	100	110	206	241	390
Main activity	3849	3877	3711	3809	3838	3970
Combustible fuels	3150	3175	3009	3028	3057	3082
Hydro	613	616	616	616	616	616
Nuclear	..	..	..	..	..	..
Other	86	86	86	165	165	272
Combustible fuel input	Terajoules					
Hard Coal	22250	25738	24415	25026	26458	25143
Biogas	*76	*98	*137	*157	*157	*157
Motor gasoline	687	647	656	660	647	638
Gas-diesel oil	16009	17311	20160	19774	13077	15240
Fuel oil	49276	55667	64644	67117	55756	69764
Natural gas	36481	35750	36429	34241	40211	39774
Bagasse	657	657	657	755	1958	2640
Vegetal waste	129	128	129	134	142	151
Total input	125565	135996	147226	147863	138406	153507
Total production	55876	56283	59956	60384	58714	61717
Estimated efficiency (% of production to input)	44	41	41	41	42	40

Ecuador

Item	2013	2014	2015	2016	2017	2018
Production, trade and consumption	Million kilowatt-hours					
Total main activity and autoproducer	23260	24307	25950	27314	28033	29198
Combustible fuels	12161	12753	12719	11357	7833	8402
Hydro	11039	11458	13096	15834	20089	20678
Nuclear	..	..	..	..	..	..
Other	60	96	135	123	111	118
Main activity	19369	20476	21756	22543	22891	23613
Combustible fuels	8783	9445	9223	7316	3772	4191
Hydro	10525	10935	12399	15104	19008	19304
Nuclear	..	..	..	..	..	..
Other	60	96	135	123	111	118
Own use in electricity, CHP and heat plants	417	528	522	456	383	369
Net production	22843	23779	25428	26858	27650	28829
Imports	662	837	512	82	19	..
Exports	29	47	46	402	212	..
Losses	3057	3165	3344	3499	3516	3790
Consumption	20090	21403	22549	23038	23972	24908
Energy industries own use	..	..	..	..	..	..
By industry and construction	8031	8419	8580	8919	9469	10559
By transport	10	10	10	10	10	11
By households and other cons.	12049	12974	13960	14109	14493	14339
Net installed capacity	Thousand kilowatts					
Total main activity and autoproducer	5897	6165	6545	8697	8385	9028
Combustible fuels	3562	3801	3969	4105	3702	3764
Hydro	2312	2316	2529	4545	4636	5216
Nuclear	..	..	..	..	..	..
Other	23	48	47	47	47	48
Main activity	5103	5299	5557	7607	7435	8048
Combustible fuels	2843	3011	3109	3142	2902	2964
Hydro	2237	2241	2402	4418	4486	5036
Nuclear	..	..	..	..	..	..
Other	23	48	47	47	47	48
Combustible fuel input	Terajoules					
Biogas	216	342	479	282	567	925
Crude oil	10476	10680	10408	13559	14061	15659
Motor gasoline	334	0	..	..	..	..
Gas-diesel oil	24503	25709	29423	25669	14995	15622
Fuel oil	48964	52566	47857	35453	19477	28707
Liquefied petroleum gas	543	587	676	770	657	763
Other oil products	4578	5165	8377	7067	4056	3970
Natural gas	25451	26224	25306	25757	23151	19889
Bagasse	2308	3185	3481	3797	4466	3951
Total input	117373	124459	126007	112354	81430	89486
Total production	43780	45911	45789	40886	28198	30246
Estimated efficiency (% of production to input)	37	37	36	36	35	34

Statistics on electricity

Egypt

Item	2013	2014	2015	2016	2017	2018
Production, trade and consumption			Million kilowatt-hours			
Total main activity and autoproducer	168050	173552	180377	191920	195150	202838
Combustible fuels	153252	158039	165347	176234	179520	187341
Hydro	13352	13822	13432	13460	12850	12726
Nuclear	..	..	..	..	..	..
Other	1446	1691	1598	2226	2780	2771
Main activity	162548	168050	174875	186320	189550	196760
Combustible fuels	147750	152537	159845	170634	173920	181263
Hydro	13352	13822	13432	13460	12850	12726
Nuclear	..	..	..	..	..	..
Other	1446	1691	1598	2226	2780	2771
Own use in electricity, CHP and heat plants	5502	4582	4738	4068	17903	12156
Net production	162548	168970	175639	187852	177247	190682
Imports	61	51	43	54	65	81
Exports	460	730	1158	747	333	425
Losses	24224	20724	20389	23037	*25373	22056
Consumption	137591	146645	154205	162275	151606	165610
Energy industries own use	..	..	..	..	..	..
By industry and construction	37320	38242	39187	40316	41479	43623
By transport	441	515	601	582	534	321
By households and other cons.	99830	107888	114417	121377	109593	121666
Net installed capacity			Thousand kilowatts			
Total main activity and autoproducer	32702	32702	35907	39544	45695	55413
Combustible fuels	29215	29215	32420	35857	42008	51424
Hydro	2800	2800	2800	2800	2800	2832
Nuclear	..	..	..	..	..	..
Other	687	687	687	887	887	1157
Main activity	32015	32015	35220	38857	45008	54526
Combustible fuels	28528	28528	31733	35170	41321	50537
Hydro	2800	2800	2800	2800	2800	2832
Nuclear	..	..	..	..	..	..
Other	687	687	687	887	887	1157
Combustible fuel input			Terajoules			
Gas-diesel oil	*4257	19479	50654	23779	24024	8729
Fuel oil	315686	348612	361903	294152	243208	228826
Natural gas	1009816	1023897	1067300	1182860	1312666	1303341
Bagasse	*5691	*5776	*5722	*5668	*5668	*5730
Total input	1335450	1397764	1485579	1506459	1585567	1546625
Total production	551707	568940	595249	634442	646272	674428
Estimated efficiency (% of production to input)	41	41	40	42	41	44

El Salvador

Item	2013	2014	2015	2016	2017	2018
Production, trade and consumption	Million kilowatt-hours					
Total main activity and autoproducer	6272	6263	6065	6083	5615	5402
Combustible fuels	2922	2913	3095	3139	2077	1937
Hydro	1790	1793	1423	1344	1704	1631
Nuclear	..	..	..	..	..	..
Other	1560	1558	1547	1600	1834	1835
Main activity	5616	5784	5425	5342	4682	4422
Combustible fuels	2266	2508	2532	2505	1399	1200
Hydro	1790	1718	1353	1261	1619	1548
Nuclear	..	..	..	..	..	..
Other	1560	1558	1540	1576	1664	1675
Own use in electricity, CHP and heat plants	363	144	233	238	356	164
Net production	5909	6119	5832	5846	5259	5238
Imports	283	589	963	1066	1675	1824
Exports	91	208	64	77	90	65
Losses	455	*504	*708	*695	*651	*719
Consumption	5647	5950	5999	6073	6153	6221
Energy industries own use	..	..	..	..	..	..
By industry and construction	2197	2104	2005	2020	2057	2147
By transport	..	..	..	..	..	..
By households and other cons.	3450	3846	3994	4053	4096	4074
Net installed capacity	Thousand kilowatts					
Total main activity and autoproducer	1585	*1587	*1671	*1727	*1923	*2009
Combustible fuels	892	*893	*959	*1016	*1034	*1063
Hydro	488	490	497	495	575	575
Nuclear	..	..	..	..	..	..
Other	204	204	215	216	314	371
Main activity	1455	*1447	*1453	*1459	1607	1604
Combustible fuels	763	*770	*776	*782	*790	*787
Hydro	488	473	473	473	553	553
Nuclear	..	..	..	..	..	..
Other	204	204	204	204	264	264
Combustible fuel input	Terajoules					
Biogas	526	412	589	531	510	495
Gas-diesel oil	86	..	..	..	..	43
Fuel oil	21008	21372	21331	20685	11554	10019
Bagasse	7495	7637	9876	11424	14073	14053
Total input	29115	29421	31796	32640	26137	24610
Total production	10519	10487	11142	11299	7476	6972
Estimated efficiency (% of production to input)	36	36	35	35	29	28

Equatorial Guinea

Item	2013	2014	2015	2016	2017	2018
Production, trade and consumption			Million kilowatt-hours			
Total main activity and autoproducer	726	833	848	*850	*850	*736
Combustible fuels	599	633	648	*650	*650	*536
Hydro	127	*200	*200	*200	*200	*200
Nuclear	..	..	..	..	..	..
Other	..	..	..	..	..	..
Main activity	726	833	848	*850	*850	*736
Combustible fuels	599	633	648	*650	*650	*536
Hydro	127	*200	*200	*200	*200	*200
Nuclear	..	..	..	..	..	..
Other	..	..	..	..	..	..
Own use in electricity, CHP and heat plants	0	0	0	0	0	0
Net production	726	833	848	*850	*850	*736
Imports	..	..	..	..	..	..
Exports	..	..	..	..	..	..
Losses	*73	*90	*95	*96	*96	*75
Consumption	*653	*743	*753	*754	*754	*661
Energy industries own use	*35	*35	*35	*35	*35	*35
By industry and construction	*150	*190	*210	*231	*231	*201
By transport	..	..	..	..	..	..
By households and other cons.	*468	*518	*508	*488	*488	*425
Net installed capacity			Thousand kilowatts			
Total main activity and autoproducer	349	349	349	349	554	*554
Combustible fuels	222	222	222	222	222	*222
Hydro	127	127	127	127	327	*327
Nuclear	..	..	..	..	..	..
Other	..	..	..	..	5	*5
Main activity	349	349	349	349	554	*554
Combustible fuels	222	222	222	222	222	*222
Hydro	127	127	127	127	327	*327
Nuclear	..	..	..	..	..	..
Other	..	..	..	..	5	*5
Combustible fuel input			Terajoules			
Gas-diesel oil	*86	*86	*86	*86	*86	*86
Natural gas	*5500	*5700	*5900	*5900	*6000	*6000
Total input	*5586	*5786	*5986	*5986	*6086	*6086
Total production	2155	2279	2334	*2340	*2340	*1930
Estimated efficiency (% of production to input)	39	39	39	39	38	32

Statistics on electricity

Eritrea

Item	2013	2014	2015	2016	2017	2018
Production, trade and consumption			**Million kilowatt-hours**			
Total main activity and autoproducer	342	349	356	363	391	495
Combustible fuels	338	345	352	359	378	450
Hydro	..	..	..	..	..	..
Nuclear	..	..	..	..	..	..
Other	4	4	4	4	13	45
Main activity	331	338	345	352	377	481
Combustible fuels	327	334	341	348	364	436
Hydro	..	..	..	..	..	..
Nuclear	..	..	..	..	..	..
Other	4	4	4	4	13	45
Own use in electricity, CHP and heat plants	17	17	17	17	18	22
Net production	325	332	339	346	373	473
Imports	..	..	..	..	..	..
Exports	..	..	..	..	..	..
Losses	42	43	44	45	48	61
Consumption	292	298	303	308	318	404
Energy industries own use	..	..	..	..	..	..
By industry and construction	78	80	82	84	88	112
By transport	..	..	..	..	..	..
By households and other cons.	214	218	221	224	230	292
Net installed capacity			**Thousand kilowatts**			
Total main activity and autoproducer	*141	*141	*161	*161	*216	*226
Combustible fuels	*139	*139	*159	*159	*205	*205
Hydro	..	..	..	..	..	..
Nuclear	..	..	..	..	..	..
Other	2	2	2	2	*11	*21
Main activity	*135	*135	*151	*151	*206	*216
Combustible fuels	*133	*133	*149	*149	*195	*195
Hydro	..	..	..	..	..	..
Nuclear	..	..	..	..	..	..
Other	2	2	2	2	*11	*21
Combustible fuel input			**Terajoules**			
Gas-diesel oil	1462	1505	1548	1591	2021	2064
Fuel oil	2384	2424	2464	2505	2343	3070
Total input	3846	3929	4012	4096	4364	5134
Total production	1217	1242	1267	1292	1361	1620
Estimated efficiency (% of production to input)	32	32	32	32	31	32

Estonia

Item	2013	2014	2015	2016	2017	2018
Production, trade and consumption	Million kilowatt-hours					
Total main activity and autoproducer	13275	12446	10398	12186	12918	12360
Combustible fuels	12720	11815	9656	11547	12155	11678
Hydro	26	27	27	35	26	15
Nuclear	..	..	..	..	..	..
Other	529	604	715	604	737	667
Main activity	13184	12389	10241	11947	12798	12241
Combustible fuels	12634	11773	9513	11321	12035	11560
Hydro	26	26	27	35	26	15
Nuclear	..	..	..	..	..	..
Other	524	590	701	591	737	666
Own use in electricity, CHP and heat plants	1452	1433	1336	1752	1670	1427
Net production	11823	11013	9062	10434	11248	10933
Imports	2712	3730	5452	3577	2281	3053
Exports	6300	6484	6377	5614	5015	4950
Losses	903	842	697	723	779	744
Consumption	7332	7417	7440	7824	7735	7985
Energy industries own use	512	511	588	525	503	494
By industry and construction	2156	2117	2059	2152	2281	2360
By transport	63	50	47	48	46	43
By households and other cons.	4601	4739	4746	5099	4905	5088
Net installed capacity	Thousand kilowatts					
Total main activity and autoproducer	2910	3030	2857	2577	2542	2819
Combustible fuels	2654	2750	2551	2251	2208	2470
Hydro	8	5	6	6	7	7
Nuclear	..	..	..	..	..	..
Other	248	275	300	320	327	342
Main activity	2892	3006	2826	2546	2515	2793
Combustible fuels	2637	2733	2526	2226	2183	2445
Hydro	8	5	6	6	7	7
Nuclear	..	..	..	..	..	..
Other	247	268	294	314	325	341
Combustible fuel input	Terajoules					
Peat	920	690	759	1090	1109	504
Biogas	200	191	367	233	214	242
Oil shale	137372	129157	108702	105702	107364	114688
Fuel oil	929	485	687	1656	768	566
Natural gas	779	564	526	575	527	615
Gasworks gas	3899	5228	6317	5250	6615	1416
Coke-oven gas	..	..	..	..	..	8301
Fuelwood	*9108	*9940	*10240	*11282	*12219	*17578
Municipal waste	1336	1455	1760	1945	2218	1970
Industrial waste	..	..	..	..	..	259
Others	54	54	0	..	88	..
Total input	154597	147764	129358	127734	131121	146139
Total production	45792	42534	34762	41569	43758	42041
Estimated efficiency (% of production to input)	30	29	27	33	33	29

Statistics on electricity

Eswatini

Item	2013	2014	2015	2016	2017	2018
Production, trade and consumption	Million kilowatt-hours					
Total main activity and autoproducer	*590	567	*496	388	414	519
Combustible fuels	*350	265	*265	265	297	311
Hydro	240	302	231	123	117	208
Nuclear	..	..	..	..	..	..
Other	..	..	..	..	0	0
Main activity	248	302	231	123	117	208
Combustible fuels	*8	0	0	0	..	..
Hydro	240	302	231	123	117	208
Nuclear	..	..	..	..	..	..
Other	..	..	..	..	..	..
Own use in electricity, CHP and heat plants	15	0	*10	31	0	0
Net production	*575	567	*486	357	414	519
Imports	822	860	980	1077	1048	1020
Exports	..	..	..	..	..	..
Losses	169	171	181	172	169	195
Consumption	1227	1256	1296	1262	1387	1323
Energy industries own use	..	..	..	..	..	..
By industry and construction	319	336	366	364	541	433
By transport	..	..	..	..	..	..
By households and other cons.	909	920	930	899	846	890
Net installed capacity	Thousand kilowatts					
Total main activity and autoproducer	*179	*188	*188	*188	*188	192
Combustible fuels	*115	*115	*115	*115	*115	119
Hydro	64	73	*73	73	*73	*73
Nuclear	..	..	..	..	..	..
Other	..	..	..	..	0	0
Main activity	70	79	*79	79	*79	*79
Combustible fuels	10	10	10	10	*10	*10
Hydro	60	69	*69	69	*69	*69
Nuclear	..	..	..	..	..	..
Other	..	..	..	..	..	..
Combustible fuel input	Terajoules					
Hard Coal	0	0	155	258	181	108
Gas-diesel oil	*473	0	0	..	..	..
Fuelwood	0	0	0	0	..	..
Bagasse	*13606	*13637	*13830	*11776	2400	2439
Black liquor	0	..	..	..	..	..
Total input	*14079	*13637	*13985	*12034	2581	2547
Total production	*1260	954	*954	954	1069	1120
Estimated efficiency (% of production to input)	9	7	7	8	41	44

Ethiopia

Item	2013	2014	2015	2016	2017	2018
Production, trade and consumption	Million kilowatt-hours					
Total main activity and autoproducer	8744	9569	10493	12596	13276	13612
Combustible fuels	44	41	42	40	40	41
Hydro	8338	9013	9674	11753	12681	13018
Nuclear	..	..	..	..	..	..
Other	362	515	777	803	555	553
Main activity	8708	9531	10455	12560	13240	13576
Combustible fuels	8	3	4	4	4	5
Hydro	8338	9013	9674	11753	12681	13018
Nuclear	..	..	..	..	..	..
Other	362	515	777	803	555	553
Own use in electricity, CHP and heat plants	41	48	76	86	56	59
Net production	8703	9521	10417	12510	13220	13553
Imports	..	..	..	..	..	..
Exports	642	761	700	1303	1432	1470
Losses	1655	2149	2085	2597	2945	3019
Consumption	6087	6660	7470	8586	8854	9090
Energy industries own use	..	..	..	..	..	..
By industry and construction	2032	2556	2278	2141	2344	2407
By transport	..	..	..	..	..	..
By households and other cons.	4055	4104	5192	6445	6510	6683
Net installed capacity	Thousand kilowatts					
Total main activity and autoproducer	2314	2320	2424	4252	4261	4260
Combustible fuels	190	190	143	99	104	104
Hydro	1943	1943	1940	3808	3814	3814
Nuclear	..	..	..	..	..	..
Other	181	187	341	345	343	342
Main activity	2314	2320	2424	4252	4261	4260
Combustible fuels	190	190	143	99	104	104
Hydro	1943	1943	1940	3808	3814	3814
Nuclear	..	..	..	..	..	..
Other	181	187	341	345	343	342
Combustible fuel input	Terajoules					
Gas-diesel oil	129	43	43	43	43	43
Naphtha	..	45	..	..	..	..
Bagasse	*649	*556	*541	*502	*502	*502
Total input	*778	*643	*584	*545	*545	*545
Total production	158	148	151	144	144	148
Estimated efficiency (% of production to input)	20	23	26	26	26	27

Faeroe Islands

Item	2013	2014	2015	2016	2017	2018
Production, trade and consumption			**Million kilowatt-hours**			
Total main activity and autoproducer	293	305	314	317	334	352
Combustible fuels	180	150	126	159	163	180
Hydro	91	121	133	106	111	108
Nuclear	..	..	..	..	..	..
Other	22	34	56	52	60	64
Main activity	293	305	314	317	334	352
Combustible fuels	180	150	126	159	163	180
Hydro	91	121	133	106	111	108
Nuclear	..	..	..	..	..	..
Other	22	34	56	52	60	64
Own use in electricity, CHP and heat plants	8	7	7	7	10	11
Net production	285	298	308	310	325	341
Imports	..	..	..	..	..	..
Exports	..	..	..	..	..	..
Losses	*10	*15	*20	*19	*18	*20
Consumption	275	284	288	291	306	321
Energy industries own use	..	..	..	..	..	..
By industry and construction	60	76	76	74	86	82
By transport	..	..	..	..	..	..
By households and other cons.	214	208	212	218	221	238
Net installed capacity			**Thousand kilowatts**			
Total main activity and autoproducer	*115	*124	*128	*129	125	125
Combustible fuels	*65	*68	*69	*70	69	69
Hydro	*39	*39	39	*39	40	40
Nuclear	..	..	..	..	..	..
Other	*11	*16	20	*20	16	16
Main activity	*115	*124	*128	*129	125	125
Combustible fuels	*65	*68	*69	*70	69	69
Hydro	*39	*39	39	*39	40	40
Nuclear	..	..	..	..	..	..
Other	*11	*16	20	*20	16	16
Combustible fuel input			**Terajoules**			
Gas-diesel oil	44	50	56	80	46	64
Fuel oil	1506	1248	1040	1301	1318	1453
Total input	1549	1298	1096	1381	1364	1517
Total production	648	541	452	572	588	648
Estimated efficiency (% of production to input)	42	42	41	41	43	43

Falkland Is. (Malvinas)

Item	2013	2014	2015	2016	2017	2018
Production, trade and consumption	**Million kilowatt-hours**					
Total main activity and autoproducer	18	18	19	21	20	19
Combustible fuels	13	13	14	15	14	14
Hydro	..	..	..	..	..	..
Nuclear	..	..	..	..	..	..
Other	5	5	5	6	5	5
Main activity	16	16	17	19	18	17
Combustible fuels	11	11	12	13	12	12
Hydro	..	..	..	..	..	..
Nuclear	..	..	..	..	..	..
Other	5	5	5	6	5	5
Own use in electricity, CHP and heat plants	0	*1	*1	*3	*2	*2
Net production	18	18	18	18	18	18
Imports	..	..	..	..	..	..
Exports	..	..	..	..	..	..
Losses	..	..	..	..	..	..
Consumption	*18	*18	*18	*18	*18	*18
Energy industries own use	..	..	..	..	..	..
By industry and construction	*7	*7	*7	*7	*7	*7
By transport	..	..	..	..	..	..
By households and other cons.	*10	*10	*10	*10	*10	*10
Net installed capacity	**Thousand kilowatts**					
Total main activity and autoproducer	11	11	11	11	11	11
Combustible fuels	9	9	9	9	9	9
Hydro	..	..	..	..	..	..
Nuclear	..	..	..	..	..	..
Other	2	2	2	2	2	2
Main activity	9	9	9	9	9	9
Combustible fuels	7	7	7	7	7	7
Hydro	..	..	..	..	..	..
Nuclear	..	..	..	..	..	..
Other	2	2	2	2	2	2
Combustible fuel input	**Terajoules**					
Gas-diesel oil	110	111	125	118	114	122
Total input	110	111	125	118	114	122
Total production	47	47	49	53	52	50
Estimated efficiency (% of production to input)	42	42	39	45	45	41

Fiji

Item	2013	2014	2015	2016	2017	2018
Production, trade and consumption	**Million kilowatt-hours**					
Total main activity and autoproducer	859	862	919	941	1017	1042
Combustible fuels	325	454	503	435	514	464
Hydro	527	401	406	495	491	567
Nuclear	..	..	..	..	..	..
Other	7	7	10	11	11	12
Main activity	812	812	896	931	994	1003
Combustible fuels	278	404	480	425	491	424
Hydro	527	401	406	495	491	567
Nuclear	..	..	..	..	..	..
Other	7	7	10	11	11	12
Own use in electricity, CHP and heat plants	11	26	12	18	33	49
Net production	848	836	906	924	984	993
Imports	..	..	..	..	..	..
Exports	..	..	..	..	..	..
Losses	*68	*54	75	*77	*82	*86
Consumption	780	783	826	842	902	*907
Energy industries own use	..	..	..	..	..	..
By industry and construction	202	200	206	211	222	*222
By transport	..	..	..	..	..	..
By households and other cons.	578	583	620	631	681	*685
Net installed capacity	**Thousand kilowatts**					
Total main activity and autoproducer	302	303	304	*328	*360	*363
Combustible fuels	156	156	156	*172	*194	*194
Hydro	135	135	135	130	138	138
Nuclear	..	..	..	..	..	..
Other	12	12	14	26	*28	*31
Main activity	261	261	263	286	*306	*309
Combustible fuels	114	114	114	*130	*140	*140
Hydro	135	135	135	130	138	138
Nuclear	..	..	..	..	..	..
Other	12	12	14	26	*28	*31
Combustible fuel input	**Terajoules**					
Hard coal briquettes	0	0	0	0	0	0
Gas-diesel oil	1291	2560	2602	1262	*1826	*1720
Fuel oil	1616	1535	1758	2511	*2424	*2222
Total input	2907	4095	4360	3773	*4251	*3942
Total production	1169	1634	1810	1566	1852	1669
Estimated efficiency (% of production to input)	40	40	42	42	44	42

Finland

Item	2013	2014	2015	2016	2017	2018
Production, trade and consumption	Million kilowatt-hours					
Total main activity and autoproducer	71257	68094	68599	68757	67523	70263
Combustible fuels	33744	29712	25999	26399	25030	27959
Hydro	12838	13397	16769	15799	14772	13301
Nuclear	23606	23580	23245	23203	22477	22793
Other	1069	1405	2586	3356	5244	6210
Main activity	61135	58000	58575	59239	57690	59552
Combustible fuels	24784	20735	17226	18122	16459	18484
Hydro	11859	12470	15690	14764	13769	12357
Nuclear	23606	23580	23245	23203	22477	22793
Other	886	1215	2414	3150	4985	5918
Own use in electricity, CHP and heat plants	2904	2636	2444	2554	2480	2730
Net production	68353	65458	66155	66203	65043	67533
Imports	17591	21622	21459	22110	22204	22548
Exports	1876	3655	5122	3159	1779	2612
Losses	2602	2766	2435	2586	2768	3024
Consumption	81292	80435	79686	82180	82275	84021
Energy industries own use	1331	1284	1189	1227	1236	1252
By industry and construction	38705	38173	37893	38503	38709	39487
By transport	734	724	706	708	775	843
By households and other cons.	40522	40254	39898	41742	41555	42439
Net installed capacity	Thousand kilowatts					
Total main activity and autoproducer	16655	16247	16616	16289	17174	17154
Combustible fuels	10223	9609	9593	8672	8997	8902
Hydro	3224	3248	3249	3249	3272	3287
Nuclear	2752	2752	2752	2764	2779	2784
Other	456	638	1022	1604	2126	2181
Main activity	14586	14176	14564	14221	14868	14790
Combustible fuels	8349	7735	7743	6826	6958	6864
Hydro	3038	3062	3063	3063	3084	3098
Nuclear	2752	2752	2752	2764	2779	2784
Other	447	627	1006	1568	2047	2044
Combustible fuel input	Terajoules					
Hard Coal	110621	83563	59016	78495	68510	66280
Peat	43441	43898	40652	38934	37002	43281
Biogas	2387	2800	3000	3361	3500	3600
Fuel oil	2707	2707	2949	1576	3757	1252
Natural gas	59170	46749	42836	33907	31361	38536
Blast furnace gas	4597	5597	5302	5234	5407	5989
Fuelwood	*97627	*93962	*90537	*94823	*95514	*97021
Municipal waste	12215	13568	14985	16759	18058	19776
Industrial waste	1071	1083	893	840	1033	986
Black liquor	*20040	*13943	*11248	*7397	*7854	*9808
Others	2609	2500	2306	1796	2733	2829
Total input	356485	310371	273724	283122	274729	289358
Total production	121478	106963	93596	95036	90108	100652
Estimated efficiency (% of production to input)	34	34	34	34	33	35

France

Item	2013	2014	2015	2016	2017	2018
Production, trade and consumption	Million kilowatt-hours					
Total main activity and autoproducer	582170	572522	579542	564181	561935	581943
Combustible fuels	58779	41480	51131	64098	72871	57967
Hydro	77073	69571	60514	65685	55135	70590
Nuclear	423685	436479	437428	403195	398359	412942
Other	22633	24992	30469	31203	35570	40444
Main activity	564536	554569	560560	545647	542524	561848
Combustible fuels	46012	28761	37726	51290	59798	44752
Hydro	76413	68904	59977	65091	54608	69983
Nuclear	423685	436479	437428	403195	398359	412942
Other	18426	20425	25429	26071	29759	34171
Own use in electricity, CHP and heat plants	24399	24016	24415	23840	23842	23856
Net production	557771	548506	555127	540341	538093	558087
Imports	11687	7873	9961	19903	21119	13562
Exports	60148	75063	74024	61404	61248	76534
Losses	38785	34527	36140	37478	38599	38604
Consumption	468667	443780	452088	460234	456914	455142
Energy industries own use	14199	15130	13895	14255	14212	14856
By industry and construction	125544	123928	122763	124718	123818	123837
By transport	11124	10828	10988	10801	10863	10360
By households and other cons.	317800	293894	304442	310460	308021	306089
Net installed capacity	Thousand kilowatts					
Total main activity and autoproducer	130053	130098	132219	133150	133089	133457
Combustible fuels	27608	25918	25867	24895	21907	19783
Hydro	25646	25577	25552	25620	25707	25793
Nuclear	63130	63130	63130	63130	63130	63130
Other	13669	15473	17670	19505	22345	24751
Main activity	122688	122456	124301	124816	124406	124247
Combustible fuels	23722	22180	22162	21065	18204	16063
Hydro	25458	25398	25368	25435	25518	25609
Nuclear	63130	63130	63130	63130	63130	63130
Other	10378	11748	13641	15186	17554	19445
Combustible fuel input	Terajoules					
Hard Coal	246221	123069	122996	109194	133727	88801
Biogas	20711	21083	23493	24205	24563	25881
Gas-diesel oil	14835	16813	18017	18748	19135	17200
Fuel oil	32199	35229	35390	36481	36683	29856
Refinery gas	13662	9999	8415	10148	10346	11880
Natural gas	161579	117532	178404	270476	308539	239987
Blast furnace gas	19034	24117	22150	16741	17911	25733
Fuelwood	*28434	*30179	*32571	*43201	*42650	*45397
Municipal waste	77784	81572	80370	84430	86648	89576
Black liquor	*7045	*15434	*19734	*19343	*19467	*18136
Others	28601	20298	19952	17727	17357	6697
Total input	650104	495324	561492	650693	717026	599143
Total production	211604	149328	184072	230753	262336	208681
Estimated efficiency (% of production to input)	33	30	33	35	37	35

French Polynesia

Item	2013	2014	2015	2016	2017	2018
Production, trade and consumption			**Million kilowatt-hours**			
Total main activity and autoproducer	681	675	697	700	698	696
Combustible fuels	511	483	499	484	487	494
Hydro	152	165	166	183	175	164
Nuclear	..	..	..	..	..	..
Other	18	27	32	33	36	37
Main activity	681	675	697	700	698	696
Combustible fuels	511	483	499	484	487	494
Hydro	152	165	166	183	175	164
Nuclear	..	..	..	..	..	..
Other	18	27	32	33	36	37
Own use in electricity, CHP and heat plants	19	10	29	13	13	10
Net production	662	665	668	687	685	686
Imports	..	..	..	..	..	..
Exports	..	..	..	..	..	..
Losses	74	70	68	64	64	67
Consumption	*589	*595	*600	*623	*621	*608
Energy industries own use	..	..	..	..	..	..
By industry and construction	..	..	..	..	..	..
By transport	..	..	..	..	..	..
By households and other cons.	*589	*595	*600	*623	*621	*608
Net installed capacity			**Thousand kilowatts**			
Total main activity and autoproducer	*241	*248	*252	*263	*267	*268
Combustible fuels	*177	*177	*177	*185	*185	*186
Hydro	47	47	47	47	47	47
Nuclear	..	..	..	..	..	..
Other	17	25	28	32	35	35
Main activity	*241	*248	*252	*263	*267	*268
Combustible fuels	*177	*177	*177	*185	*185	*186
Hydro	47	47	47	47	47	47
Nuclear	..	..	..	..	..	..
Other	17	25	28	32	35	35
Combustible fuel input			**Terajoules**			
Gas-diesel oil	2110	2293	2319	1401	1750	1830
Fuel oil	3027	2779	2776	2715	2638	2714
Total input	5137	5073	5095	4116	4388	4544
Total production	1840	1739	1797	1743	1754	1780
Estimated efficiency (% of production to input)	36	34	35	42	40	39

Gabon

Item	2013	2014	2015	2016	2017	2018
Production, trade and consumption	**Million kilowatt-hours**					
Total main activity and autoproducer	2101	1998	2127	2338	2277	2614
Combustible fuels	1163	1202	1207	1383	1346	1555
Hydro	936	794	918	953	929	1057
Nuclear	..	..	..	..	..	..
Other	2	2	2	2	2	*2
Main activity	1891	1784	1907	2112	2039	2443
Combustible fuels	955	990	989	1159	1115	1392
Hydro	936	794	918	953	924	1052
Nuclear	..	..	..	..	..	..
Other	..	..	..	..	..	..
Own use in electricity, CHP and heat plants	74	99	95	102	102	27
Net production	2027	1899	2032	2236	2175	2587
Imports	184	388	337	344	346	349
Exports	..	..	..	..	..	..
Losses	454	452	476	518	321	288
Consumption	1757	1835	1893	2062	2199	2518
Energy industries own use	38	40	41	45	44	44
By industry and construction	466	487	502	547	648	652
By transport	7	7	7	8	8	8
By households and other cons.	1246	1301	1343	1462	1499	1814
Net installed capacity	**Thousand kilowatts**					
Total main activity and autoproducer	514	509	511	523	533	751
Combustible fuels	343	338	340	352	359	418
Hydro	170	170	170	170	173	332
Nuclear	..	..	..	..	..	..
Other	*1	*1	*1	*1	*1	*1
Main activity	443	438	440	452	460	663
Combustible fuels	273	268	270	282	289	333
Hydro	170	170	170	170	171	330
Nuclear	..	..	..	..	..	..
Other	..	..	..	..	..	..
Combustible fuel input	**Terajoules**					
Gas-diesel oil	3053	2580	2709	2666	2881	2881
Fuel oil	40	81	..	..	..	..
Natural gas	10970	12146	13264	15030	15253	15381
Fuelwood	*299	*301	*320	332	334	*336
Total input	14362	15108	16293	18028	18468	18598
Total production	4187	4327	4345	4979	4846	5599
Estimated efficiency (% of production to input)	29	29	27	28	26	30

Statistics on electricity

Gambia

Item	2013	2014	2015	2016	2017	2018
Production, trade and consumption			Million kilowatt-hours			
Total main activity and autoproducer	255	258	286	302	317	*321
Combustible fuels	251	254	283	299	314	*318
Hydro	..	..	..	..	..	..
Nuclear	..	..	..	..	..	..
Other	*3	*4	*4	*4	*4	*4
Main activity	220	222	250	265	280	*284
Combustible fuels	217	219	246	262	277	*280
Hydro	..	..	..	..	..	..
Nuclear	..	..	..	..	..	..
Other	*3	*4	*4	*4	*4	*4
Own use in electricity, CHP and heat plants	*12	*11	*11	*11	*12	*13
Net production	243	247	275	291	305	*309
Imports	..	..	..	..	..	..
Exports	..	..	..	..	..	..
Losses	*52	*52	*55	*58	*68	*69
Consumption	*191	*195	*220	*233	*237	*239
Energy industries own use	..	..	..	..	..	..
By industry and construction	*35	*35	*37	*39	*40	*41
By transport	..	..	..	..	..	..
By households and other cons.	*156	*160	*183	*193	*197	*199
Net installed capacity			Thousand kilowatts			
Total main activity and autoproducer	*95	117	*120	*121	*121	*126
Combustible fuels	*91	114	*116	*117	*118	*123
Hydro	..	..	..	..	..	..
Nuclear	..	..	..	..	..	..
Other	3	3	3	3	3	*3
Main activity	*61	83	*85	*86	*86	*90
Combustible fuels	*57	80	*81	*82	*82	*87
Hydro	..	..	..	..	..	..
Nuclear	..	..	..	..	..	..
Other	3	3	3	3	3	*3
Combustible fuel input			Terajoules			
Gas-diesel oil	*2137	*2146	*2417	*2507	*2593	*2627
Fuel oil	*929	*889	*889	*889	*929	*941
Total input	*3066	*3035	*3305	*3396	*3522	*3569
Total production	905	915	1018	1075	1129	*1144
Estimated efficiency (% of production to input)	30	30	31	32	32	32

Georgia

Item	2013	2014	2015	2016	2017	2018
Production, trade and consumption	**Million kilowatt-hours**					
Total main activity and autoproducer	10059	10371	10833	11574	11531	12149
Combustible fuels	1788	2036	2379	2236	2233	2115
Hydro	8271	8335	8454	9329	9210	9949
Nuclear	..	..	..	..	..	..
Other	..	..	..	9	88	84
Main activity	10059	10371	10833	11574	11531	12149
Combustible fuels	1788	2036	2379	2236	2233	2115
Hydro	8271	8335	8454	9329	9210	9949
Nuclear	..	..	..	..	..	..
Other	..	..	..	9	88	84
Own use in electricity, CHP and heat plants	199	217	240	209	215	215
Net production	9860	10154	10592	11365	11316	11934
Imports	484	853	699	1329	1751	1522
Exports	450	604	660	1409	940	602
Losses	805	600	711	784	904	886
Consumption	9089	9801	9921	10501	11224	11950
Energy industries own use	15	17	14	14	15	13
By industry and construction	2327	2816	2752	2902	3295	3306
By transport	282	267	294	301	337	366
By households and other cons.	6465	6701	6861	7284	7578	8266
Net installed capacity	**Thousand kilowatts**					
Total main activity and autoproducer	3471	2995	2993	3299	3592	3591
Combustible fuels	680	615	615	849	849	876
Hydro	2791	2380	2378	2430	2723	2695
Nuclear	..	..	..	..	..	..
Other	..	..	..	20	20	20
Main activity	3471	2995	2993	3299	3592	3591
Combustible fuels	680	615	615	849	849	876
Hydro	2791	2380	2378	2430	2723	2695
Nuclear	..	..	..	..	..	..
Other	..	..	..	20	20	20
Combustible fuel input	**Terajoules**					
Brown Coal	..	..	..	451	634	359
Gas-diesel oil	0	0	0	0	..	..
Natural gas	18869	21963	24976	20080	20408	19304
Total input	18869	21963	24976	20530	21042	19662
Total production	6437	7330	8563	8048	8039	7614
Estimated efficiency (% of production to input)	34	33	34	39	38	39

Germany

Item	2013	2014	2015	2016	2017	2018
Production, trade and consumption			**Million kilowatt-hours**			
Total main activity and autoproducer	638701	627806	648310	650450	653723	643159
Combustible fuels	427037	408559	410318	419596	404286	385531
Hydro	28782	25444	24898	26135	26155	24143
Nuclear	97290	97129	91786	84634	76324	76005
Other	85592	96674	121308	120085	146958	157480
Main activity	593810	582357	598096	595587	596946	588202
Combustible fuels	383572	364685	361485	366199	348797	331746
Hydro	28600	25282	24741	25959	25983	24056
Nuclear	97290	97129	91786	84634	76324	76005
Other	84348	95261	120084	118795	145842	156395
Own use in electricity, CHP and heat plants	37775	36933	38018	36717	34670	33968
Net production	600926	590873	610292	613733	619053	609191
Imports	39222	40435	37008	28338	27842	31727
Exports	71415	74320	85290	78863	80301	80463
Losses	24474	24159	25605	25759	27024	26661
Consumption	544259	532829	536405	537449	539570	533794
Energy industries own use	21949	21072	21457	20494	20617	20860
By industry and construction	227850	232862	228825	230574	232227	230527
By transport	11925	11523	11148	11739	11957	12087
By households and other cons.	282535	267372	274975	274642	274769	270320
Net installed capacity			**Thousand kilowatts**			
Total main activity and autoproducer	185306	197504	203255	208215	215324	229195
Combustible fuels	91368	97203	96967	95716	95134	103030
Hydro	11239	11234	11255	11207	11120	10940
Nuclear	12068	12074	10799	10799	10799	10799
Other	70631	76993	84234	90493	98271	104426
Main activity	175687	187697	192537	197627	203745	217207
Combustible fuels	82072	87747	86552	85409	83824	91301
Hydro	11197	11190	11212	11164	11078	10908
Nuclear	12068	12074	10799	10799	10799	10799
Other	70350	76686	83974	90255	98044	104199
Combustible fuel input			**Terajoules**			
Hard Coal	1254261	1162815	1127187	1090750	875477	801479
Brown Coal	1509182	1468554	1460006	1411719	1394434	1354287
Lignite briquettes	20807	18068	19628	18666	15754	17253
Biogas	212161	224008	235765	238590	238280	239453
Other oil products	28462	22110	26452	21507	21467	18974
Natural gas	614480	554407	555457	707551	749713	720855
Coke-oven gas	19258	17522	22759	24647	27371	27192
Blast furnace gas	73193	69845	69659	73166	71768	66613
Fuelwood	*121028	*125897	*127292	*121485	*119451	*123695
Municipal waste	177360	189580	179782	194092	196030	186036
Others	60251	61319	60340	63641	63472	51099
Total input	4090442	3914125	3884326	3965815	3773217	3606936
Total production	1537333	1470812	1477145	1510546	1455430	1387912
Estimated efficiency (% of production to input)	38	38	38	38	39	38

Ghana

Item	2013	2014	2015	2016	2017	2018
Production, trade and consumption	**Million kilowatt-hours**					
Total main activity and autoproducer	13050	13143	11672	13203	14248	16425
Combustible fuels	4814	4752	5824	7615	8604	10375
Hydro	8233	8387	5845	5561	5616	6017
Nuclear	..	..	..	..	..	..
Other	3	4	3	27	28	33
Main activity	12870	12963	11492	13023	14068	16245
Combustible fuels	4634	4572	5644	7435	8424	10195
Hydro	8233	8387	5845	5561	5616	6017
Nuclear	..	..	..	..	..	..
Other	3	4	3	27	28	33
Own use in electricity, CHP and heat plants	67	58	38	71	251	229
Net production	12983	13085	11634	13132	13997	16196
Imports	27	51	223	745	320	140
Exports	530	522	587	187	268	740
Losses	1661	1739	1406	1845	1920	2403
Consumption	10636	10694	9778	11523	12120	13185
Energy industries own use	..	..	..	..	..	..
By industry and construction	3284	3262	2659	3088	3078	4062
By transport	4	4	9	6	6	8
By households and other cons.	7348	7428	7110	8429	9036	9115
Net installed capacity	**Thousand kilowatts**					
Total main activity and autoproducer	3041	3041	3866	4005	4609	5099
Combustible fuels	1458	1458	2263	2402	3006	3476
Hydro	1580	1580	1580	1580	1580	1580
Nuclear	..	..	..	..	..	..
Other	3	3	23	23	23	43
Main activity	2831	2831	3656	3795	4399	4889
Combustible fuels	1248	1248	2053	2192	2796	3266
Hydro	1580	1580	1580	1580	1580	1580
Nuclear	..	..	..	..	..	..
Other	3	3	23	23	23	43
Combustible fuel input	**Terajoules**					
Crude oil	37393	25211	12394	25380	10448	42
Gas-diesel oil	228	65	43	1871	1484	473
Fuel oil	..	..	..	14920	4775	4173
Liquefied petroleum gas	..	..	..	..	3888	5132
Natural gas	11815	25805	46315	21658	43517	55852
Total input	49437	51080	58752	63828	64112	65673
Total production	17330	17107	20966	27414	30974	37350
Estimated efficiency (% of production to input)	35	33	36	43	48	57

Gibraltar

Item	2013	2014	2015	2016	2017	2018
Production, trade and consumption			Million kilowatt-hours			
Total main activity and autoproducer	189	198	224	214	180	215
Combustible fuels	189	198	224	214	180	215
Hydro	..	..	..	..	..	..
Nuclear	..	..	..	..	..	..
Other	..	..	..	0	0	0
Main activity	189	198	224	214	180	215
Combustible fuels	189	198	224	214	180	215
Hydro	..	..	..	..	..	..
Nuclear	..	..	..	..	..	..
Other	..	..	..	0	0	0
Own use in electricity, CHP and heat plants	4	4	4	4	4	4
Net production	185	194	220	210	176	211
Imports	..	..	..	..	..	..
Exports	..	..	..	..	..	..
Losses	6	6	7	6	6	7
Consumption	179	188	213	204	171	204
Energy industries own use	..	..	..	..	..	..
By industry and construction	..	..	..	..	..	..
By transport	..	..	..	..	..	..
By households and other cons.	179	188	213	204	171	204
Net installed capacity			Thousand kilowatts			
Total main activity and autoproducer	43	43	*43	*43	*43	*43
Combustible fuels	43	43	*43	*43	*43	*43
Hydro	..	..	..	..	..	..
Nuclear	..	..	..	..	..	..
Other	..	..	..	0	0	0
Main activity	43	43	*43	*43	*43	*43
Combustible fuels	43	43	*43	*43	*43	*43
Hydro	..	..	..	..	..	..
Nuclear	..	..	..	..	..	..
Other	..	..	..	0	0	0
Combustible fuel input			Terajoules			
Fuel oil	1858	1939	2182	2060	1737	2101
Total input	1858	1939	2182	2060	1737	2101
Total production	680	713	806	770	648	774
Estimated efficiency (% of production to input)	37	37	37	37	37	37

Greece

Item	2013	2014	2015	2016	2017	2018
Production, trade and consumption	**Million kilowatt-hours**					
Total main activity and autoproducer	57152	50474	51874	54439	55266	53263
Combustible fuels	42981	38386	37203	39798	41698	37412
Hydro	6384	4607	6150	5565	4040	5760
Nuclear	..	..	..	..	..	..
Other	7787	7481	8521	9076	9528	10091
Main activity	55267	48682	49534	52492	53333	51048
Combustible fuels	41096	36594	34863	37851	39765	35197
Hydro	6384	4607	6150	5565	4040	5760
Nuclear	..	..	..	..	..	..
Other	7787	7481	8521	9076	9528	10091
Own use in electricity, CHP and heat plants	4592	3772	4068	4212	4677	3179
Net production	52560	46702	47806	50227	50589	50084
Imports	5788	9461	11081	9833	8696	8550
Exports	3901	642	1473	1037	2459	2272
Losses	3895	4149	4895	3957	1102	5242
Consumption	50552	51372	52519	55066	55726	51120
Energy industries own use	1761	1872	1732	1703	1755	1650
By industry and construction	11366	12869	12668	11285	12286	12413
By transport	267	343	388	186	188	202
By households and other cons.	37158	36288	37731	41892	41497	36855
Net installed capacity	**Thousand kilowatts**					
Total main activity and autoproducer	18855	18895	18942	19165	19427	19582
Combustible fuels	11229	10932	10855	10799	10805	10644
Hydro	3238	3389	3392	3392	3392	3409
Nuclear	..	..	..	..	..	..
Other	4388	4574	4695	4974	5230	5529
Main activity	18328	18390	18381	18597	18856	19014
Combustible fuels	10702	10427	10294	10231	10234	10076
Hydro	3238	3389	3392	3392	3392	3409
Nuclear	..	..	..	..	..	..
Other	4388	4574	4695	4974	5230	5529
Combustible fuel input	**Terajoules**					
Hard Coal	27	..	..	..	..	..
Brown Coal	283513	271373	226190	174176	192614	185399
Biogas	2975	2961	3138	3623	3711	3791
Gas-diesel oil	10019	10320	11137	11911	13932	11782
Fuel oil	34623	35754	35592	25816	36683	36360
Liquefied petroleum gas	189	142	0	2034	189	..
Refinery gas	9455	11435	16781	14850	6633	7128
Natural gas	91617	59593	61257	103888	132678	125276
Fuelwood	..	..	*19	*138	*145	*205
Industrial waste	883	868	1030	1364	0	1213
Total input	433301	392445	355144	337800	386586	371154
Total production	154732	138190	133931	143273	150113	134683
Estimated efficiency (% of production to input)	36	35	38	42	39	36

Greenland

Item	2013	2014	2015	2016	2017	2018
Production, trade and consumption	Million kilowatt-hours					
Total main activity and autoproducer	473	488	520	490	518	*530
Combustible fuels	95	92	97	89	130	*130
Hydro	378	396	423	401	388	*400
Nuclear	..	..	..	..	..	..
Other	..	..	..	..	..	..
Main activity	473	488	520	490	518	*530
Combustible fuels	95	92	97	89	130	*130
Hydro	378	396	423	401	388	*400
Nuclear	..	..	..	..	..	..
Other	..	..	..	..	..	..
Own use in electricity, CHP and heat plants	17	16	17	15	16	*15
Net production	456	472	504	476	502	*515
Imports	..	..	..	..	..	..
Exports	..	..	..	..	..	..
Losses	*10	*12	*12	*12	13	*10
Consumption	309	319	331	320	328	*334
Energy industries own use	..	..	..	..	..	..
By industry and construction	44	45	47	51	52	*53
By transport	..	..	..	..	..	..
By households and other cons.	265	274	284	269	275	*281
Net installed capacity	Thousand kilowatts					
Total main activity and autoproducer	*187	187	*187	*187	187	*187
Combustible fuels	*96	96	*96	*96	96	*96
Hydro	91	91	91	91	91	*91
Nuclear	..	..	..	..	..	..
Other	..	..	..	..	..	..
Main activity	171	171	171	171	171	*171
Combustible fuels	*80	80	*80	*80	80	*80
Hydro	91	91	91	91	91	*91
Nuclear	..	..	..	..	..	..
Other	..	..	..	..	..	..
Combustible fuel input	Terajoules					
Gas-diesel oil	1103	1138	1321	1074	1107	*1118
Municipal waste	117	92	98	94	94	*94
Total input	1220	1230	1419	1168	1201	*1212
Total production	343	330	350	322	467	*468
Estimated efficiency (% of production to input)	28	27	25	28	39	39

Grenada

Item	2013	2014	2015	2016	2017	2018
Production, trade and consumption	**Million kilowatt-hours**					
Total main activity and autoproducer	197	201	207	218	227	*231
Combustible fuels	197	200	207	218	227	*231
Hydro	..	..	..	..	..	..
Nuclear	..	..	..	..	..	..
Other	0	0	0	0	0	0
Main activity	197	200	206	217	225	*228
Combustible fuels	197	200	206	217	225	*228
Hydro	..	..	..	..	..	..
Nuclear	..	..	..	..	..	..
Other	0	0	0	0	0	0
Own use in electricity, CHP and heat plants	6	6	6	12	12	6
Net production	191	195	201	207	215	*224
Imports	..	..	..	..	..	..
Exports	..	..	..	..	..	..
Losses	15	15	17	18	19	16
Consumption	176	179	184	189	196	208
Energy industries own use	..	..	..	..	..	..
By industry and construction	6	6	6	5	6	6
By transport	..	..	..	..	..	..
By households and other cons.	170	173	178	184	190	202
Net installed capacity	**Thousand kilowatts**					
Total main activity and autoproducer	49	49	49	49	50	53
Combustible fuels	48	48	48	48	50	52
Hydro	..	..	..	..	..	..
Nuclear	..	..	..	..	..	..
Other	0	0	0	0	0	0
Main activity	49	48	48	48	50	52
Combustible fuels	48	48	48	48	50	52
Hydro	..	..	..	..	..	..
Nuclear	..	..	..	..	..	..
Other	0	0	0	0	0	0
Combustible fuel input	**Terajoules**					
Gas-diesel oil	2558	1642	1823	1944	2016	2173
Total input	2558	1642	1823	1944	2016	2173
Total production	708	721	745	786	815	*831
Estimated efficiency (% of production to input)	28	44	41	40	40	38

Guam

Item	2013	2014	2015	2016	2017	2018
Production, trade and consumption			Million kilowatt-hours			
Total main activity and autoproducer	1736	*1703	1702	1720	1760	1715
Combustible fuels	1736	*1703	1681	1668	1708	1663
Hydro	..	..	..	..	..	..
Nuclear	..	..	..	..	..	..
Other	..	..	22	52	52	52
Main activity	1736	*1703	1702	1720	1760	1715
Combustible fuels	1736	*1703	1681	1668	1708	1663
Hydro	..	..	..	..	..	..
Nuclear	..	..	..	..	..	..
Other	..	..	22	52	52	52
Own use in electricity, CHP and heat plants	86	*86	83	65	66	63
Net production	1650	*1618	1619	1655	1694	1652
Imports	..	..	..	..	..	..
Exports	..	..	..	..	..	..
Losses	101	*84	79	81	84	85
Consumption	1565	1533	1540	1574	1610	1567
Energy industries own use	..	..	..	..	..	..
By industry and construction	..	..	..	..	..	..
By transport	..	..	..	..	..	..
By households and other cons.	1565	1533	1540	1574	1610	1567
Net installed capacity			Thousand kilowatts			
Total main activity and autoproducer	552	552	498	498	446	446
Combustible fuels	552	552	472	472	420	420
Hydro	..	..	..	..	..	..
Nuclear	..	..	..	..	..	..
Other	..	..	26	26	26	26
Main activity	552	552	498	498	446	446
Combustible fuels	552	552	472	472	420	420
Hydro	..	..	..	..	..	..
Nuclear	..	..	..	..	..	..
Other	..	..	26	26	26	26
Combustible fuel input			Terajoules			
Total input	..	..	..	..	..	..
Total production	6251	*6132	6050	6004	6148	5985
Estimated efficiency (% of production to input)	..	..	..	..	..	..

Guatemala

Item	2013	2014	2015	2016	2017	2018
Production, trade and consumption			**Million kilowatt-hours**			
Total main activity and autoproducer	10125	10638	11157	11789	12272	13568
Combustible fuels	5254	5531	6769	7122	5816	7572
Hydro	4659	4853	3880	3971	5787	5218
Nuclear	..	..	..	..	..	..
Other	212	254	508	696	669	778
Main activity	9270	9782	10302	10878	11490	12522
Combustible fuels	4427	4703	5942	6231	5055	6554
Hydro	4631	4825	3852	3951	5765	5191
Nuclear	..	..	..	..	..	..
Other	212	254	508	696	669	778
Own use in electricity, CHP and heat plants	754	855	747	868	886	775
Net production	9371	9783	10410	10921	11386	12793
Imports	267	708	585	747	891	825
Exports	588	1207	1087	1335	1858	2500
Losses	314	330	333	383	373	903
Consumption	8635	8953	9466	9907	10115	10220
Energy industries own use	..	..	..	..	..	..
By industry and construction	3093	3329	3547	3621	3707	3695
By transport	..	..	..	..	..	..
By households and other cons.	5542	5624	5919	6286	6408	6525
Net installed capacity			**Thousand kilowatts**			
Total main activity and autoproducer	2525	2626	3139	3442	3356	3499
Combustible fuels	1537	1624	1905	1942	1845	1770
Hydro	955	964	1039	1306	1311	1492
Nuclear	..	..	..	..	..	..
Other	34	39	194	194	200	237
Main activity	1926	2152	2449	2737	2677	2846
Combustible fuels	942	1154	1219	1241	1170	1122
Hydro	950	959	1035	1302	1307	1487
Nuclear	..	..	..	..	..	..
Other	34	39	194	194	200	237
Combustible fuel input			**Terajoules**			
Hard Coal	28600	30931	44340	52079	43218	51029
Biogas	..	..	212	199	329	459
Gas-diesel oil	96	69	137	80	114	62
Fuel oil	17856	11165	12644	8707	4074	3423
Petroleum coke	..	..	..	..	..	1751
Fuelwood	..	..	37	12	5	2
Bagasse	52353	56283	55979	85152	53779	51340
Total input	98906	98448	113349	146228	101519	108066
Total production	18914	19911	24370	25638	20939	27259
Estimated efficiency (% of production to input)	19	20	21	18	21	25

Guernsey

Item	2013	2014	2015	2016	2017	2018
Production, trade and consumption	Million kilowatt-hours					
Total main activity and autoproducer	289	227	157	87	77	54
Combustible fuels	289	227	157	87	77	54
Hydro	..	..	..	..	..	..
Nuclear	..	..	..	..	..	..
Other	..	..	..	..	..	..
Main activity	289	227	157	87	77	54
Combustible fuels	289	227	157	87	77	54
Hydro	..	..	..	..	..	..
Nuclear	..	..	..	..	..	..
Other	..	..	..	..	..	..
Own use in electricity, CHP and heat plants	0	0	0	0	0	0
Net production	289	227	157	87	77	54
Imports	111	156	218	285	294	319
Exports	..	..	..	..	..	..
Losses	36	19	28	23	17	25
Consumption	365	365	347	349	354	348
Energy industries own use	..	..	..	..	..	..
By industry and construction	..	..	..	..	..	..
By transport	..	..	..	..	..	..
By households and other cons.	365	365	347	349	354	348
Net installed capacity	Thousand kilowatts					
Total main activity and autoproducer	*115	*115	*115	*115	*132	*132
Combustible fuels	*115	*115	*115	*115	*132	*132
Hydro	..	..	..	..	..	..
Nuclear	..	..	..	..	..	..
Other	..	..	..	..	..	0
Main activity	*115	*115	*115	*115	*132	*132
Combustible fuels	*115	*115	*115	*115	*132	*132
Hydro	..	..	..	..	..	..
Nuclear	..	..	..	..	..	..
Other	..	..	..	..	..	0
Combustible fuel input	Terajoules					
Gas-diesel oil	*49	*49	*49	*43	*43	*43
Fuel oil	*2424	*1903	*1329	*727	*646	*444
Total input	*2473	*1951	*1378	*770	*689	*487
Total production	1040	818	565	315	277	194
Estimated efficiency (% of production to input)	42	42	41	41	40	40

Guinea

Item	2013	2014	2015	2016	2017	2018
Production, trade and consumption			**Million kilowatt-hours**			
Total main activity and autoproducer	654	713	1118	1596	1753	1914
Combustible fuels	172	287	238	512	541	732
Hydro	482	426	881	1084	1212	1182
Nuclear	..	..	..	..	..	..
Other	..	..	..	..	..	..
Main activity	624	552	945	1117	1288	1295
Combustible fuels	141	126	64	34	76	114
Hydro	482	426	881	1084	1212	1182
Nuclear	..	..	..	..	..	..
Other	..	..	..	..	..	..
Own use in electricity, CHP and heat plants	10	14	22	32	35	38
Net production	644	698	1096	1564	1718	1876
Imports	..	..	..	..	..	..
Exports	..	..	..	..	..	..
Losses	*103	*107	*168	*239	*263	*287
Consumption	*541	*591	*928	*1324	*1455	1588
Energy industries own use	..	..	..	..	..	..
By industry and construction	*197	*239	*432	*617	*620	*676
By transport	..	..	..	..	..	..
By households and other cons.	*344	*352	*496	*707	*835	912
Net installed capacity			**Thousand kilowatts**			
Total main activity and autoproducer	390	279	596	593	640	610
Combustible fuels	263	153	228	226	*273	*243
Hydro	127	125	367	367	367	367
Nuclear	..	..	..	..	..	..
Other	..	..	..	..	..	..
Main activity	338	227	496	444	460	462
Combustible fuels	211	101	128	77	*93	*95
Hydro	127	125	367	367	367	367
Nuclear	..	..	..	..	..	..
Other	..	..	..	..	..	..
Combustible fuel input			**Terajoules**			
Gas-diesel oil	*860	*1032	*538	*237	*516	*731
Fuel oil	*1010	*2060	*1899	*5010	*5131	*6626
Total input	*1870	*3092	*2436	*5246	*5647	*7357
Total production	619	1032	855	1842	1947	2636
Estimated efficiency (% of production to input)	33	33	35	35	34	36

Guinea-Bissau

Item	2013	2014	2015	2016	2017	2018
Production, trade and consumption	Million kilowatt-hours					
Total main activity and autoproducer	*23	*28	*58	*84	*86	*87
Combustible fuels	*23	*28	*58	*79	*79	*80
Hydro	..	..	..	..	..	..
Nuclear	..	..	..	..	..	..
Other	..	..	..	*6	*7	*7
Main activity	*18	*22	*45	*66	*67	*68
Combustible fuels	*18	*22	*45	*60	*60	*61
Hydro	..	..	..	..	..	..
Nuclear	..	..	..	..	..	..
Other	..	..	..	*6	*7	*7
Own use in electricity, CHP and heat plants	0	0	0	0	0	0
Net production	*23	*28	*58	*84	*86	*87
Imports	..	..	..	..	..	..
Exports	..	..	..	..	..	..
Losses	..	..	..	..	..	..
Consumption	*23	*28	*58	*84	*86	*87
Energy industries own use	..	..	..	..	..	..
By industry and construction	*6	*8	*15	*22	*23	*23
By transport	..	..	..	..	..	..
By households and other cons.	*17	*21	*43	*62	*63	*64
Net installed capacity	Thousand kilowatts					
Total main activity and autoproducer	*20	*24	*23	*31	*31	*32
Combustible fuels	*20	*24	*23	*27	*26	*26
Hydro	..	..	..	..	..	..
Nuclear	..	..	..	..	..	..
Other	..	..	..	*5	*5	*5
Main activity	*18	*22	*19	*26	*26	*26
Combustible fuels	*18	*22	*19	*21	*21	*21
Hydro	..	..	..	..	..	..
Nuclear	..	..	..	..	..	..
Other	..	..	..	*5	*5	*5
Combustible fuel input	Terajoules					
Gas-diesel oil	*245	*305	*576	*800	*796	*843
Total input	*245	*305	*576	*800	*796	*843
Total production	*83	*102	*209	*283	*284	*287
Estimated efficiency (% of production to input)	34	34	36	35	36	34

Guyana

Item	2013	2014	2015	2016	2017	2018
Production, trade and consumption	**Million kilowatt-hours**					
Total main activity and autoproducer	962	979	1004	1081	1105	1136
Combustible fuels	960	977	999	1076	1098	1125
Hydro	..	..	..	..	..	..
Nuclear	..	..	..	..	..	..
Other	2	2	5	5	7	11
Main activity	878	901	941	999	1022	1054
Combustible fuels	877	899	935	994	1015	1043
Hydro	..	..	..	..	..	..
Nuclear	..	..	..	..	..	..
Other	2	2	5	5	7	11
Own use in electricity, CHP and heat plants	28	29	6	31	12	33
Net production	933	950	998	1050	1092	1103
Imports	..	..	..	..	..	..
Exports	..	..	..	..	..	..
Losses	230	215	219	224	233	235
Consumption	704	735	789	826	859	868
Energy industries own use	..	..	..	..	..	..
By industry and construction	235	306	307	321	334	337
By transport	..	..	..	..	..	..
By households and other cons.	468	430	483	505	526	531
Net installed capacity	**Thousand kilowatts**					
Total main activity and autoproducer	337	359	369	360	348	348
Combustible fuels	336	358	366	356	343	340
Hydro	..	..	..	..	..	..
Nuclear	..	..	..	..	..	..
Other	1	1	3	3	5	8
Main activity	283	305	315	306	298	297
Combustible fuels	282	304	312	302	293	289
Hydro	..	..	..	..	..	..
Nuclear	..	..	..	..	..	..
Other	1	1	3	3	5	8
Combustible fuel input	**Terajoules**					
Gas-diesel oil	3106	2819	2532	2635	3096	3335
Fuel oil	7183	7137	7502	8118	7908	8356
Bagasse	512	480	621	448	327	231
Total input	10802	10436	10655	11200	11331	11921
Total production	3457	3518	3595	3874	3951	4049
Estimated efficiency (% of production to input)	32	34	34	35	35	34

Haiti

Item	2013	2014	2015	2016	2017	2018
Production, trade and consumption	Million kilowatt-hours					
Total main activity and autoproducer	1055	1033	1038	1084	1056	1046
Combustible fuels	914	943	955	1013	928	848
Hydro	141	90	83	71	127	197
Nuclear	..	..	..	..	..	..
Other	..	..	..	..	1	1
Main activity	990	983	994	1047	1033	1025
Combustible fuels	849	893	911	976	905	827
Hydro	141	90	83	71	127	197
Nuclear	..	..	..	..	..	..
Other	..	..	..	..	1	1
Own use in electricity, CHP and heat plants	19	11	17	17	17	18
Net production	1036	1022	1021	1067	1039	1028
Imports	..	..	..	..	..	..
Exports	..	..	..	..	..	..
Losses	630	613	608	617	624	634
Consumption	456	410	411	417	422	429
Energy industries own use	..	..	..	..	..	..
By industry and construction	171	184	184	187	189	192
By transport	..	..	..	..	..	..
By households and other cons.	285	226	227	230	233	237
Net installed capacity	Thousand kilowatts					
Total main activity and autoproducer	*340	*321	*333	*336	*344	*352
Combustible fuels	*262	*259	*271	*274	*282	*290
Hydro	77	61	61	61	61	61
Nuclear	..	..	..	..	..	..
Other	1	1	1	1	1	1
Main activity	*246	*228	*237	*240	*245	*250
Combustible fuels	*168	*166	*175	*178	*183	*188
Hydro	77	61	61	61	61	61
Nuclear	..	..	..	..	..	..
Other	1	1	1	1	1	1
Combustible fuel input	Terajoules					
Gas-diesel oil	5633	5418	5461	5289	3870	3483
Fuel oil	6343	6908	6908	7797	8282	7716
Total input	11976	12326	12369	13086	12152	11199
Total production	3290	3395	3438	3647	3341	3053
Estimated efficiency (% of production to input)	27	28	28	28	27	27

Honduras

Item	2013	2014	2015	2016	2017	2018
Production, trade and consumption	**Million kilowatt-hours**					
Total main activity and autoproducer	8274	8421	9167	9150	9251	9526
Combustible fuels	5225	5421	5745	5345	4568	4045
Hydro	2739	2602	2340	2350	3088	3262
Nuclear	..	..	..	..	..	..
Other	310	398	1082	1455	1595	2219
Main activity	7549	7650	8284	8603	8211	8125
Combustible fuels	4500	4650	4862	4798	3528	2644
Hydro	2739	2602	2340	2350	3088	3262
Nuclear	..	..	..	..	..	..
Other	310	398	1082	1455	1595	2219
Own use in electricity, CHP and heat plants	13	14	15	17	12	20
Net production	8261	8407	9152	9133	9239	9506
Imports	115	827	679	607	329	368
Exports	8	505	536	553	25	8
Losses	2672	2885	3004	3143	2995	2970
Consumption	5696	5844	6291	6044	6641	6886
Energy industries own use	..	..	..	..	..	..
By industry and construction	1683	1837	2112	1681	1849	2126
By transport	..	..	..	..	..	..
By households and other cons.	4013	4007	4179	4363	4792	4760
Net installed capacity	**Thousand kilowatts**					
Total main activity and autoproducer	1743	1897	2250	2439	2562	2637
Combustible fuels	1083	1121	1078	1185	1185	1171
Hydro	558	624	632	670	666	696
Nuclear	..	..	..	..	..	..
Other	102	152	540	584	711	771
Main activity	1619	1755	2081	2229	2352	2428
Combustible fuels	959	979	909	975	975	961
Hydro	558	624	632	670	666	696
Nuclear	..	..	..	..	..	..
Other	102	152	540	584	711	771
Combustible fuel input	**Terajoules**					
Hard Coal	1238	1445	1058	1496	26	..
Gas-diesel oil	2107	1161	1591	1204	344	1290
Fuel oil	35269	38501	41289	33734	25169	25331
Liquefied petroleum gas	..	..	..	..	..	899
Petroleum coke	..	..	..	..	6273	9360
Fuelwood	*10872	*7002	*10378	*16705	*18075	*16959
Total input	49487	48109	54316	53139	49886	53839
Total production	18810	19516	20682	19242	16445	14562
Estimated efficiency (% of production to input)	38	41	38	36	33	27

Hungary

Item	2013	2014	2015	2016	2017	2018
Production, trade and consumption	Million kilowatt-hours					
Total main activity and autoproducer	30294	29403	30360	31902	32885	32004
Combustible fuels	13936	12674	13395	14583	15377	14671
Hydro	213	301	234	259	220	222
Nuclear	15370	15649	15834	16054	16098	15733
Other	775	779	897	1006	1190	1378
Main activity	29679	28737	29554	30893	31616	30362
Combustible fuels	13378	12130	12792	13863	14502	13722
Hydro	213	301	234	259	220	222
Nuclear	15370	15649	15834	16054	16098	15733
Other	718	657	694	717	796	685
Own use in electricity, CHP and heat plants	2263	2262	2210	2354	2186	2172
Net production	28031	27141	28150	29548	30699	29832
Imports	16635	19079	19935	17951	19803	18613
Exports	4758	5689	6249	5240	6925	4265
Losses	3663	3631	3695	3566	3456	3357
Consumption	36241	35899	37439	38262	39647	40595
Energy industries own use	1368	1162	1148	1110	1154	1169
By industry and construction	14840	14696	15403	16002	16735	17257
By transport	1227	1156	1171	1177	1208	1204
By households and other cons.	18806	18885	19717	19973	20550	20965
Net installed capacity	Thousand kilowatts					
Total main activity and autoproducer	8418	8667	8634	8758	8860	9249
Combustible fuels	5987	6179	6062	6100	6090	6083
Hydro	57	57	57	57	57	57
Nuclear	2000	2000	2000	2000	2000	2013
Other	374	431	515	601	713	1096
Main activity	8217	8393	8258	8290	8268	8350
Combustible fuels	5831	6007	5856	5878	5837	5837
Hydro	57	57	57	57	57	57
Nuclear	2000	2000	2000	2000	2000	2013
Other	329	329	345	355	374	443
Combustible fuel input	Terajoules					
Hard Coal	0	29	0	2989	1001	869
Brown Coal	68609	64078	63146	60077	53838	54874
Biogas	2269	2113	2202	2529	2612	2516
Fuel oil	566	525	444	404	566	606
Natural gas	57584	44671	49177	59535	69551	64381
Coke-oven gas	1596	1786	1284	2021	1722	2055
Blast furnace gas	1246	2141	2894	2130	2895	3056
Fuelwood	*17663	*21531	*21071	*19129	*20873	*21957
Municipal waste	3923	4096	4827	5194	4314	4398
Industrial waste	296	398	807	1782	938	1222
Others	262	305	354	305	424	351
Total input	154014	141674	146207	156094	158734	156285
Total production	50170	45626	48222	52499	55357	52816
Estimated efficiency (% of production to input)	33	32	33	34	35	34

Iceland

Item	2013	2014	2015	2016	2017	2018
Production, trade and consumption			Million kilowatt-hours			
Total main activity and autoproducer	18116	18123	18799	18550	19239	19830
Combustible fuels	5	3	4	3	2	2
Hydro	12863	12873	13781	13470	14059	13814
Nuclear	..	..	..	..	..	..
Other	5248	5247	5014	5077	5178	6014
Main activity	18116	18123	18799	18550	19239	19830
Combustible fuels	5	3	4	3	2	2
Hydro	12863	12873	13781	13470	14059	13814
Nuclear	..	..	..	..	..	..
Other	5248	5247	5014	5077	5178	6014
Own use in electricity, CHP and heat plants	116	320	241	378	392	397
Net production	18000	17803	18558	18172	18847	19433
Imports	..	..	..	..	..	..
Exports	..	..	..	..	..	..
Losses	374	498	576	489	591	554
Consumption	16989	17009	17665	17479	18062	18664
Energy industries own use	166	179	195	176	169	177
By industry and construction	14678	14682	15129	14840	15389	15524
By transport	2	4	19	66	76	89
By households and other cons.	2143	2144	2322	2397	2428	2874
Net installed capacity			Thousand kilowatts			
Total main activity and autoproducer	2765	2766	2772	2772	2823	2973
Combustible fuels	114	114	117	117	116	116
Hydro	1984	1984	1987	1987	1995	2099
Nuclear	..	..	..	..	..	..
Other	667	668	668	668	712	758
Main activity	2765	2766	2772	2772	2823	2973
Combustible fuels	114	114	117	117	116	116
Hydro	1984	1984	1987	1987	1995	2099
Nuclear	..	..	..	..	..	..
Other	667	668	668	668	712	758
Combustible fuel input			Terajoules			
Gas-diesel oil	86	86	86	86	43	43
Total input	86	86	86	86	43	43
Total production	18	11	14	11	7	7
Estimated efficiency (% of production to input)	21	13	17	13	17	17

India

Item	2013	2014	2015	2016	2017	2018
Production, trade and consumption			Million kilowatt-hours			
Total main activity and autoproducer	1193480	1308873	1354382	1432358	1490293	1521785
Combustible fuels	980599	1111341	1158338	1188280	1217575	1244959
Hydro	141637	129353	121546	122507	126271	134991
Nuclear	34228	36102	37414	37916	38346	37813
Other	37016	32077	37084	83655	108101	*104022
Main activity	1002743	1146816	1135434	1233926	1305954	1346325
Combustible fuels	792477	951504	943013	993516	1037184	1072314
Hydro	141508	129244	121377	122378	126123	134894
Nuclear	34228	36102	37414	37916	38346	37813
Other	34530	29966	33630	80116	104301	*101304
Own use in electricity, CHP and heat plants	81588	90857	79302	95931	100862	108124
Net production	1111892	1218016	1275080	1336427	1389431	1413661
Imports	5598	4998	5244	5617	5611	4657
Exports	..	4433	5150	6710	7203	8494
Losses	220257	228325	240864	248834	259827	269165
Consumption	897233	955927	1034374	1071213	1135284	1163990
Energy industries own use	7178	*7600	*5294	*4945	*4956	*5679
By industry and construction	374278	*418346	*451412	426665	*468909	484843
By transport	15447	16177	16594	17217	14356	16823
By households and other cons.	500330	513804	561074	622386	647063	656645
Net installed capacity			Thousand kilowatts			
Total main activity and autoproducer	*294879	*316382	287134	374789	400701	411773
Combustible fuels	*226449	*241396	210430	267129	276294	282350
Hydro	*40067	*40064	40337	44591	45358	45447
Nuclear	4780	5780	5780	6780	6780	6780
Other	*23583	29142	*30587	56289	72269	77196
Main activity	*256786	*271722	205114	322506	343824	352179
Combustible fuels	*190000	*198745	130475	218330	222907	226279
Hydro	*40000	*40000	40272	44532	45293	45399
Nuclear	4780	5780	5780	6780	6780	6780
Other	*22006	27197	*28587	52864	68844	73721
Combustible fuel input			Terajoules			
Hard Coal	8249905	8625865	9353251	9407701	10218153	*10158212
Brown Coal	*346863	376809	360925	434150	368083	361622
Gas-diesel oil	290293	*281048	9632	16426	15222	21457
Fuel oil	34906	84234	19432	15231	12362	14059
Liquefied petroleum gas	142	142	142	95	..	95
Naphtha	9568	8856	2225	2670	2982	223
Natural gas	642401	418305	*634158	654623	632575	468447
Coke-oven gas	25477	*29968	*30881	*33073	*36321	*38643
Fuelwood	*275463	*222700	*225409	*749011	*783371	*790000
Vegetal waste	*225681	*327716	*349703	*231629	*242255	*236504
Total input	10100698	10375642	10985758	11544609	12311325	*12089261
Total production	3530156	4000828	4170017	4277808	4383270	4481852
Estimated efficiency (% of production to input)	35	39	38	37	36	37

Indonesia

Item	2013	2014	2015	2016	2017	2018
Production, trade and consumption	Million kilowatt-hours					
Total main activity and autoproducer	222017	234549	267287	233367	*283647	293203
Combustible fuels	192591	199993	240698	201209	*251766	260211
Hydro	15710	18800	17595	21475	18632	19774
Nuclear	..	..	..	..	..	..
Other	13717	15756	8995	10683	13249	13218
Main activity	169254	175297	157027	166458	*224746	276881
Combustible fuels	146602	150478	142227	148606	*207769	243889
Hydro	13014	14816	10005	13885	12425	19774
Nuclear	..	..	..	..	..	..
Other	9638	10003	4796	3967	4552	13218
Own use in electricity, CHP and heat plants	10842	10012	12838	9912	*14068	19410
Net production	211175	224537	254449	223455	*269579	273793
Imports	3	9	13	1	1120	..
Exports	..	..	..	..	..	..
Losses	20701	22006	22057	22706	24887	25093
Consumption	196967	198355	212767	215781	244637	251796
Energy industries own use	..	..	..	..	..	..
By industry and construction	72153	65909	72541	68145	93465	92968
By transport	129	155	257	..	240	266
By households and other cons.	124685	132291	139969	147636	150932	158562
Net installed capacity	Thousand kilowatts					
Total main activity and autoproducer	56315	61689	74448	59305	*60980	64265
Combustible fuels	48875	53692	65967	52622	*53517	56383
Hydro	5191	5655	6186	4868	*5190	5741
Nuclear	..	..	..	..	..	..
Other	2249	2342	2295	*1815	*2273	2141
Main activity	46427	51651	55394	39980	*41099	43241
Combustible fuels	40441	45258	48967	35622	*36228	37520
Hydro	4491	4805	4886	3568	*3804	3582
Nuclear	..	..	..	..	..	..
Other	1495	1588	1541	790	*1067	2139
Combustible fuel input	Terajoules					
Hard Coal	1562018	1711643	1850002	1854221	2013593	2393869
Motor gasoline	..	..	7664	7752	6867	8284
Gas-diesel oil	258129	253528	155316	130333	97653	123109
Fuel oil	44521	24725	20200	21129	16483	22180
Natural gas	533975	509724	777817	452991	559508	465092
Fuelwood	2592	3690	8298	10512	0	..
Charcoal	2183	*266	266	*266	*266	..
Biodiesel	..	*6698	*5814	*10378	*6734	..
Total input	2403418	2510273	2825377	2487582	2701103	3012533
Total production	693326	719976	866513	724352	*906357	936761
Estimated efficiency (% of production to input)	29	29	31	29	34	31

Statistics on electricity

Iran (Islamic Rep. of)

Item	2013	2014	2015	2016	2017	2018
Production, trade and consumption	**Million kilowatt-hours**					
Total main activity and autoproducer	262434	274437	280635	289116	307992	307968
Combustible fuels	242909	255870	263393	265799	285012	284508
Hydro	14582	13862	14090	16421	15051	15051
Nuclear	4546	4472	2914	6620	7514	7514
Other	397	233	238	276	415	895
Main activity	255885	268167	274195	282634	300087	300063
Combustible fuels	236360	249600	256953	259317	277107	276603
Hydro	14582	13862	14090	16421	15051	15051
Nuclear	4546	4472	2914	6620	7514	7514
Other	397	233	238	276	415	895
Own use in electricity, CHP and heat plants	9137	8717	8132	8205	8833	11639
Net production	253297	265720	272503	280911	299159	296329
Imports	3707	3772	4148	4221	3852	2587
Exports	11586	9660	6822	6688	8172	6295
Losses	38049	34610	33818	33513	33722	32853
Consumption	208168	224136	235555	243468	254942	262929
Energy industries own use	2705	2797	2915	3016	3225	3176
By industry and construction	72852	75689	77186	80860	80749	88541
By transport	286	363	549	436	477	477
By households and other cons.	132325	145287	154905	159156	170491	170735
Net installed capacity	**Thousand kilowatts**					
Total main activity and autoproducer	70236	73148	74185	74106	*76569	*78794
Combustible fuels	58833	61174	61632	61262	*63145	*65241
Hydro	10266	10789	11354	11578	11949	11953
Nuclear	1020	1020	1020	1020	1020	1020
Other	117	166	179	246	455	580
Main activity	64655	67568	68604	68525	*70816	*72889
Combustible fuels	53252	55593	56051	55681	*57392	*59336
Hydro	10266	10789	11354	11578	11949	11953
Nuclear	1020	1020	1020	1020	1020	1020
Other	117	166	179	246	455	580
Combustible fuel input	**Terajoules**					
Biogas	127	127	127	282	288	288
Gas-diesel oil	290783	332024	227649	219566	181176	216419
Fuel oil	585589	394140	266494	171999	141457	131664
Other kerosene	..	..	..	..	175	175
Natural gas	1430042	1957762	2279763	2431484	2730586	2650863
Coke-oven gas	35	186	88	169	2181	2518
Blast furnace gas	9088	10284	9064	9474	7739	8191
Total input	2315664	2694523	2783185	2832973	3063602	3010118
Total production	874472	921132	948215	956876	1026043	1024229
Estimated efficiency (% of production to input)	38	34	34	34	33	34

Iraq

Item	2013	2014	2015	2016	2017	2018
Production, trade and consumption	**Million kilowatt-hours**					
Total main activity and autoproducer	58468	67825	*68745	80087	83947	82507
Combustible fuels	53665	64837	*66116	76659	81714	80312
Hydro	4757	2931	*2572	3371	2176	1818
Nuclear	..	..	..	..	..	..
Other	46	57	57	57	57	377
Main activity	58422	67768	*68688	80030	83890	82130
Combustible fuels	53665	64837	*66116	76659	81714	80312
Hydro	4757	2931	*2572	3371	2176	1818
Nuclear	..	..	..	..	..	..
Other	..	..	..	..	..	..
Own use in electricity, CHP and heat plants	2356	1770	*977	2080	3947	2076
Net production	56112	66055	*67768	78007	80000	80431
Imports	12202	12251	13104	11965	11787	21793
Exports	..	..	..	..	..	..
Losses	23285	34312	31967	48958	52767	55472
Consumption	45042	43993	42035	38733	38377	39594
Energy industries own use	..	..	..	..	..	..
By industry and construction	9867	10071	*8665	5180	5160	4784
By transport	..	..	..	..	..	..
By households and other cons.	35175	33922	33370	33553	33217	34810
Net installed capacity	**Thousand kilowatts**					
Total main activity and autoproducer	27140	25626	31148	32214	26133	27412
Combustible fuels	24597	23076	28598	29664	24300	25400
Hydro	2513	2513	2513	2513	1796	1796
Nuclear	..	..	..	..	..	..
Other	30	37	37	37	37	216
Main activity	27110	25589	31111	32177	26096	27196
Combustible fuels	24597	23076	28598	29664	24300	25400
Hydro	2513	2513	2513	2513	1796	1796
Nuclear	..	..	..	..	..	..
Other	..	..	..	..	..	..
Combustible fuel input	**Terajoules**					
Crude oil	191788	283114	348044	380489	338781	345929
Gas-diesel oil	333508	426345	359738	360340	360684	270814
Fuel oil	289506	229674	201071	233795	121523	217958
Naphtha	0	0	0	..	..	..
Natural gas	152218	183234	207313	225878	353870	460255
Total input	967021	1122367	1116166	1200501	1174858	1294956
Total production	193194	233413	*238018	275972	294170	289123
Estimated efficiency (% of production to input)	20	21	21	23	25	22

Ireland

Item	2013	2014	2015	2016	2017	2018
Production, trade and consumption			Million kilowatt-hours			
Total main activity and autoproducer	25933	26110	28420	30539	30898	31118
Combustible fuels	20435	19958	20716	23385	22522	21546
Hydro	944	988	1095	973	895	932
Nuclear	..	..	..	..	..	..
Other	4554	5164	6609	6181	7481	8640
Main activity	23864	24014	26227	28308	28673	28925
Combustible fuels	18378	17886	18559	21186	20333	19393
Hydro	944	988	1095	973	895	932
Nuclear	..	..	..	..	..	..
Other	4542	5140	6573	6149	7445	8600
Own use in electricity, CHP and heat plants	818	798	802	849	811	765
Net production	25115	25312	27618	29690	30087	30353
Imports	2625	2853	1752	871	1116	1622
Exports	383	704	1079	1583	1795	1649
Losses	2017	2028	2084	2135	2176	2236
Consumption	24991	24815	25729	26221	26368	27774
Energy industries own use	789	678	656	647	517	629
By industry and construction	9287	9396	9844	10143	10255	10890
By transport	43	40	44	49	52	61
By households and other cons.	14872	14701	15185	15382	15544	16194
Net installed capacity			Thousand kilowatts			
Total main activity and autoproducer	8972	9260	9679	10017	10608	10981
Combustible fuels	6434	6446	6697	6696	6745	6752
Hydro	529	529	529	529	529	529
Nuclear	..	..	..	..	..	..
Other	2009	2285	2453	2792	3334	3700
Main activity	8628	8901	9318	9650	10222	10578
Combustible fuels	6098	6105	6354	6351	6395	6396
Hydro	529	529	529	529	529	529
Nuclear	..	..	..	..	..	..
Other	2001	2267	2435	2770	3298	3653
Combustible fuel input			Terajoules			
Hard Coal	42334	40473	48423	46439	37510	21262
Peat	22070	24120	24635	23893	22476	20985
Biogas	1764	1846	1917	1904	1878	1699
Gas-diesel oil	172	301	774	473	301	344
Fuel oil	1414	1980	2424	2182	1091	1091
Liquefied petroleum gas	47	0	47	47	47	47
Refinery gas	198	198	396	198	0	..
Natural gas	97410	91598	88183	108711	112511	114233
Fuelwood	*2130	*2431	*1794	*3675	*3561	*3074
Municipal waste	2044	2096	2120	2132	4596	7958
Total input	169583	165043	170713	189654	183971	170693
Total production	73566	71849	74578	84186	81079	77566
Estimated efficiency (% of production to input)	43	44	44	44	44	45

Isle of Man

Item	2013	2014	2015	2016	2017	2018
Production, trade and consumption			**Million kilowatt-hours**			
Total main activity and autoproducer	443	465	435	433	467	493
Combustible fuels	440	462	431	430	463	490
Hydro	*3	3	4	3	4	*3
Nuclear	..	..	..	..	..	..
Other	..	..	..	..	..	..
Main activity	418	442	411	408	443	460
Combustible fuels	415	439	407	405	439	457
Hydro	*3	3	4	3	4	*3
Nuclear	..	..	..	..	..	..
Other	..	..	..	..	..	..
Own use in electricity, CHP and heat plants	0	0	0	0	0	36
Net production	443	465	435	433	467	457
Imports	58	42	63	65	41	*65
Exports	77	93	87	105	95	131
Losses	*30	*30	*30	*30	*30	*25
Consumption	373	368	367	362	363	362
Energy industries own use	..	..	..	..	..	..
By industry and construction	137	137	141	139	133	135
By transport	..	..	..	..	..	..
By households and other cons.	236	231	226	223	230	227
Net installed capacity			**Thousand kilowatts**			
Total main activity and autoproducer	194	194	194	184	187	187
Combustible fuels	193	193	193	183	186	186
Hydro	1	1	1	1	1	1
Nuclear	..	..	..	..	..	..
Other	..	..	..	..	..	..
Main activity	186	186	186	176	180	180
Combustible fuels	185	185	185	175	179	179
Hydro	1	1	1	1	1	1
Nuclear	..	..	..	..	..	..
Other	..	..	..	..	..	..
Combustible fuel input			**Terajoules**			
Fuel oil	149	81	108	105	48	35
Natural gas	3317	3587	3165	3668	3587	3587
Municipal waste	*409	*380	*389	*411	*396	*546
Total input	3875	4048	3662	4184	4031	4168
Total production	1584	1664	1551	1548	1666	1765
Estimated efficiency (% of production to input)	41	41	42	37	41	42

Israel

Item	2013	2014	2015	2016	2017	2018
Production, trade and consumption	Million kilowatt-hours					
Total main activity and autoproducer	61322	60813	64226	66976	67675	68893
Combustible fuels	60794	59954	63080	65432	65742	66977
Hydro	28	13	24	0	0	0
Nuclear	..	..	..	..	..	..
Other	500	846	1122	1544	1933	1916
Main activity	59026	57478	60483	62907	63409	63846
Combustible fuels	58997	57464	60461	62907	63409	63846
Hydro	23	8	15	0	0	0
Nuclear	..	..	..	..	..	..
Other	6	6	7	0	0	0
Own use in electricity, CHP and heat plants	2140	1989	1928	2441	2200	2303
Net production	59182	58824	62298	64535	65475	66590
Imports	..	..	..	..	..	..
Exports	4675	4844	5197	5553	5649	5863
Losses	2567	1738	2472	2535	2387	2514
Consumption	52118	52201	54791	56443	57148	58307
Energy industries own use	478	883	769	755	855	826
By industry and construction	13181	15211	12746	13444	12942	13996
By transport	..	..	..	..	..	..
By households and other cons.	38459	36107	41276	42244	43351	43485
Net installed capacity	Thousand kilowatts					
Total main activity and autoproducer	14985	16220	17221	17585	17827	18019
Combustible fuels	14491	15526	16466	16689	16813	16617
Hydro	7	7	7	7	9	9
Nuclear	..	..	..	..	..	..
Other	487	687	748	889	1005	1393
Main activity	14091	15075	15986	16198	16236	16001
Combustible fuels	14080	15064	15975	16166	16205	15964
Hydro	5	5	5	5	4	2
Nuclear	..	..	..	..	..	..
Other	6	6	6	27	27	35
Combustible fuel input	Terajoules					
Hard Coal	289694	273447	266209	227233	206952	195461
Brown Coal	3573	..	..	..	..	..
Biogas	353	593	559	795	960	878
Oil shale	1671	1572	1667	1679	1783	647
Gas-diesel oil	12900	731	3913	2193	6579	2623
Fuel oil	7070	525	848	848	1293	970
Other oil products	1930	1568	0	..	..	..
Natural gas	223101	245137	262263	317669	342459	300611
Total input	540291	523573	535460	550418	560026	501190
Total production	218858	215834	227088	235555	236671	241117
Estimated efficiency (% of production to input)	41	41	42	43	42	48

Italy

Item	2013	2014	2015	2016	2017	2018
Production, trade and consumption			Million kilowatt-hours			
Total main activity and autoproducer	289807	279827	282994	289768	295833	289710
Combustible fuels	192237	175510	191458	198693	208826	192131
Hydro	54672	60256	46970	44257	38025	50503
Nuclear	..	..	..	..	..	..
Other	42898	44061	44566	46818	48982	47076
Main activity	273734	264085	263912	271301	276051	266924
Combustible fuels	177113	160761	173249	181006	189676	170015
Hydro	54045	59518	46361	43695	37536	50037
Nuclear	..	..	..	..	..	..
Other	42576	43806	44302	46600	48839	46872
Own use in electricity, CHP and heat plants	10973	10679	10566	10065	10567	9866
Net production	278834	269148	272428	279703	285266	279844
Imports	44338	46747	50849	43181	42895	47170
Exports	2200	3031	4471	6154	5134	3271
Losses	21187	19451	19717	18753	18668	17988
Consumption	299784	293414	299089	297977	304359	305754
Energy industries own use	12386	11916	11606	11950	12393	12674
By industry and construction	114981	112918	112665	113257	115610	116070
By transport	10775	10463	10856	11162	11383	11539
By households and other cons.	161642	158117	163962	161608	164973	165471
Net installed capacity			Thousand kilowatts			
Total main activity and autoproducer	124515	121747	116964	114162	114240	115220
Combustible fuels	74733	71272	65617	62096	61289	61276
Hydro	22009	22098	22220	22298	22426	22498
Nuclear	..	..	..	..	..	..
Other	27773	28377	29127	29768	30525	31446
Main activity	120213	117673	111706	109328	109206	109699
Combustible fuels	70664	67419	60575	57438	56426	55929
Hydro	21890	21979	22099	22181	22307	22393
Nuclear	..	..	..	..	..	..
Other	27659	28275	29032	29709	30473	31377
Combustible fuel input			Terajoules			
Hard Coal	427786	408150	414451	342425	304051	266911
Biogas	74133	80223	76475	76651	77413	76494
Fuel oil	41006	32401	37532	20281	20038	12484
Refinery gas	32274	26978	28958	31581	30839	30393
Other oil products	105163	106811	118188	125022	119474	125585
Natural gas	938888	829412	947225	1057652	1162357	1075137
Blast furnace gas	23404	25051	15672	23686	16953	17987
Fuelwood	*78399	*82397	*70047	*73136	*72332	*72080
Municipal waste	69302	71882	70840	72908	71442	70894
Other liquid biofuels	22632	26386	29400	28277	26907	26140
Others	34787	29970	26071	17982	18042	15992
Total input	1847774	1719661	1834857	1869601	1919848	1790096
Total production	692053	631836	689249	715295	751774	691672
Estimated efficiency (% of production to input)	37	37	38	38	39	39

Statistics on electricity

Jamaica

Item	2013	2014	2015	2016	2017	2018
Production, trade and consumption			Million kilowatt-hours			
Total main activity and autoproducer	4163	4123	4206	4342	4360	4402
Combustible fuels	3924	3869	3953	4002	3873	3875
Hydro	124	135	128	118	154	179
Nuclear	..	..	..	..	..	..
Other	115	119	125	222	333	348
Main activity	2365	2462	2528	2556	2533	2561
Combustible fuels	2241	2327	2400	2438	2379	2382
Hydro	124	135	128	118	154	179
Nuclear	..	..	..	..	..	..
Other	..	..	..	..	..	..
Own use in electricity, CHP and heat plants	22	12	12	13	18	19
Net production	4141	4111	4194	4329	4342	4383
Imports	..	..	..	..	..	..
Exports	..	..	..	..	..	..
Losses	1097	1103	1137	1160	1152	1144
Consumption	3038	3011	3073	3184	3191	3299
Energy industries own use	..	..	..	..	..	..
By industry and construction	1365	1357	1379	1410	1358	1800
By transport	..	..	..	..	..	..
By households and other cons.	1673	1654	1694	1774	1833	1499
Net installed capacity			Thousand kilowatts			
Total main activity and autoproducer	939	939	965	1031	1041	1045
Combustible fuels	874	874	871	871	871	874
Hydro	23	23	29	29	29	29
Nuclear	..	..	..	..	..	..
Other	42	42	65	131	141	142
Main activity	638	638	641	661	661	665
Combustible fuels	612	612	609	609	609	612
Hydro	23	23	29	29	29	29
Nuclear	..	..	..	..	..	..
Other	3	3	3	23	23	24
Combustible fuel input			Terajoules			
Gas-diesel oil	7645	7886	7835	9507	1587	1419
Fuel oil	26433	24433	26337	26296	29007	29169
Natural gas	..	..	..	*355	*4089	3789
Bagasse	*2471	*2317	*2626	*2703	*1853	*309
Total input	36550	34636	36797	38861	36536	34686
Total production	14126	13928	14231	14407	13943	13950
Estimated efficiency (% of production to input)	39	40	39	37	38	40

Japan

Item	2013	2014	2015	2016	2017	2018
Production, trade and consumption	Million kilowatt-hours					
Total main activity and autoproducer	1104249	1076066	1058748	1061874	1071200	1057755
Combustible fuels	967639	937239	894376	883161	862526	812737
Hydro	84886	86942	91270	85666	91060	88348
Nuclear	9303	0	9437	18060	32912	64929
Other	42421	51885	63665	74987	84702	91741
Main activity	888559	854703	824252	913763	919425	895973
Combustible fuels	808007	781906	737465	799505	781222	726604
Hydro	68564	70255	74801	81919	88356	85058
Nuclear	9303	0	9437	18060	32912	64929
Other	2685	2542	2549	14279	16935	19382
Own use in electricity, CHP and heat plants	37379	33794	31058	31060	31055	31059
Net production	1066870	1042272	1027690	1030814	1040145	1026696
Imports	..	..	..	..	..	..
Exports	..	..	..	..	..	..
Losses	47518	43334	40587	45600	40642	44999
Consumption	1012006	992537	969590	972905	989627	970436
Energy industries own use	22445	18876	20098	23120	24895	24902
By industry and construction	361038	355110	344897	342707	346630	344320
By transport	17721	17604	17551	17460	17460	17460
By households and other cons.	610802	600947	587044	589618	600642	583754
Net installed capacity	Thousand kilowatts					
Total main activity and autoproducer	306789	319625	326444	338210	342198	347368
Combustible fuels	194337	196664	194388	198299	197092	196656
Hydro	48932	49597	50034	50117	50014	50037
Nuclear	44264	44264	42048	41482	39132	38042
Other	19256	29100	39974	48312	55960	62633
Main activity	231467	234028	231484	274454	272831	271643
Combustible fuels	141901	143777	143040	174392	173261	171469
Hydro	44676	45403	45786	49521	49562	49582
Nuclear	44264	44264	42048	41482	39132	38042
Other	626	584	610	9059	10876	12550
Combustible fuel input	Terajoules					
Hard Coal	2942216	2925909	2901200	2875960	2973094	2868155
Fuel oil	614969	468074	364650	305666	226482	163014
Refinery gas	116622	113652	119840	133403	152807	129789
Natural gas	3530817	3585183	3342273	3420877	3292214	3109123
Coke-oven gas	68596	64203	65612	64667	62449	60176
Blast furnace gas	210199	233959	224408	217389	196630	191141
Fuelwood	*9779	*17750	*30356	*46170	*63997	*75388
Vegetal waste	*66970	*60216	*60615	*62214	*66646	*66643
Industrial waste	74538	73127	73631	135435	149680	167878
Bitumen	45788	39919	36904	60983	57004	55757
Others	666222	478154	433458	264404	222675	175704
Total input	8346716	8060146	7652947	7587169	7463678	7062768
Total production	3483500	3374060	3219754	3179380	3105094	2925853
Estimated efficiency (% of production to input)	42	42	42	42	42	41

Jersey

Item	2013	2014	2015	2016	2017	2018
Production, trade and consumption	**Million kilowatt-hours**					
Total main activity and autoproducer	157	108	48	70	49	*45
Combustible fuels	157	108	48	70	49	*45
Hydro	..	..	..	..	..	..
Nuclear	..	..	..	..	..	..
Other	..	..	..	..	..	..
Main activity	123	71	7	24	4	*4
Combustible fuels	123	71	7	24	4	*4
Hydro	..	..	..	..	..	..
Nuclear	..	..	..	..	..	..
Other	..	..	..	..	..	..
Own use in electricity, CHP and heat plants	0	0	0	0	0	*2
Net production	157	108	48	70	49	*43
Imports	568	566	625	614	626	637
Exports	..	..	..	..	..	..
Losses	71	60	52	47	53	48
Consumption	656	615	622	637	620	633
Energy industries own use	..	..	..	..	..	..
By industry and construction	256	253	242	*249	*239	*239
By transport	..	..	..	..	..	..
By households and other cons.	400	362	380	387	381	395
Net installed capacity	**Thousand kilowatts**					
Total main activity and autoproducer	*240	*240	78	78	78	78
Combustible fuels	*240	*240	78	78	78	78
Hydro	..	..	..	..	..	..
Nuclear	..	..	..	..	..	..
Other	..	..	..	..	..	..
Main activity	*212	*212	50	50	50	50
Combustible fuels	*212	*212	50	50	50	50
Hydro	..	..	..	..	..	..
Nuclear	..	..	..	..	..	..
Other	..	..	..	..	..	..
Combustible fuel input	**Terajoules**					
Gas-diesel oil	1428	744	103	259	58	32
Municipal waste	*616	*658	*732	*813	*799	*760
Total input	2044	1402	*835	*1072	*857	*792
Total production	564	388	173	250	176	*160
Estimated efficiency (% of production to input)	28	28	21	23	20	20

Jordan

Item	2013	2014	2015	2016	2017	2018
Production, trade and consumption	**Million kilowatt-hours**					
Total main activity and autoproducer	17263	18270	19012	*19627	19432	18859
Combustible fuels	17205	18210	18834	*18704	18354	17293
Hydro	55	58	53	42	38	23
Nuclear	..	..	..	..	..	..
Other	3	2	125	882	1040	1543
Main activity	16977	17887	18540	*19427	19232	18720
Combustible fuels	16919	17827	18363	*18504	18154	17154
Hydro	55	58	53	42	38	23
Nuclear	..	..	..	..	..	..
Other	3	2	125	882	1040	1543
Own use in electricity, CHP and heat plants	616	632	676	614	600	520
Net production	16647	17638	18336	*19013	18832	18339
Imports	381	435	604	334	51	188
Exports	59	64	50	46	57	94
Losses	2406	2569	2190	2072	2029	2094
Consumption	14571	15419	16282	16805	17605	17594
Energy industries own use	99	98	105	105	101	100
By industry and construction	3425	3780	3823	3763	3910	3861
By transport	..	..	..	..	..	..
By households and other cons.	11047	11541	12354	12937	13594	13632
Net installed capacity	**Thousand kilowatts**					
Total main activity and autoproducer	3385	4199	4455	4475	4506	4736
Combustible fuels	3372	4186	4320	3969	3890	3745
Hydro	12	12	12	12	12	12
Nuclear	..	..	..	..	..	..
Other	1	1	123	494	604	979
Main activity	3186	4000	4256	4276	4307	4537
Combustible fuels	3173	3987	4121	3770	3691	3546
Hydro	12	12	12	12	12	12
Nuclear	..	..	..	..	..	..
Other	1	1	123	494	604	979
Combustible fuel input	**Terajoules**					
Biogas	72	72	90	100	100	*100
Gas-diesel oil	58961	70258	24079	569	398	181
Fuel oil	53887	69561	63227	15473	12874	5252
Natural gas	37961	*12590	81400	141902	163276	159917
Total input	150881	152480	168797	158044	176648	165450
Total production	61938	65556	67803	*67333	66073	62254
Estimated efficiency (% of production to input)	41	43	40	43	37	38

Kazakhstan

Item	2013	2014	2015	2016	2017	2018
Production, trade and consumption	Million kilowatt-hours					
Total main activity and autoproducer	103086	105068	106468	106626	103128	107060
Combustible fuels	95349	96791	97020	94644	91485	96187
Hydro	7731	8263	9269	11620	11210	10330
Nuclear	..	..	..	..	..	..
Other	6	14	179	362	433	543
Main activity	103085	105067	106467	106625	103127	107059
Combustible fuels	95349	96791	97020	94644	91485	96187
Hydro	7731	8263	9269	11620	11210	10330
Nuclear	..	..	..	..	..	..
Other	5	13	178	361	432	542
Own use in electricity, CHP and heat plants	17337	19778	25201	23968	20846	12436
Net production	85749	85290	81267	82658	82282	94624
Imports	2147	1749	1618	1319	1327	1561
Exports	2996	2917	1614	2572	5692	5042
Losses	11174	7082	5181	5349	6411	2248
Consumption	73338	76676	76407	76064	79533	89114
Energy industries own use	7611	7776	8209	10166	9957	8786
By industry and construction	44280	45529	45110	44244	47406	50397
By transport	2960	2511	3573	3245	4019	3234
By households and other cons.	18487	20860	19515	18409	18151	26697
Net installed capacity	Thousand kilowatts					
Total main activity and autoproducer	*22222	*25011	*25149	*25223	*25256	24658
Combustible fuels	*20000	*22500	*22500	*22500	*22500	21902
Hydro	*2217	*2500	*2500	*2500	*2500	*2500
Nuclear	..	..	..	..	..	..
Other	*5	*11	*149	*223	*256	*256
Main activity	*22221	*25010	*25148	*25222	*25255	24657
Combustible fuels	*20000	*22500	*22500	*22500	*22500	21902
Hydro	*2217	*2500	*2500	*2500	*2500	*2500
Nuclear	..	..	..	..	..	..
Other	*4	*10	*148	*222	*255	*255
Combustible fuel input	Terajoules					
Hard Coal	305992	307125	292391	282264	315914	346903
Brown Coal	161	161	166	1560	2023	2626
Biogas	..	..	..	..	..	19
Fuel oil	7151	12201	16241	23028	8888	8601
Natural gas	194836	233178	225843	257658	261839	313105
Total input	508140	552665	534641	564510	588664	671254
Total production	343256	348448	349272	340718	329346	346273
Estimated efficiency (% of production to input)	68	63	65	60	56	52

Kenya

Item	2013	2014	2015	2016	2017	2018
Production, trade and consumption	Million kilowatt-hours					
Total main activity and autoproducer	8448	9139	9515	9971	10129	11163
Combustible fuels	2218	2635	1462	1471	2534	1673
Hydro	4435	3569	*3472	3960	2777	3986
Nuclear	..	..	..	..	..	..
Other	1796	2934	4580	4541	4818	5504
Main activity	8448	9139	9515	9971	10129	11036
Combustible fuels	2218	2635	1462	1471	2534	1546
Hydro	4435	3569	*3472	3960	2777	3986
Nuclear	..	..	..	..	..	..
Other	1796	2934	4580	4541	4818	5504
Own use in electricity, CHP and heat plants	49	43	48	50	50	110
Net production	8399	9095	9467	9921	10079	11053
Imports	49	158	59	86	230	130
Exports	36	27	46	39	12	69
Losses	1476	1662	1642	1965	1965	2244
Consumption	7296	7786	7732	8346	8741	8702
Energy industries own use	..	..	..	..	..	..
By industry and construction	4438	3988	4426	5257	5398	4337
By transport	..	..	..	..	..	..
By households and other cons.	2858	3798	3306	3089	3343	4366
Net installed capacity	Thousand kilowatts					
Total main activity and autoproducer	1724	2115	2263	2254	2270	2647
Combustible fuels	715	734	819	786	766	864
Hydro	767	797	800	798	826	821
Nuclear	..	..	..	..	..	..
Other	242	584	645	670	678	963
Main activity	1724	2115	2263	2254	2270	2628
Combustible fuels	715	734	819	786	766	845
Hydro	767	797	800	798	826	821
Nuclear	..	..	..	..	..	..
Other	242	584	645	670	678	963
Combustible fuel input	Terajoules					
Biogas	..	..	..	..	..	6
Gas-diesel oil	12943	7310	3612	2263	1196	12470
Fuel oil	6464	6399	7874	5484	11009	12605
Vegetal waste	16800	16800	16800	15460	16800	*16500
Total input	36207	30509	28286	23207	29005	41581
Total production	7984	9487	5264	5295	9123	6023
Estimated efficiency (% of production to input)	22	31	19	23	31	14

Kiribati

Item	2013	2014	2015	2016	2017	2018
Production, trade and consumption	**Million kilowatt-hours**					
Total main activity and autoproducer	26	*27	*29	*31	*31	*31
Combustible fuels	25	*26	*26	*26	*26	*27
Hydro	..	..	..	..	..	..
Nuclear	..	..	..	..	..	..
Other	1	1	4	5	5	*5
Main activity	24	*25	*27	*29	*29	*29
Combustible fuels	23	*24	*24	*24	*24	*24
Hydro	..	..	..	..	..	..
Nuclear	..	..	..	..	..	..
Other	1	1	4	5	5	*5
Own use in electricity, CHP and heat plants	1	1	2	2	2	*2
Net production	25	*26	*28	*30	*30	*30
Imports	..	..	..	..	..	..
Exports	..	..	..	..	..	..
Losses	5	4	*5	*5	*5	*5
Consumption	20	21	*23	*25	*25	*24
Energy industries own use	..	..	..	..	..	..
By industry and construction	*2	*2	*2	*2	*2	*2
By transport	..	..	..	..	..	..
By households and other cons.	18	19	*21	*23	*23	*22
Net installed capacity	**Thousand kilowatts**					
Total main activity and autoproducer	7	*7	*10	*11	*11	*11
Combustible fuels	6	*6	*8	*8	*8	*8
Hydro	..	..	..	..	..	..
Nuclear	..	..	..	..	..	..
Other	1	1	2	3	3	3
Main activity	6	*6	*9	*10	*10	*10
Combustible fuels	5	*5	*7	*7	*7	*7
Hydro	..	..	..	..	..	..
Nuclear	..	..	..	..	..	..
Other	1	1	2	3	3	3
Combustible fuel input	**Terajoules**					
Gas-diesel oil	301	292	*280	*241	*301	*301
Total input	301	292	*280	*241	*301	*301
Total production	91	*92	*92	*94	*94	*95
Estimated efficiency (% of production to input)	30	31	33	39	31	32

Korea, Dem.Ppl's.Rep.

Item	2013	2014	2015	2016	2017	2018
Production, trade and consumption	Million kilowatt-hours					
Total main activity and autoproducer	18337	17916	13748	16939	14915	15431
Combustible fuels	4432	4909	3737	4126	3001	2616
Hydro	13900	13000	10000	12800	11900	12800
Nuclear	..	..	..	..	..	..
Other	5	7	11	13	14	15
Main activity	18337	17916	13748	16939	14915	15431
Combustible fuels	4432	4909	3737	4126	3001	2616
Hydro	13900	13000	10000	12800	11900	12800
Nuclear	..	..	..	..	..	..
Other	5	7	11	13	14	15
Own use in electricity, CHP and heat plants	1738	1698	1303	1605	1413	1461
Net production	16599	16218	12445	15334	13502	13970
Imports	..	..	..	..	..	..
Exports	..	..	..	..	..	..
Losses	2899	2832	2173	2677	2357	2439
Consumption	13700	13386	10272	12657	11146	11530
Energy industries own use	..	..	..	..	..	..
By industry and construction	6850	6693	5136	6329	5573	5765
By transport	..	..	..	..	..	..
By households and other cons.	6850	6693	5136	6328	5573	5765
Net installed capacity	Thousand kilowatts					
Total main activity and autoproducer	7249	7260	7435	7671	7731	8160
Combustible fuels	2960	2960	2960	2960	2960	3360
Hydro	4283	4293	4467	4701	4761	4790
Nuclear	..	..	..	..	..	..
Other	6	*7	*8	*10	*10	*10
Main activity	7249	7260	7435	7671	7731	8160
Combustible fuels	2960	2960	2960	2960	2960	3360
Hydro	4283	4293	4467	4701	4761	4790
Nuclear	..	..	..	..	..	..
Other	6	*7	*8	*10	*10	*10
Combustible fuel input	Terajoules					
Hard Coal	28716	33948	22517	28976	20195	16849
Brown Coal	5504	6155	4168	4537	3165	2638
Fuel oil	10342	10625	14706	17049	14140	13857
Total input	44563	50728	41390	50561	37500	33344
Total production	15955	17672	13453	14854	10804	9418
Estimated efficiency (% of production to input)	36	35	33	29	29	28

Korea, Republic of

Item	2013	2014	2015	2016	2017	2018
Production, trade and consumption	**Million kilowatt-hours**					
Total main activity and autoproducer	541996	550934	552697	562603	566881	590108
Combustible fuels	390858	381511	375110	385386	400148	435290
Hydro	8394	7820	5796	6634	7006	7270
Nuclear	138784	156407	164762	161995	148427	133505
Other	3960	5196	7029	8588	11300	14043
Main activity	513833	517962	522835	527590	533229	554384
Combustible fuels	363146	349044	345891	351162	367461	400689
Hydro	8394	7820	5796	6634	7006	7270
Nuclear	138784	156407	164762	161995	148427	133505
Other	3509	4691	6386	7799	10335	12920
Own use in electricity, CHP and heat plants	20526	20927	23733	22519	21085	23263
Net production	521470	530007	528964	540084	545796	566845
Imports	..	..	..	..	..	..
Exports	..	..	..	..	..	..
Losses	18311	18270	17979	18475	18790	18183
Consumption	503570	505690	511469	534858	543862	550589
Energy industries own use	16445	18856	16158	17587	20624	19216
By industry and construction	255697	259606	262369	265383	274429	278813
By transport	2168	2003	2217	2689	2865	2967
By households and other cons.	229260	225225	230725	249199	245944	249593
Net installed capacity	**Thousand kilowatts**					
Total main activity and autoproducer	91478	99817	103191	111203	122950	127475
Combustible fuels	61795	69122	70108	75559	86377	89013
Hydro	6452	6467	6471	6485	6489	6490
Nuclear	20716	20716	21716	23116	22529	21850
Other	2515	3512	4896	6043	7555	10122
Main activity	85145	92115	95695	103742	113913	117613
Combustible fuels	55960	62121	63704	68903	78130	80138
Hydro	6452	6467	6471	6485	6489	6490
Nuclear	20716	20716	21716	23116	22529	21850
Other	2017	2811	3804	5238	6765	9135
Combustible fuel input	**Terajoules**					
Hard Coal	2135854	2049054	2106320	2107076	2117889	2113883
Brown Coal	38499	103882	145713	140268	208597	209857
Fuel oil	139663	66741	76073	112070	44642	48844
Naphtha	46903	47882	63680	55136	45657	47571
Petroleum coke	8840	11050	15925	10628	20573	21125
Natural gas	1054747	933846	889749	952847	993522	1204484
Coke-oven gas	23544	38166	35247	35474	39417	41092
Blast furnace gas	102556	127625	124623	120427	121844	121419
Fuelwood	*6776	*4613	*10176	*38807	*41348	*52535
Other recovered gases	14983	20893	22509	23676	23219	23176
Others	28989	42111	38246	36358	45759	49292
Total input	3601355	3445863	3528261	3632766	3702467	3933277
Total production	1407089	1373440	1350396	1387390	1440533	1567044
Estimated efficiency (% of production to input)	39	40	38	38	39	40

Kosovo

Item	2013	2014	2015	2016	2017	2018
Production, trade and consumption	Million kilowatt-hours					
Total main activity and autoproducer	6525	5436	6119	5981	5919	5917
Combustible fuels	6382	5285	5979	5736	5739	5612
Hydro	143	151	140	245	179	273
Nuclear	..	..	..	..	..	..
Other	..	..	..	..	1	32
Main activity	6525	5436	6119	5981	5919	5917
Combustible fuels	6382	5285	5979	5736	5739	5612
Hydro	143	151	140	245	179	273
Nuclear	..	..	..	..	..	..
Other	..	..	..	..	1	32
Own use in electricity, CHP and heat plants	664	434	618	430	618	537
Net production	5861	5002	5501	5551	5301	5380
Imports	2551	966	684	557	1242	825
Exports	2893	475	553	1064	880	677
Losses	879	818	999	1174	1317	1125
Consumption	4645	4674	4622	3871	4337	4398
Energy industries own use	0	0	0	0	..	..
By industry and construction	1255	1311	1368	1048	1062	979
By transport	..	..	..	..	..	..
By households and other cons.	3390	3363	3254	2823	3275	3419
Net installed capacity	Thousand kilowatts					
Total main activity and autoproducer	959	959	959	1009	1409	1409
Combustible fuels	915	915	915	915	1288	1288
Hydro	43	43	43	86	80	80
Nuclear	..	..	..	..	..	..
Other	1	1	1	8	40	40
Main activity	959	959	959	1009	1409	1409
Combustible fuels	915	915	915	915	1288	1288
Hydro	43	43	43	86	80	80
Nuclear	..	..	..	..	..	..
Other	1	1	1	8	40	40
Combustible fuel input	Terajoules					
Brown Coal	63142	54598	63532	66473	55792	59498
Gas-diesel oil	86	86	86	86	86	43
Fuel oil	121	121	121	121	81	81
Total input	63349	54806	63739	66680	55959	59622
Total production	22975	19026	21524	20650	20660	20203
Estimated efficiency (% of production to input)	36	35	34	31	37	34

Kuwait

Item	2013	2014	2015	2016	2017	2018
Production, trade and consumption			**Million kilowatt-hours**			
Total main activity and autoproducer	60982	65140	68288	70085	72790	74107
Combustible fuels	60982	65140	68288	70085	72788	74103
Hydro	..	..	..	..	..	..
Nuclear	..	..	..	..	..	..
Other	..	..	..	0	2	4
Main activity	60982	65140	68288	70085	72788	74103
Combustible fuels	60982	65140	68288	70085	72788	74103
Hydro	..	..	..	..	..	..
Nuclear	..	..	..	..	..	..
Other	..	..	..	..	..	..
Own use in electricity, CHP and heat plants	7398	7597	7878	8168	7921	8316
Net production	53584	57543	60410	61917	64869	65791
Imports	124	136	133	171	553	202
Exports	164	178	175	213	390	535
Losses	5354	5750	6037	6188	6503	6546
Consumption	48190	51751	54331	55688	58529	58912
Energy industries own use	13211	14188	14895	15267	16046	16151
By industry and construction	..	..	..	..	..	..
By transport	..	..	..	..	..	..
By households and other cons.	34978	37563	39436	40421	42483	42762
Net installed capacity			**Thousand kilowatts**			
Total main activity and autoproducer	15639	15739	18279	18892	18765	18867
Combustible fuels	15639	15739	18279	18890	18763	18863
Hydro	..	..	..	..	..	..
Nuclear	..	..	..	..	..	..
Other	..	..	..	*2	*2	*4
Main activity	15619	15719	18259	18870	18743	18793
Combustible fuels	15619	15719	18259	18870	18743	18793
Hydro	..	..	..	..	..	..
Nuclear	..	..	..	..	..	..
Other	..	..	..	..	..	..
Combustible fuel input			**Terajoules**			
Crude oil	66538	84642	28510	23857	54017	36632
Gas-diesel oil	53234	64285	49407	33024	29971	20898
Fuel oil	284901	230240	283406	293950	252298	260580
Natural gas	272734	337808	377668	407319	403477	434116
Total input	677407	716975	738991	758151	739763	752226
Total production	219535	234504	245837	252306	262037	266771
Estimated efficiency (% of production to input)	32	33	33	33	35	35

Kyrgyzstan

Item	2013	2014	2015	2016	2017	2018
Production, trade and consumption			Million kilowatt-hours			
Total main activity and autoproducer	14011	14572	13030	13262	15514	15728
Combustible fuels	914	1274	1930	1768	1311	1410
Hydro	13097	13298	11100	11494	14203	14318
Nuclear	..	..	..	..	..	..
Other	..	..	..	..	..	..
Main activity	14004	14552	13006	13236	15499	15689
Combustible fuels	907	1254	1906	1742	1296	1371
Hydro	13097	13298	11100	11494	14203	14318
Nuclear	..	..	..	..	..	..
Other	..	..	..	..	..	..
Own use in electricity, CHP and heat plants	199	270	244	182	136	194
Net production	13812	14302	12786	13080	15378	15534
Imports	0	286	729	330	..	..
Exports	377	72	184	199	1215	755
Losses	2841	3458	2668	2655	2844	2814
Consumption	10322	11058	10663	10428	11190	11965
Energy industries own use	55	74	76	268	182	101
By industry and construction	1464	1175	2356	1709	1763	2510
By transport	41	232	174	45	46	44
By households and other cons.	8762	9577	8057	8406	9199	9310
Net installed capacity			Thousand kilowatts			
Total main activity and autoproducer	*3861	*3864	*3865	*3786	3869	*3869
Combustible fuels	*797	*800	*801	*722	*734	*734
Hydro	*3064	*3064	*3064	*3064	3135	*3135
Nuclear	..	..	..	..	..	..
Other	..	..	..	..	..	..
Main activity	*3859	*3859	*3859	*3780	3863	*3863
Combustible fuels	*795	*795	*795	*716	*728	*728
Hydro	*3064	*3064	*3064	*3064	3135	*3135
Nuclear	..	..	..	..	..	..
Other	..	..	..	..	..	..
Combustible fuel input			Terajoules			
Hard Coal	9840	11838	18775	9922	6120	4043
Brown Coal	4645	7298	5334	6389	6462	8367
Gas-diesel oil	0	0	0	0	..	..
Fuel oil	1252	1050	646	364	566	1010
Natural gas	382	1651	2419	2710	1697	1142
Total input	16120	21837	27175	19385	14845	14563
Total production	3290	4586	6948	6365	4720	5076
Estimated efficiency (% of production to input)	20	21	26	33	32	35

Lao People's Dem. Rep.

Item	2013	2014	2015	2016	2017	2018
Production, trade and consumption	Million kilowatt-hours					
Total main activity and autoproducer	15512	15640	16730	25068	31550	*34410
Combustible fuels	5	6	2476	7120	*11683	*12555
Hydro	15506	15633	14252	17946	19858	*21844
Nuclear	..	..	..	..	..	..
Other	0	1	2	2	9	*12
Main activity	15512	15640	16730	25068	31550	*34410
Combustible fuels	5	6	2476	7120	*11683	*12555
Hydro	15506	15633	14252	17946	19858	*21844
Nuclear	..	..	..	..	..	..
Other	0	1	2	2	9	*12
Own use in electricity, CHP and heat plants	0	350	229	2	*320	*360
Net production	15512	15290	16501	25066	31230	*34050
Imports	1272	1559	2050	787	500	302
Exports	12494	11936	11559	19650	24901	27216
Losses	907	1106	2565	1673	1799	1994
Consumption	3381	3791	4239	4660	*5030	*5142
Energy industries own use	..	..	..	..	..	..
By industry and construction	1118	1564	1745	1916	*2069	*2115
By transport	..	..	..	..	..	..
By households and other cons.	2263	2228	2494	2744	*2962	*3028
Net installed capacity	Thousand kilowatts					
Total main activity and autoproducer	3020	3098	5813	6457	6916	7171
Combustible fuels	40	40	1918	1918	1903	1909
Hydro	2980	3058	3894	4538	5006	5256
Nuclear	..	..	..	..	..	..
Other	0	1	2	2	7	7
Main activity	3020	3098	5813	6457	6916	7171
Combustible fuels	40	40	1918	1918	1903	1909
Hydro	2980	3058	3894	4538	5006	5256
Nuclear	..	..	..	..	..	..
Other	0	1	2	2	7	7
Combustible fuel input	Terajoules					
Brown Coal	..	..	41605	*92617	*124378	*131235
Bagasse	*77	*77	*54	*77	*425	*421
Total input	*77	*77	41659	*92695	*124803	*131656
Total production	19	20	8914	25632	*42060	*45197
Estimated efficiency (% of production to input)	25	26	21	28	34	34

Latvia

Item	2013	2014	2015	2016	2017	2018
Production, trade and consumption	**Million kilowatt-hours**					
Total main activity and autoproducer	6209	5139	5533	6425	7531	6725
Combustible fuels	3177	3006	3526	3767	3000	4170
Hydro	2912	1994	1860	2530	4381	2432
Nuclear	..	..	..	..	..	..
Other	120	139	147	128	150	123
Main activity	5954	4884	5276	6214	7337	6535
Combustible fuels	2926	2760	3273	3560	2812	3984
Hydro	2909	1987	1858	2528	4377	2430
Nuclear	..	..	..	..	..	..
Other	119	137	145	126	148	121
Own use in electricity, CHP and heat plants	409	407	440	498	506	522
Net production	5800	4732	5093	5927	7025	6203
Imports	5005	5340	5246	4828	4073	5174
Exports	3650	3023	3425	3795	4137	4265
Losses	575	465	451	476	474	448
Consumption	6576	6582	6461	6482	6485	6661
Energy industries own use	..	..	..	..	..	..
By industry and construction	1808	1667	1703	1667	1763	1842
By transport	124	117	106	105	104	103
By households and other cons.	4644	4798	4652	4710	4618	4716
Net installed capacity	**Thousand kilowatts**					
Total main activity and autoproducer	2908	2922	2931	2927	2942	2915
Combustible fuels	1255	1265	1275	1292	1299	1269
Hydro	1587	1588	1588	1564	1564	1565
Nuclear	..	..	..	..	..	..
Other	66	69	68	71	79	81
Main activity	2857	2880	2889	2883	2908	2880
Combustible fuels	1205	1224	1234	1251	1268	1239
Hydro	1586	1587	1587	1563	1563	1563
Nuclear	..	..	..	..	..	..
Other	66	69	68	69	77	78
Combustible fuel input	**Terajoules**					
Hard Coal	446	169	96	143	48	96
Peat	40	0	0	0	..	80
Biogas	2365	2780	3310	3424	3568	3291
Gas-diesel oil	0	0	0	0	..	0
Fuel oil	121	0	0	0	0	0
Natural gas	33458	29896	32244	32978	18586	27058
Fuelwood	5256	7097	8359	10331	11095	11693
Vegetal waste	0	0	0	0	0	0
Biodiesel	0	0	0	0	..	..
Total input	41687	39942	44009	46876	33297	42219
Total production	11437	10822	12694	13561	10800	15012
Estimated efficiency (% of production to input)	27	27	29	29	32	36

Statistics on electricity

Lebanon

Item	2013	2014	2015	2016	2017	2018
Production, trade and consumption			**Million kilowatt-hours**			
Total main activity and autoproducer	17490	19777	20720	21457	23411	23150
Combustible fuels	16218	19578	20226	21047	22955	22754
Hydro	1269	193	479	382	415	348
Nuclear	..	..	..	..	..	..
Other	3	6	15	28	41	48
Main activity	10487	12387	12253	13060	14498	15234
Combustible fuels	9218	12194	11774	12678	14083	14886
Hydro	1269	193	479	382	415	348
Nuclear	..	..	..	..	..	..
Other	..	..	..	..	..	..
Own use in electricity, CHP and heat plants	3	6	15	28	41	48
Net production	17487	19771	20705	21429	23370	23102
Imports	522	136	268	69	534	11
Exports	..	..	..	..	..	..
Losses	1651	*1792	*1888	*1935	*2151	*2080
Consumption	16358	*18116	*19085	*19563	*21753	*21033
Energy industries own use	..	..	..	..	..	..
By industry and construction	4294	*4747	*5001	*5126	*5700	*5511
By transport	..	..	..	..	..	..
By households and other cons.	12064	*13369	*14084	*14437	*16053	*15522
Net installed capacity			**Thousand kilowatts**			
Total main activity and autoproducer	3535	3537	3643	3662	3698	3704
Combustible fuels	3259	3259	3359	3359	3409	3409
Hydro	*274	*274	*274	280	*253	*253
Nuclear	..	..	..	..	..	..
Other	2	4	10	23	36	42
Main activity	2583	2583	2583	2589	2562	2562
Combustible fuels	2309	2309	2309	2309	2309	2309
Hydro	*274	*274	*274	280	*253	*253
Nuclear	..	..	..	..	..	..
Other	..	..	..	..	..	..
Combustible fuel input			**Terajoules**			
Gas-diesel oil	109646	116949	126631	126133	124593	122210
Fuel oil	47811	57087	57173	62844	77415	75581
Natural gas	0	0	0	..	..	..
Total input	157457	174036	183804	188976	202007	197791
Total production	58385	70481	72814	75769	82638	81914
Estimated efficiency (% of production to input)	37	40	40	40	41	41

Lesotho

Item	2013	2014	2015	2016	2017	2018
Production, trade and consumption	**Million kilowatt-hours**					
Total main activity and autoproducer	515	515	532	508	502	517
Combustible fuels	..	..	..	0	*1	1
Hydro	515	515	532	508	501	517
Nuclear	..	..	..	..	..	..
Other	..	..	..	..	..	..
Main activity	515	515	532	508	502	517
Combustible fuels	..	..	..	0	*1	1
Hydro	515	515	532	508	501	517
Nuclear	..	..	..	..	..	..
Other	..	..	..	..	..	..
Own use in electricity, CHP and heat plants	0	0	0	0	1	1
Net production	515	515	532	508	501	517
Imports	285	271	261	373	387	397
Exports	2	3	4	3	1	3
Losses	88	98	122	154	116	115
Consumption	711	675	*694	*765	700	807
Energy industries own use	..	..	..	..	..	..
By industry and construction	236	233	*225	*267	309	320
By transport	..	..	..	..	..	..
By households and other cons.	475	442	*469	*498	391	487
Net installed capacity	**Thousand kilowatts**					
Total main activity and autoproducer	80	80	80	81	75	75
Combustible fuels	..	..	..	*1	*1	1
Hydro	80	80	80	80	74	74
Nuclear	..	..	..	..	..	..
Other	0	0	0	0	0	0
Main activity	80	80	80	81	75	75
Combustible fuels	..	..	..	*1	*1	1
Hydro	80	80	80	80	74	74
Nuclear	..	..	..	..	..	..
Other	0	0	0	0	0	0
Combustible fuel input	**Terajoules**					
Gas-diesel oil	..	..	..	*4	*4	*4
Total input	..	..	..	*4	*4	*4
Total production	..	..	..	*1	*2	2
Estimated efficiency (% of production to input)	..	..	..	35	56	54

Liberia

Item	2013	2014	2015	2016	2017	2018
Production, trade and consumption	**Million kilowatt-hours**					
Total main activity and autoproducer	*340	*340	*350	*440	*440	*444
Combustible fuels	*300	*300	*310	*400	*397	*318
Hydro	*40	*40	*40	*40	*40	*122
Nuclear	..	..	..	..	..	..
Other	..	..	..	..	*3	*4
Main activity	*140	*140	*145	*175	*160	*234
Combustible fuels	*100	*100	*105	*135	*117	*108
Hydro	*40	*40	*40	*40	*40	*122
Nuclear	..	..	..	..	..	..
Other	..	..	..	..	*3	*4
Own use in electricity, CHP and heat plants	*60	*60	*60	*135	*124	*117
Net production	*280	*280	*290	*305	*316	*327
Imports	..	..	..	..	..	..
Exports	..	..	..	..	..	..
Losses	*24	*24	*25	*30	*30	*27
Consumption	*256	*256	*265	*275	*285	*300
Energy industries own use	..	..	..	..	..	..
By industry and construction	..	..	..	..	..	..
By transport	..	..	..	..	..	..
By households and other cons.	*256	*256	*265	*275	*285	*300
Net installed capacity	**Thousand kilowatts**					
Total main activity and autoproducer	*102	*102	*102	*107	*111	*195
Combustible fuels	*93	*93	*93	*98	*100	*100
Hydro	*9	*9	*9	*9	*9	*92
Nuclear	..	..	..	..	..	..
Other	..	..	..	0	*2	*3
Main activity	32	*32	*32	37	*41	*125
Combustible fuels	23	*23	*23	28	*30	*30
Hydro	*9	*9	*9	*9	*9	*92
Nuclear	..	..	..	..	..	..
Other	..	..	..	0	*2	*3
Combustible fuel input	**Terajoules**					
Gas-diesel oil	*2709	*2752	*3225	*4160	*3870	*3311
Fuel oil	*404	*404	0	0	..	..
Total input	*3113	*3156	*3225	*4160	*3870	*3311
Total production	*1080	*1080	*1116	*1440	*1429	*1145
Estimated efficiency (% of production to input)	35	34	35	35	37	35

Libya

Item	2013	2014	2015	2016	2017	2018
Production, trade and consumption	**Million kilowatt-hours**					
Total main activity and autoproducer	37921	37731	37511	31420	33282	34171
Combustible fuels	37913	37723	37503	31412	33274	34163
Hydro	..	..	..	..	..	..
Nuclear	..	..	..	..	..	..
Other	8	8	8	8	8	8
Main activity	37921	37731	37511	31420	33282	34171
Combustible fuels	37913	37723	37503	31412	33274	34163
Hydro	..	..	..	..	..	..
Nuclear	..	..	..	..	..	..
Other	8	8	8	8	8	8
Own use in electricity, CHP and heat plants	609	632	731	1004	999	842
Net production	37312	37099	36780	30416	32283	33329
Imports	64	88	..	376	302	465
Exports	1	0	..	..	..	..
Losses	7215	7186	7127	6327	6683	6893
Consumption	18995	17019	15282	13988	14132	17605
Energy industries own use	..	..	..	..	..	..
By industry and construction	1892	1560	1892	1213	1225	1169
By transport	..	..	..	..	..	..
By households and other cons.	17103	15459	13390	12775	12907	16436
Net installed capacity	**Thousand kilowatts**					
Total main activity and autoproducer	9460	9460	9460	10249	10243	10516
Combustible fuels	9455	9455	9455	10244	10238	10511
Hydro	..	..	..	..	..	..
Nuclear	..	..	..	..	..	..
Other	5	5	5	5	5	5
Main activity	9460	9460	9460	10249	10243	10516
Combustible fuels	9455	9455	9455	10244	10238	10511
Hydro	..	..	..	..	..	..
Nuclear	..	..	..	..	..	..
Other	5	5	5	5	5	5
Combustible fuel input	**Terajoules**					
Gas-diesel oil	134246	134246	134246	52632	79206	85140
Fuel oil	36602	36602	36602	32845	24280	31431
Natural gas	236429	216420	231270	266071	266448	261466
Total input	407277	387268	402118	351548	369934	378037
Total production	136487	135803	135011	113083	119786	122987
Estimated efficiency (% of production to input)	34	35	34	32	32	33

Liechtenstein

Item	2013	2014	2015	2016	2017	2018
Production, trade and consumption	**Million kilowatt-hours**					
Total main activity and autoproducer	85	41	70	90	93	89
Combustible fuels	3	3	2	2	2	2
Hydro	69	22	49	68	69	62
Nuclear	..	..	..	..	..	..
Other	13	17	19	20	22	25
Main activity	85	41	70	90	93	89
Combustible fuels	3	3	2	2	2	2
Hydro	69	22	49	68	69	62
Nuclear	..	..	..	..	..	..
Other	13	17	19	20	22	25
Own use in electricity, CHP and heat plants	0	0	0	0	0	0
Net production	85	41	70	90	93	89
Imports	319	355	325	309	314	321
Exports	..	..	..	..	..	..
Losses	..	..	..	..	..	..
Consumption	404	396	395	399	407	410
Energy industries own use	..	..	..	..	..	..
By industry and construction	..	..	..	..	..	..
By transport	..	..	..	..	..	..
By households and other cons.	404	396	395	399	407	410
Net installed capacity	**Thousand kilowatts**					
Total main activity and autoproducer	*14	*15	*16	*16	*16	*16
Combustible fuels	*1	1	*1	*1	*1	*1
Hydro	*10	*10	*10	*10	*10	*10
Nuclear	..	..	..	..	..	..
Other	*3	*4	*5	*5	*5	*5
Main activity	*14	*15	*16	*16	*16	*16
Combustible fuels	*1	1	*1	*1	*1	*1
Hydro	*10	*10	*10	*10	*10	*10
Nuclear	..	..	..	..	..	..
Other	*3	*4	*5	*5	*5	*5
Combustible fuel input	**Terajoules**					
Biogas	*13	0	0	*1	*1	*1
Natural gas	*28	*28	*25	*26	*25	*20
Municipal waste	0	0	0	0	0	0
Total input	*41	*28	*25	*27	*26	*21
Total production	12	9	8	9	8	7
Estimated efficiency (% of production to input)	30	32	32	32	32	32

Lithuania

Item	2013	2014	2015	2016	2017	2018
Production, trade and consumption	**Million kilowatt-hours**					
Total main activity and autoproducer	4762	4397	4933	4266	4187	3514
Combustible fuels	2808	2354	2761	1750	1324	1091
Hydro	1069	1088	1024	1044	1181	960
Nuclear	..	..	..	..	..	..
Other	885	955	1148	1472	1682	1463
Main activity	4141	3661	4002	3378	3361	2865
Combustible fuels	2424	1861	2095	1132	748	674
Hydro	1069	1088	1024	1044	1181	960
Nuclear	..	..	..	..	..	..
Other	648	712	883	1202	1432	1231
Own use in electricity, CHP and heat plants	311	253	257	215	191	200
Net production	4451	4144	4676	4051	3996	3314
Imports	8073	8521	7938	11106	11926	12848
Exports	1127	898	730	2831	3249	3215
Losses	872	815	793	907	914	935
Consumption	10522	10949	11089	11416	11755	12013
Energy industries own use	1567	1712	1747	1666	1697	1610
By industry and construction	2986	3119	3313	3417	3634	3688
By transport	74	63	67	72	74	81
By households and other cons.	5895	6055	5962	6261	6350	6634
Net installed capacity	**Thousand kilowatts**					
Total main activity and autoproducer	4323	4037	3587	3665	3326	3354
Combustible fuels	3075	2778	2180	2184	1832	1837
Hydro	876	877	877	877	877	877
Nuclear	..	..	..	..	..	..
Other	372	382	530	604	617	640
Main activity	4053	3764	3313	3387	3046	3074
Combustible fuels	2830	2530	1931	1931	1577	1582
Hydro	876	877	877	877	877	877
Nuclear	..	..	..	..	..	..
Other	347	357	505	579	592	615
Combustible fuel input	**Terajoules**					
Hard Coal	0	0	0	0	0	0
Peat	0	35	0	0	0	0
Biogas	473	603	669	996	1004	1209
Gas-diesel oil	0	0	0	0	0	0
Fuel oil	2666	1414	2060	1091	646	606
Refinery gas	149	99	198	396	297	347
Natural gas	30737	24187	21472	14542	11180	9045
Fuelwood	6075	6060	6365	5911	7192	7887
Municipal waste	929	975	1312	2480	2443	1678
Industrial waste	155	258	290	486	182	584
Others	0	0	0	0	0	0
Total input	41184	33631	32366	25902	22944	21355
Total production	10109	8474	9940	6300	4766	3928
Estimated efficiency (% of production to input)	25	25	31	24	21	18

Luxembourg

Item	2013	2014	2015	2016	2017	2018
Production, trade and consumption	**Million kilowatt-hours**					
Total main activity and autoproducer	2888	2966	2766	2196	2235	2201
Combustible fuels	1573	1622	1030	467	470	490
Hydro	1158	1169	1530	1528	1422	1336
Nuclear	..	..	..	..	..	..
Other	157	175	206	201	343	375
Main activity	2623	2695	2492	1911	1957	1918
Combustible fuels	1388	1452	866	290	304	331
Hydro	1152	1163	1524	1520	1418	1332
Nuclear	..	..	..	..	..	..
Other	83	80	102	101	235	255
Own use in electricity, CHP and heat plants	28	28	28	28	30	30
Net production	2860	2938	2738	2168	2205	2171
Imports	6852	6961	7519	7718	7567	7553
Exports	1908	2067	1919	1420	1389	1392
Losses	153	153	158	158	156	155
Consumption	7668	7677	8175	8309	8228	8141
Energy industries own use	1468	1496	1951	1943	1834	1717
By industry and construction	3053	3075	3145	3431	3004	3061
By transport	129	124	132	131	135	137
By households and other cons.	3018	2982	2947	2804	3255	3226
Net installed capacity	**Thousand kilowatts**					
Total main activity and autoproducer	1813	2022	2024	1710	1711	1718
Combustible fuels	526	524	514	138	133	134
Hydro	1134	1330	1330	1330	1330	1330
Nuclear	..	..	..	..	..	..
Other	153	168	180	242	248	254
Main activity	1657	1851	1844	1509	1523	1530
Combustible fuels	467	465	452	61	75	79
Hydro	1132	1328	1328	1328	1328	1328
Nuclear	..	..	..	..	..	..
Other	58	58	64	120	120	123
Combustible fuel input	**Terajoules**					
Biogas	307	384	395	448	447	485
Gas-diesel oil	0	0	0	43	0	..
Natural gas	13481	12598	7918	3620	3216	2769
Fuelwood	*49	*525	*598	*612	*1122	1976
Municipal waste	1225	1171	1365	1400	1557	1552
Total input	15062	14678	10276	6123	6342	6782
Total production	5663	5839	3708	1681	1692	1764
Estimated efficiency (% of production to input)	38	40	36	27	27	26

Madagascar

Item	2013	2014	2015	2016	2017	2018
Production, trade and consumption	Million kilowatt-hours					
Total main activity and autoproducer	1593	1658	1712	1867	1971	2072
Combustible fuels	784	774	777	980	1182	1104
Hydro	809	884	935	887	789	968
Nuclear	..	..	..	..	..	..
Other	0	0	0	0	0	0
Main activity	1423	1488	1542	1652	1702	1797
Combustible fuels	614	604	607	765	913	829
Hydro	809	884	935	887	789	968
Nuclear	..	..	..	..	..	..
Other	0	0	0	0	0	0
Own use in electricity, CHP and heat plants	*24	*25	*25	*27	26	*25
Net production	1569	1633	1687	1840	1945	2047
Imports	..	..	..	..	..	..
Exports	..	..	..	..	..	..
Losses	*100	*105	*110	116	128	*130
Consumption	1469	1527	1577	1738	1802	1917
Energy industries own use	..	..	..	..	..	..
By industry and construction	*511	*537	*544	416	442	608
By transport	..	..	..	..	..	..
By households and other cons.	958	990	1033	1322	1361	1309
Net installed capacity	Thousand kilowatts					
Total main activity and autoproducer	*541	*542	*543	526	663	*663
Combustible fuels	*379	*379	*379	366	496	*496
Hydro	162	163	164	159	166	*166
Nuclear	..	..	..	..	..	..
Other	0	0	0	*1	*1	*1
Main activity	*509	*510	*511	486	603	*603
Combustible fuels	*347	*347	*347	326	436	*436
Hydro	162	163	164	159	166	*166
Nuclear	..	..	..	..	..	..
Other	0	0	0	*1	*1	*1
Combustible fuel input	Terajoules					
Hard Coal	*774	*697	*722	712	963	*1032
Gas-diesel oil	*5160	3474	4795	5865	4687	*4257
Fuel oil	*2505	*1939	*606	2182	5090	*4604
Bagasse	..	..	..	336	368	*324
Total input	*8439	6110	6123	9095	11108	*10217
Total production	2824	2786	2799	3528	4255	3973
Estimated efficiency (% of production to input)	33	46	46	39	38	39

Malawi

Item	2013	2014	2015	2016	2017	2018
Production, trade and consumption	Million kilowatt-hours					
Total main activity and autoproducer	*2046	*2151	*2136	*2160	*1991	*2266
Combustible fuels	*181	*181	*183	*183	*183	*185
Hydro	*1865	*1970	*1953	*1977	*1809	*2081
Nuclear	..	..	..	..	..	..
Other	..	..	..	..	..	..
Main activity	*1865	*1970	*1953	*1977	*1809	*2081
Combustible fuels	*5	*5	*5	*5	*5	*5
Hydro	*1860	*1965	*1948	*1972	*1804	*2076
Nuclear	..	..	..	..	..	..
Other	..	..	..	..	..	..
Own use in electricity, CHP and heat plants	*97	*100	*101	*102	*192	*210
Net production	*1949	*2051	*2035	*2058	*1799	*2056
Imports	..	..	..	..	..	..
Exports	32	39	22	24	20	82
Losses	*389	*294	*437	*179	*450	*460
Consumption	1529	1718	1559	1855	1329	*1513
Energy industries own use	..	..	..	..	..	..
By industry and construction	661	709	691	971	573	*743
By transport	..	..	..	..	..	..
By households and other cons.	868	1009	868	884	756	*771
Net installed capacity	Thousand kilowatts					
Total main activity and autoproducer	503	567	567	567	567	661
Combustible fuels	*212	*212	*211	*211	*211	*211
Hydro	291	355	356	356	356	450
Nuclear	..	..	..	..	..	..
Other	..	..	..	..	..	..
Main activity	288	353	352	352	352	446
Combustible fuels	*2	*2	*1	*1	*1	*1
Hydro	286	351	351	351	351	445
Nuclear	..	..	..	..	..	..
Other	..	..	..	..	..	..
Combustible fuel input	Terajoules					
Gas-diesel oil	*2002	*1886	*1829	*1904	*1905	*1943
Bagasse	*903	*1116	*934	*903	*903	*903
Total input	*2906	*3002	*2764	*2808	*2808	*2847
Total production	*652	*652	*658	*658	*658	*666
Estimated efficiency (% of production to input)	22	22	24	23	23	23

Statistics on electricity

Malaysia

Item	2013	2014	2015	2016	2017	2018
Production, trade and consumption	**Million kilowatt-hours**					
Total main activity and autoproducer	138331	147461	150123	156665	164509	170578
Combustible fuels	127604	133846	135926	136336	137599	143621
Hydro	10586	13388	13924	20019	26580	26325
Nuclear	..	..	..	..	..	..
Other	141	227	273	310	330	632
Main activity	133311	142788	145137	150442	159257	163415
Combustible fuels	122584	129173	130940	130113	132352	136517
Hydro	10586	13388	13924	20019	26575	26325
Nuclear	..	..	..	..	..	..
Other	141	227	273	310	330	573
Own use in electricity, CHP and heat plants	5835	2885	4043	1317	4588	696
Net production	132496	144576	146080	155348	159921	169882
Imports	221	23	13	33	7	20
Exports	23	12	3	694	1124	1509
Losses	11366	15585	12535	10102	12288	14109
Consumption	123076	128333	132199	144024	146520	152866
Energy industries own use	..	..	..	..	..	..
By industry and construction	55886	58948	60641	67664	71417	76088
By transport	241	256	266	340	459	482
By households and other cons.	66949	69129	71292	76020	74644	76296
Net installed capacity	**Thousand kilowatts**					
Total main activity and autoproducer	31817	29974	30440	33090	33334	34389
Combustible fuels	27725	25040	23519	25732	26848	26432
Hydro	3931	4773	5716	6137	6128	6168
Nuclear	..	..	..	..	..	..
Other	*161	161	1205	1220	358	1790
Main activity	28780	27623	27368	29789	30892	31714
Combustible fuels	24688	22695	21309	23226	24410	24479
Hydro	3931	4768	5714	6135	6126	6168
Nuclear	..	..	..	..	..	..
Other	*161	160	345	427	356	1066
Combustible fuel input	**Terajoules**					
Hard Coal	566362	571404	654254	710051	794090	857092
Gas-diesel oil	27348	27391	13975	8944	15781	14448
Fuel oil	15958	10948	4121	6302	4040	687
Natural gas	634711	650113	711320	600958	540161	536208
Vegetal waste	*15955	9346	9878	9878	*8196	12581
Total input	1260334	1269202	1393548	1336134	1362268	1421016
Total production	459374	481846	489334	490810	495356	517036
Estimated efficiency (% of production to input)	36	38	35	37	36	36

Maldives

Item	2013	2014	2015	2016	2017	2018
Production, trade and consumption			**Million kilowatt-hours**			
Total main activity and autoproducer	425	543	619	672	725	772
Combustible fuels	420	535	611	660	709	756
Hydro	..	..	..	..	..	..
Nuclear	..	..	..	..	..	..
Other	5	8	8	12	16	16
Main activity	308	335	394	432	465	492
Combustible fuels	303	327	386	420	449	476
Hydro	..	..	..	..	..	..
Nuclear	..	..	..	..	..	..
Other	5	8	8	12	16	16
Own use in electricity, CHP and heat plants	*18	*18	*19	*21	*21	*21
Net production	407	525	600	651	704	751
Imports	..	..	..	..	..	..
Exports	..	..	..	..	..	..
Losses	*16	*16	*18	*20	*20	*21
Consumption	*390	*509	*582	*631	*684	*730
Energy industries own use	..	..	..	..	..	..
By industry and construction	*19	*33	*33	*35	*37	*39
By transport	..	..	..	..	..	..
By households and other cons.	*371	*476	*549	*596	*647	*691
Net installed capacity			**Thousand kilowatts**			
Total main activity and autoproducer	157	271	271	274	*277	*277
Combustible fuels	154	266	266	266	*266	*266
Hydro	..	..	..	..	..	..
Nuclear	..	..	..	..	..	..
Other	3	5	5	8	11	11
Main activity	84	146	146	149	*152	*152
Combustible fuels	81	141	141	141	*141	*141
Hydro	..	..	..	..	..	..
Nuclear	..	..	..	..	..	..
Other	3	5	5	8	11	11
Combustible fuel input			**Terajoules**			
Gas-diesel oil	*4911	*6695	*7310	*7433	*8109	*8790
Total input	*4911	*6695	*7310	*7433	*8109	*8790
Total production	1512	1926	2201	2376	2552	2722
Estimated efficiency (% of production to input)	31	29	30	32	31	31

Mali

Item	2013	2014	2015	2016	2017	2018
Production, trade and consumption	**Million kilowatt-hours**					
Total main activity and autoproducer	2017	2104	2370	2613	*3068	*3261
Combustible fuels	1058	1107	1356	1509	*1935	*2128
Hydro	959	997	1012	1102	1130	*1130
Nuclear	..	..	..	..	..	..
Other	..	..	2	2	3	*3
Main activity	1382	1574	1712	1905	2082	*2083
Combustible fuels	423	577	698	801	949	*950
Hydro	959	997	1012	1102	1130	*1130
Nuclear	..	..	..	..	..	..
Other	..	..	2	2	3	*3
Own use in electricity, CHP and heat plants	8	*9	*10	*11	*12	*13
Net production	2009	2095	2360	2602	*3056	*3248
Imports	*349	*512	317	113	*117	*198
Exports	*460	*479	*486	*529	*535	*550
Losses	*318	*339	*288	*311	*318	*356
Consumption	*1580	1785	*1903	*1875	*2320	*2540
Energy industries own use	..	..	..	..	..	..
By industry and construction	*730	810	*823	*715	*920	*1010
By transport	..	..	..	..	..	..
By households and other cons.	*850	975	*1080	*1160	*1400	*1530
Net installed capacity	**Thousand kilowatts**					
Total main activity and autoproducer	811	*894	*895	1011	*1112	*1112
Combustible fuels	363	*404	*404	*490	*560	*560
Hydro	448	*490	*490	520	550	*550
Nuclear	..	..	..	..	..	..
Other	..	..	*1	*1	*2	*2
Main activity	714	*780	*781	811	852	*852
Combustible fuels	266	*290	*290	*290	*300	*300
Hydro	448	*490	*490	520	550	*550
Nuclear	..	..	..	..	..	..
Other	..	..	*1	*1	*2	*2
Combustible fuel input	**Terajoules**					
Gas-diesel oil	*14706	18275	*19350	*13115	*17200	*19608
Bagasse	*1457	1457	*1457	1457	*1457	*1457
Total input	*16163	19732	*20807	*14572	*18657	*21065
Total production	3807	3984	4882	5432	*6965	*7661
Estimated efficiency (% of production to input)	24	20	23	37	37	36

Malta

Item	2013	2014	2015	2016	2017	2018
Production, trade and consumption			**Million kilowatt-hours**			
Total main activity and autoproducer	2251	2245	1305	857	1652	1962
Combustible fuels	2222	2177	1210	729	1490	1772
Hydro	..	..	..	..	..	..
Nuclear	..	..	..	..	..	..
Other	29	68	95	128	162	190
Main activity	2216	2170	1203	721	1480	1763
Combustible fuels	2216	2170	1203	721	1480	1763
Hydro	..	..	..	..	..	..
Nuclear	..	..	..	..	..	..
Other	0	..	..	..	..	..
Own use in electricity, CHP and heat plants	114	108	64	50	49	50
Net production	2137	2137	1241	807	1603	1912
Imports	..	..	1054	1525	897	631
Exports	..	..	..	..	36	11
Losses	187	132	179	216	144	143
Consumption	1950	2005	2114	2116	2319	2391
Energy industries own use	..	..	..	..	..	..
By industry and construction	404	406	415	411	459	480
By transport	..	..	..	..	..	..
By households and other cons.	1546	1599	1699	1705	1860	1911
Net installed capacity			**Thousand kilowatts**			
Total main activity and autoproducer	652	678	668	573	707	726
Combustible fuels	623	623	593	480	595	595
Hydro	..	..	..	..	..	..
Nuclear	..	..	..	..	..	..
Other	29	55	75	94	112	131
Main activity	620	620	590	475	590	590
Combustible fuels	620	620	590	475	590	590
Hydro	..	..	..	..	..	..
Nuclear	..	..	..	..	..	..
Other	..	..	..	..	..	..
Combustible fuel input			**Terajoules**			
Biogas	34	37	46	42	46	42
Gas-diesel oil	2494	2322	860	129	258	215
Fuel oil	18988	18665	10262	7151	1899	0
Natural gas	..	..	..	..	10776	13602
Total input	21516	21024	11168	7322	12979	13859
Total production	7999	7837	4356	2624	5364	6379
Estimated efficiency (% of production to input)	37	37	39	36	41	46

Marshall Islands

Item	2013	2014	2015	2016	2017	2018
Production, trade and consumption	Million kilowatt-hours					
Total main activity and autoproducer	84	*86	*87	*88	*89	*90
Combustible fuels	83	*85	*86	*86	*87	*88
Hydro	..	..	..	..	..	..
Nuclear	..	..	..	..	..	..
Other	0	1	1	2	2	2
Main activity	84	*86	*87	*88	*89	*90
Combustible fuels	83	*85	*86	*86	*87	*88
Hydro	..	..	..	..	..	..
Nuclear	..	..	..	..	..	..
Other	0	1	1	2	2	2
Own use in electricity, CHP and heat plants	0	0	0	0	0	0
Net production	84	*86	*87	*88	*89	*90
Imports	..	..	..	..	..	..
Exports	..	..	..	..	..	..
Losses	*11	*11	*11	*11	*12	*12
Consumption	73	*75	*75	*76	*78	*78
Energy industries own use	..	..	..	..	..	..
By industry and construction	*3	*3	*3	*4	*4	*4
By transport	..	..	..	..	..	..
By households and other cons.	70	*72	*72	*73	*74	*74
Net installed capacity	Thousand kilowatts					
Total main activity and autoproducer	34	34	37	*38	*39	*39
Combustible fuels	33	33	36	*36	*37	*37
Hydro	..	..	..	..	..	..
Nuclear	..	..	..	..	..	..
Other	*1	1	1	2	2	2
Main activity	34	34	37	*38	*39	*39
Combustible fuels	33	33	36	*36	*37	*37
Hydro	..	..	..	..	..	..
Nuclear	..	..	..	..	..	..
Other	*1	1	1	2	2	2
Combustible fuel input	Terajoules					
Gas-diesel oil	787	*796	*817	*817	*834	*843
Total input	787	*796	*817	*817	*834	*843
Total production	300	*306	*308	*308	*314	*315
Estimated efficiency (% of production to input)	38	38	38	38	38	37

Mauritania

Item	2013	2014	2015	2016	2017	2018
Production, trade and consumption			Million kilowatt-hours			
Total main activity and autoproducer	812	851	975	1042	1183	1271
Combustible fuels	773	808	841	875	1022	1023
Hydro	..	..	..	..	..	..
Nuclear	..	..	..	..	..	..
Other	39	43	134	168	161	248
Main activity	492	525	662	683	841	925
Combustible fuels	453	482	528	515	680	677
Hydro	..	..	..	..	..	..
Nuclear	..	..	..	..	..	..
Other	39	43	134	168	161	248
Own use in electricity, CHP and heat plants	24	25	35	63	95	95
Net production	788	826	940	979	1088	1176
Imports	174	183	183	221	*185	198
Exports	..	..	..	57	..	..
Losses	164	*172	*190	*192	*210	*225
Consumption	792	844	932	951	1063	1148
Energy industries own use	..	..	..	..	..	..
By industry and construction	298	326	360	357	342	*346
By transport	..	..	..	..	..	..
By households and other cons.	494	519	572	594	721	802
Net installed capacity			Thousand kilowatts			
Total main activity and autoproducer	231	240	444	*461	*506	*570
Combustible fuels	209	218	392	*392	*421	*449
Hydro	..	..	..	..	..	..
Nuclear	..	..	..	..	..	..
Other	22	22	52	69	85	121
Main activity	161	161	364	*381	*426	*485
Combustible fuels	139	139	312	*312	*341	*364
Hydro	..	..	..	..	..	..
Nuclear	..	..	..	..	..	..
Other	22	22	52	69	85	121
Combustible fuel input			Terajoules			
Gas-diesel oil	*4532	5173	*5616	*5031	*7310	*7740
Fuel oil	*3030	*3717	*3313	*2674	*2771	*2020
Total input	*7562	8890	*8929	*7705	*10081	*9760
Total production	2783	2907	3028	3148	3678	3683
Estimated efficiency (% of production to input)	37	33	34	41	36	38

Mauritius

Item	2013	2014	2015	2016	2017	2018
Production, trade and consumption	Million kilowatt-hours					
Total main activity and autoproducer	2882	2936	2996	3042	3120	3132
Combustible fuels	2781	2817	2845	2894	2976	2943
Hydro	95	91	122	100	90	125
Nuclear	..	..	..	..	..	..
Other	6	28	29	48	54	64
Main activity	1176	1175	1258	1215	1277	1350
Combustible fuels	1078	1081	1133	1112	1184	1223
Hydro	95	91	122	100	90	125
Nuclear	..	..	..	..	..	..
Other	4	3	3	4	3	3
Own use in electricity, CHP and heat plants	39	42	44	45	44	44
Net production	2843	2894	2952	2998	3076	3088
Imports	..	..	..	..	..	..
Exports	..	..	..	..	..	..
Losses	184	182	178	172	187	182
Consumption	2657	2708	2770	2815	2880	2918
Energy industries own use	273	256	264	260	266	268
By industry and construction	*714	687	696	706	727	734
By transport	..	..	..	..	..	..
By households and other cons.	1670	1765	1809	1848	1886	1916
Net installed capacity	Thousand kilowatts					
Total main activity and autoproducer	778	782	792	847	836	874
Combustible fuels	714	702	711	749	736	737
Hydro	61	61	61	61	60	60
Nuclear	..	..	..	..	..	..
Other	4	19	20	38	40	77
Main activity	501	490	489	499	513	513
Combustible fuels	439	428	427	437	452	452
Hydro	61	61	61	61	60	60
Nuclear	..	..	..	..	..	..
Other	1	1	1	1	1	1
Combustible fuel input	Terajoules					
Hard Coal	17731	18344	17647	18091	18871	17916
Biogas	*68	*70	73	67	61	81
Gas-diesel oil	43	43	43	45	55	34
Fuel oil	8726	8928	9292	8696	9672	9991
Other kerosene	44	44	44	34	41	28
Bagasse	8155	7954	9575	8722	8324	7791
Total input	34766	35383	36675	35654	37025	35842
Total production	10012	10142	10242	10420	10714	10593
Estimated efficiency (% of production to input)	29	29	28	29	29	30

Mexico

Item	2013	2014	2015	2016	2017	2018
Production, trade and consumption	Million kilowatt-hours					
Total main activity and autoproducer	297326	301496	310712	320565	322063	335581
Combustible fuels	247163	240279	253005	262310	261726	269256
Hydro	28002	38893	30815	30698	31982	32636
Nuclear	11800	9677	11577	10567	10883	13675
Other	10361	12647	15315	16990	17472	20014
Main activity	258821	258258	262721	266201	259078	268103
Combustible fuels	211680	202346	212385	217231	209160	214880
Hydro	27444	38145	30051	29805	31040	31581
Nuclear	11800	9677	11577	10567	10883	13675
Other	7897	8090	8708	8598	7995	7967
Own use in electricity, CHP and heat plants	10235	11446	12935	17689	13130	13780
Net production	287091	290050	297777	302876	308933	321801
Imports	1210	2124	1650	2232	2151	3759
Exports	1240	2653	2320	1968	1804	2276
Losses	42520	41322	40640	40002	43915	46940
Consumption	246503	256779	261850	274210	275859	286960
Energy industries own use	5033	4559	4400	3843	3938	3552
By industry and construction	137391	142326	139990	145945	147465	149739
By transport	1130	1130	1134	1140	1077	1072
By households and other cons.	102949	108764	116326	123282	123379	132597
Net installed capacity	Thousand kilowatts					
Total main activity and autoproducer	64107	66255	67504	72574	74431	76921
Combustible fuels	48047	48893	49421	53047	54388	54388
Hydro	11633	12464	12223	12580	12628	12628
Nuclear	1400	1400	1510	1608	1608	1608
Other	3027	3498	4350	5339	5807	8297
Main activity	53497	54379	54856	55904	57536	59024
Combustible fuels	39161	39294	39735	40280	41616	41616
Hydro	11509	12269	12028	12348	12395	12395
Nuclear	1400	1400	1510	1608	1608	1608
Other	1427	1416	1583	1668	1917	3405
Combustible fuel input	Terajoules					
Hard Coal	125044	150551	146312	169061	205979	183718
Brown Coal	197886	200358	206785	198168	133446	133665
Biogas	1970	1939	1961	1912	2265	2514
Gas-diesel oil	35475	21371	21586	27606	31820	39947
Fuel oil	432522	300010	254762	282194	306838	264903
Liquefied petroleum gas	568	5061	5014	3548	2270	3595
Petroleum coke	40073	39910	39163	29803	38350	37863
Natural gas	1423071	1484833	1609427	1684576	1782417	1850149
Bagasse	*53758	*71126	*68416	*70268	*76782	*76074
Industrial waste	1690	861	473	552	897	3693
Others	5061	5263	6289	5518	3947	2578
Total input	2317117	2281284	2360188	2473205	2585012	2598698
Total production	889787	865004	910818	944316	942214	969322
Estimated efficiency (% of production to input)	38	38	39	38	36	37

Micronesia (Fed. States of)

Item	2013	2014	2015	2016	2017	2018
Production, trade and consumption	Million kilowatt-hours					
Total main activity and autoproducer	*67	69	67	*68	*67	*69
Combustible fuels	*66	68	66	*66	*65	*65
Hydro	..	0	0	0	0	0
Nuclear	..	..	..	..	..	..
Other	1	1	1	2	2	*4
Main activity	*67	69	67	*68	*67	*69
Combustible fuels	*66	68	66	*66	*65	*65
Hydro	..	0	0	0	0	0
Nuclear	..	..	..	..	..	..
Other	1	1	1	2	2	*4
Own use in electricity, CHP and heat plants	*3	3	1	2	*2	*2
Net production	*65	66	66	*65	*65	*66
Imports	..	..	..	..	..	..
Exports	..	..	..	..	..	..
Losses	*13	*15	*19	*19	*20	*21
Consumption	*51	*51	46	*46	*46	*46
Energy industries own use	..	..	..	..	..	..
By industry and construction	*11	*14	15	*15	*15	*15
By transport	..	..	..	..	..	..
By households and other cons.	*40	*38	31	*31	*31	*31
Net installed capacity	Thousand kilowatts					
Total main activity and autoproducer	32	34	*34	*34	*34	*36
Combustible fuels	32	32	*32	*32	*32	*32
Hydro	..	2	2	2	*2	*2
Nuclear	..	..	..	..	..	..
Other	1	1	1	1	1	3
Main activity	32	34	*34	*34	*34	*36
Combustible fuels	32	32	*32	*32	*32	*32
Hydro	..	2	2	2	*2	*2
Nuclear	..	..	..	..	..	..
Other	1	1	1	1	1	3
Combustible fuel input	Terajoules					
Gas-diesel oil	*753	*774	834	*834	*830	*830
Total input	*753	*774	834	*834	*830	*830
Total production	*238	243	236	*236	*235	*233
Estimated efficiency (% of production to input)	32	31	28	28	28	28

Mongolia

Item	2013	2014	2015	2016	2017	2018
Production, trade and consumption			Million kilowatt-hours			
Total main activity and autoproducer	5020	5376	5513	5667	6027	6535
Combustible fuels	5020	5376	5513	5667	6027	6535
Hydro	..	..	..	..	..	..
Nuclear	..	..	..	..	..	..
Other	..	..	..	..	..	..
Main activity	5020	5376	5513	5667	6027	6535
Combustible fuels	5020	5376	5513	5667	6027	6535
Hydro	..	..	..	..	..	..
Nuclear	..	..	..	..	..	..
Other	..	..	..	..	..	..
Own use in electricity, CHP and heat plants	725	772	778	749	816	849
Net production	4294	4603	4735	4918	5211	5686
Imports	1196	1349	1417	1446	1574	1666
Exports	18	33	51	36	26	27
Losses	740	793	783	817	811	875
Consumption	4732	5159	5284	5446	5949	6450
Energy industries own use	..	..	..	..	..	..
By industry and construction	2931	3172	3261	3356	3692	4003
By transport	197	211	217	223	248	268
By households and other cons.	1605	1776	1806	1867	2009	2178
Net installed capacity			Thousand kilowatts			
Total main activity and autoproducer	1278	*1171	*1171	*1189	1286	*1461
Combustible fuels	1200	*1092	*1092	*1103	1132	*1210
Hydro	26	26	26	29	29	31
Nuclear	..	..	..	..	..	..
Other	52	53	53	57	125	220
Main activity	1102	*1135	*1135	*1150	1247	*1420
Combustible fuels	1050	*1082	*1082	*1093	1122	*1200
Hydro	..	..	..	..	..	..
Nuclear	..	..	..	..	..	..
Other	52	53	53	57	125	220
Combustible fuel input			Terajoules			
Hard Coal	35173	38740	40417	42227	51712	63440
Brown Coal	74013	76185	75744	75391	78587	79093
Gas-diesel oil	3741	3311	3182	2662	3913	4124
Fuel oil	162	125	129	105	89	121
Total input	113088	118361	119472	120385	134301	146777
Total production	18070	19353	19848	20402	21698	23527
Estimated efficiency (% of production to input)	16	16	17	17	16	16

Montenegro

Item	2013	2014	2015	2016	2017	2018
Production, trade and consumption	**Million kilowatt-hours**					
Total main activity and autoproducer	3945	3173	3003	3141	2483	3679
Combustible fuels	1441	1421	1512	1298	1348	1444
Hydro	2504	1752	1491	1843	1040	2092
Nuclear	..	..	..	..	..	..
Other	..	..	..	..	95	143
Main activity	3945	3173	3003	3141	2483	3679
Combustible fuels	1441	1421	1512	1298	1348	1444
Hydro	2504	1752	1491	1843	1040	2092
Nuclear	..	..	..	..	..	..
Other	..	..	..	..	95	143
Own use in electricity, CHP and heat plants	136	135	131	118	119	134
Net production	3809	3038	2872	3023	2364	3546
Imports	388	903	1040	1210	1537	780
Exports	733	642	517	906	417	976
Losses	758	689	586	541	512	503
Consumption	2706	2610	2679	2671	2855	2847
Energy industries own use	..	..	..	..	..	..
By industry and construction	1326	760	767	660	732	737
By transport	20	18	20	21	20	19
By households and other cons.	1360	1832	1892	1990	2103	2090
Net installed capacity	**Thousand kilowatts**					
Total main activity and autoproducer	870	870	870	870	949	*999
Combustible fuels	219	219	219	219	225	*225
Hydro	651	651	651	651	652	*652
Nuclear	..	..	..	..	..	..
Other	..	..	..	..	72	121
Main activity	870	870	870	870	949	*999
Combustible fuels	219	219	219	219	225	*225
Hydro	651	651	651	651	652	*652
Nuclear	..	..	..	..	..	..
Other	..	..	..	..	72	121
Combustible fuel input	**Terajoules**					
Brown Coal	15178	14708	15362	12028	12341	14816
Total input	15178	14708	15362	12028	12341	14816
Total production	5188	5116	5443	4673	4853	5198
Estimated efficiency (% of production to input)	34	35	35	39	39	35

Montserrat

Item	2013	2014	2015	2016	2017	2018
Production, trade and consumption	Million kilowatt-hours					
Total main activity and autoproducer	*23	*24	*24	*20	*19	*20
Combustible fuels	*23	*24	*24	*20	*19	*20
Hydro	..	..	..	..	..	..
Nuclear	..	..	..	..	..	..
Other	..	..	..	..	..	..
Main activity	*23	*24	*24	*20	*19	*20
Combustible fuels	*23	*24	*24	*20	*19	*20
Hydro	..	..	..	..	..	..
Nuclear	..	..	..	..	..	..
Other	..	..	..	..	..	..
Own use in electricity, CHP and heat plants	*2	*2	*2	0	0	0
Net production	*21	*22	*22	*20	*19	*20
Imports	..	..	..	..	..	..
Exports	..	..	..	..	..	..
Losses	*1	*1	*1	*1	*1	*1
Consumption	20	20	20	*18	18	*19
Energy industries own use	..	..	..	..	..	..
By industry and construction	*9	*9	*9	*8	*8	*8
By transport	..	..	..	..	..	..
By households and other cons.	11	11	11	*10	10	*11
Net installed capacity	Thousand kilowatts					
Total main activity and autoproducer	*5	6	5	5	5	5
Combustible fuels	*5	6	5	5	5	5
Hydro	..	..	..	..	..	..
Nuclear	..	..	..	..	..	..
Other	..	..	..	..	..	..
Main activity	*5	6	5	5	5	5
Combustible fuels	*5	6	5	5	5	5
Hydro	..	..	..	..	..	..
Nuclear	..	..	..	..	..	..
Other	..	..	..	..	..	..
Combustible fuel input	Terajoules					
Gas-diesel oil	*237	*237	*237	*194	*172	*177
Total input	*237	*237	*237	*194	*172	*177
Total production	*83	*86	*86	*72	*68	*70
Estimated efficiency (% of production to input)	35	37	37	37	40	40

Morocco

Item	2013	2014	2015	2016	2017	2018
Production, trade and consumption	Million kilowatt-hours					
Total main activity and autoproducer	28242	29384	31217	32141	33192	35839
Combustible fuels	22594	24125	25108	25776	26875	27748
Hydro	2990	2033	2282	1662	1565	1998
Nuclear	..	..	..	..	..	..
Other	2658	3226	3827	4703	4752	6093
Main activity	26829	27945	29855	30839	31890	34537
Combustible fuels	22483	23988	25048	25776	26875	27748
Hydro	2990	2033	2282	1662	1565	1998
Nuclear	..	..	..	..	..	..
Other	1356	1924	2525	3401	3450	4791
Own use in electricity, CHP and heat plants	40	44	52	50	60	62
Net production	28202	29340	31165	32091	33132	35777
Imports	5551	6138	5138	5289	6058	3725
Exports	151	128	165	135	161	350
Losses	4915	5197	5515	5654	6066	6159
Consumption	28687	30153	30624	31592	32963	32993
Energy industries own use	654	899	685	529	510	406
By industry and construction	10303	10659	10864	11190	11826	12086
By transport	322	332	345	352	368	375
By households and other cons.	17408	18263	18730	19521	20259	20126
Net installed capacity	Thousand kilowatts					
Total main activity and autoproducer	10642	11294	11455	11561	12120	12350
Combustible fuels	8377	8727	8727	8732	9128	9151
Hydro	1770	1770	1770	1770	1770	1770
Nuclear	..	..	..	..	..	..
Other	495	797	958	1059	1222	1429
Main activity	7342	7994	8155	8261	8820	9050
Combustible fuels	5077	5427	5427	5432	5828	5851
Hydro	1770	1770	1770	1770	1770	1770
Nuclear	..	..	..	..	..	..
Other	495	797	958	1059	1222	1429
Combustible fuel input	Terajoules					
Hard Coal	126034	171048	188077	178592	185666	205976
Gas-diesel oil	774	645	430	516	430	258
Fuel oil	51106	28765	23917	31148	34704	12403
Natural gas	44285	42865	43985	45068	44651	39792
Total input	222199	243323	256409	255324	265451	258429
Total production	81338	86850	90389	92794	96750	99893
Estimated efficiency (% of production to input)	37	36	35	36	36	39

Mozambique

Item	2013	2014	2015	2016	2017	2018
Production, trade and consumption	Million kilowatt-hours					
Total main activity and autoproducer	15123	17739	19641	18697	16992	16659
Combustible fuels	318	1379	2547	3103	2930	2736
Hydro	14805	16359	17093	15592	14060	13921
Nuclear	..	..	..	..	..	..
Other	..	1	1	2	2	2
Main activity	14860	17271	19471	18620	16669	16640
Combustible fuels	318	1379	2493	3045	2891	2736
Hydro	14542	15892	16978	15575	13778	13904
Nuclear	..	..	..	..	..	..
Other	..	..	..	..	..	..
Own use in electricity, CHP and heat plants	220	238	238	58	58	109
Net production	14903	17501	19403	18639	16934	16550
Imports	8339	7656	10547	9928	9935	9899
Exports	9058	10199	12876	14269	9945	10446
Losses	2647	2612	5080	2480	2480	2480
Consumption	11605	12342	12180	11383	14443	12722
Energy industries own use	..	..	..	..	..	..
By industry and construction	9295	10651	9800	9100	12488	10332
By transport	..	..	..	..	..	..
By households and other cons.	2310	1691	2380	2283	1955	2390
Net installed capacity	Thousand kilowatts					
Total main activity and autoproducer	2646	2682	2508	2491	*2739	*2744
Combustible fuels	359	359	410	412	*413	*465
Hydro	2287	2322	2097	2078	*2311	*2239
Nuclear	..	..	..	..	..	..
Other	..	1	1	1	15	40
Main activity	2596	2596	2460	2460	*2611	*2589
Combustible fuels	359	359	385	385	*385	*435
Hydro	2237	2237	2075	2075	*2226	*2154
Nuclear	..	..	..	..	..	..
Other	..	..	..	..	..	..
Combustible fuel input	Terajoules					
Gas-diesel oil	..	..	215	215	..	..
Natural gas	3026	16137	23573	24356	23541	23016
Total input	3026	16137	23788	24571	23541	23016
Total production	1145	4964	9168	11172	10548	9850
Estimated efficiency (% of production to input)	38	31	39	45	45	43

Myanmar

Item	2013	2014	2015	2016	2017	2018
Production, trade and consumption	**Million kilowatt-hours**					
Total main activity and autoproducer	12247	14156	15970	17867	20056	26714
Combustible fuels	3424	5327	6463	8123	8865	11878
Hydro	8823	8829	9507	9744	11191	14826
Nuclear	..	..	..	..	..	..
Other	..	..	..	..	..	10
Main activity	11302	11197	14156	14390	18178	24555
Combustible fuels	2929	3046	5327	5235	7647	10419
Hydro	8373	8151	8829	9155	10531	14126
Nuclear	..	..	..	..	..	..
Other	..	..	..	..	..	10
Own use in electricity, CHP and heat plants	182	152	0	0	0	2382
Net production	12065	14005	15970	17867	20055	24332
Imports	..	..	..	..	..	..
Exports	..	..	..	..	..	2356
Losses	2452	2750	2573	2385	2803	3432
Consumption	9613	11255	13397	15355	17115	18544
Energy industries own use	..	..	..	..	..	..
By industry and construction	5849	7142	2145	2120	2773	7117
By transport	..	..	..	..	..	..
By households and other cons.	3764	4113	11252	13235	14343	11427
Net installed capacity	**Thousand kilowatts**					
Total main activity and autoproducer	4146	4805	5259	5390	5799	5828
Combustible fuels	1141	1620	2076	2135	2387	2392
Hydro	3005	3185	3183	3255	3402	3436
Nuclear	..	..	..	..	..	..
Other	..	..	..	..	*10	..
Main activity	3753	4177	4631	4590	5208	5155
Combustible fuels	920	1164	1620	1507	1973	1896
Hydro	2833	3013	3011	3083	3225	3259
Nuclear	..	..	..	..	..	..
Other	..	..	..	..	*10	..
Combustible fuel input	**Terajoules**					
Hard Coal	3056	619	465	*605	*2326	*7653
Brown Coal	..	..	..	179	3744	5589
Gas-diesel oil	2580	4300	4322	6807	4597	860
Natural gas	40331	71842	89943	123472	126111	132958
Total input	45967	76761	94730	131063	136778	147060
Total production	12326	19179	23268	29243	31912	42760
Estimated efficiency (% of production to input)	27	25	25	22	23	29

Namibia

Item	2013	2014	2015	2016	2017	2018
Production, trade and consumption	**Million kilowatt-hours**					
Total main activity and autoproducer	1740	1530	1576	1479	1772	1363
Combustible fuels	72	13	34	62	66	21
Hydro	1640	1485	1502	1359	1593	1144
Nuclear	..	..	..	..	..	..
Other	28	32	40	58	113	198
Main activity	1740	1530	1576	1479	1772	1363
Combustible fuels	72	13	34	62	66	21
Hydro	1640	1485	1502	1359	1593	1144
Nuclear	..	..	..	..	..	..
Other	28	32	40	58	113	198
Own use in electricity, CHP and heat plants	28	2	1	1	82	67
Net production	1712	1528	1575	1478	1690	1296
Imports	2916	2886	2678	3085	2939	3449
Exports	89	84	88	99	100	114
Losses	369	546	340	504	445	434
Consumption	3772	3747	3782	3909	4057	4171
Energy industries own use	..	..	..	..	..	..
By industry and construction	786	716	613	585	603	586
By transport	..	..	..	..	..	..
By households and other cons.	2986	3031	3169	3324	3454	3585
Net installed capacity	**Thousand kilowatts**					
Total main activity and autoproducer	502	504	513	529	565	582
Combustible fuels	155	155	155	143	143	143
Hydro	332	332	337	350	347	347
Nuclear	..	..	..	..	..	..
Other	15	17	21	36	75	93
Main activity	502	504	513	529	565	582
Combustible fuels	155	155	155	143	143	143
Hydro	332	332	337	350	347	347
Nuclear	..	..	..	..	..	..
Other	15	17	21	36	75	93
Combustible fuel input	**Terajoules**					
Hard Coal	590	0	91	772	953	295
Gas-diesel oil	*430	172	387	129	0	..
Total input	1020	172	478	901	953	295
Total production	259	47	122	223	238	76
Estimated efficiency (% of production to input)	25	27	26	25	25	26

Nauru

Item	2013	2014	2015	2016	2017	2018
Production, trade and consumption			**Million kilowatt-hours**			
Total main activity and autoproducer	*24	*25	31	32	35	36
Combustible fuels	*24	*25	31	31	34	35
Hydro	..	..	..	..	..	..
Nuclear	..	..	..	..	..	..
Other	0	0	0	0	1	1
Main activity	*24	*25	31	32	35	36
Combustible fuels	*24	*25	31	31	34	35
Hydro	..	..	..	..	..	..
Nuclear	..	..	..	..	..	..
Other	0	0	0	0	1	1
Own use in electricity, CHP and heat plants	0	0	0	0	0	0
Net production	*24	*25	31	31	34	36
Imports	..	..	..	..	..	..
Exports	..	..	..	..	..	..
Losses	*7	*8	12	10	9	8
Consumption	*17	*17	19	21	26	28
Energy industries own use	..	..	..	..	..	..
By industry and construction	*1	*1	1	1	1	1
By transport	..	..	..	..	..	..
By households and other cons.	*16	*16	18	20	25	27
Net installed capacity			**Thousand kilowatts**			
Total main activity and autoproducer	*6	*6	*6	*7	*8	*14
Combustible fuels	*5	*6	*6	*6	*7	*13
Hydro	..	..	..	..	..	..
Nuclear	..	..	..	..	..	..
Other	0	0	0	1	1	1
Main activity	*6	*6	*6	*7	*8	*14
Combustible fuels	*5	*6	*6	*6	*7	*13
Hydro	..	..	..	..	..	..
Nuclear	..	..	..	..	..	..
Other	0	0	0	1	1	1
Combustible fuel input			**Terajoules**			
Gas-diesel oil	*292	*305	334	343	360	344
Total input	*292	*305	334	343	360	344
Total production	*87	*90	112	113	121	126
Estimated efficiency (% of production to input)	30	29	34	33	34	37

Nepal

Item	2013	2014	2015	2016	2017	2018
Production, trade and consumption			**Million kilowatt-hours**			
Total main activity and autoproducer	3130	3508	3460	4244	4639	4913
Combustible fuels	10	10	..	..	0	0
Hydro	3120	3498	3453	4237	4632	4898
Nuclear	..	..	..	..	..	..
Other	..	..	7	7	7	15
Main activity	2993	3368	3306	4089	4483	4753
Combustible fuels	10	10	..	..	0	0
Hydro	2983	3358	3299	4082	4476	4738
Nuclear	..	..	..	..	..	..
Other	..	..	7	7	7	15
Own use in electricity, CHP and heat plants	40	15	49	48	55	59
Net production	3090	3493	3411	4196	4584	4854
Imports	1072	1319	1778	2175	2582	2813
Exports	4	3	3	3	3	35
Losses	745	*1200	1309	1433	1443	1157
Consumption	3413	3491	3867	4926	5710	6503
Energy industries own use	..	..	..	..	..	..
By industry and construction	1222	1252	1206	1719	2010	2438
By transport	6	6	6	6	5	5
By households and other cons.	2185	2233	2655	3201	3695	4060
Net installed capacity			**Thousand kilowatts**			
Total main activity and autoproducer	*772	*829	798	979	*1141	1189
Combustible fuels	53	53	53	53	53	53
Hydro	*718	*776	738	919	*1081	1129
Nuclear	..	..	..	..	..	..
Other	..	..	*7	*7	*7	*7
Main activity	*617	*654	701	701	*628	628
Combustible fuels	53	53	53	53	53	53
Hydro	*563	*601	641	641	*568	568
Nuclear	..	..	..	..	..	..
Other	..	..	*7	*7	*7	*7
Combustible fuel input			**Terajoules**			
Fuel oil	89	*89	0	0	1	1
Total input	89	*89	0	0	1	1
Total production	36	35	..	..	0	0
Estimated efficiency (% of production to input)	41	39	..	..	40	40

Netherlands

Item	2013	2014	2015	2016	2017	2018
Production, trade and consumption	**Million kilowatt-hours**					
Total main activity and autoproducer	101630	103359	110389	115211	117264	114466
Combustible fuels	92465	92488	97411	101241	100899	96520
Hydro	114	112	93	100	61	72
Nuclear	2891	4091	4077	3960	3402	3515
Other	6160	6668	8808	9910	12902	14359
Main activity	77092	81447	87496	92476	92220	87753
Combustible fuels	69467	72440	76914	81098	79075	74284
Hydro	114	112	93	100	61	72
Nuclear	2891	4091	4077	3960	3402	3515
Other	4620	4804	6412	7318	9682	9882
Own use in electricity, CHP and heat plants	4180	4645	4487	4179	3792	3421
Net production	97450	98714	105902	111032	113472	111045
Imports	33252	32855	30760	24258	22458	26755
Exports	15015	18128	22012	19343	18952	18785
Losses	5133	4934	5264	5434	5414	5334
Consumption	110321	107291	109928	111445	112274	114035
Energy industries own use	5652	5592	6095	5984	5755	6068
By industry and construction	34907	33295	34330	35846	35759	36057
By transport	1750	1716	1729	1969	1997	2122
By households and other cons.	68012	66688	67774	67646	68763	69788
Net installed capacity	**Thousand kilowatts**					
Total main activity and autoproducer	30539	31762	33866	34176	33815	35024
Combustible fuels	26520	27286	28401	27311	26150	25550
Hydro	37	37	37	37	37	37
Nuclear	485	485	485	485	485	485
Other	3497	3954	4943	6343	7143	8952
Main activity	24136	24969	26825	26730	25557	24966
Combustible fuels	21390	22092	23400	22391	21231	20106
Hydro	37	37	37	37	37	37
Nuclear	485	485	485	485	485	485
Other	2224	2355	2903	3817	3804	4338
Combustible fuel input	**Terajoules**					
Hard Coal	221265	257247	336307	306318	267981	231448
Biogas	6640	6169	6110	6245	5776	5400
Gas-diesel oil	1032	2924	946	645	559	559
Refinery gas	17375	20345	13662	13613	11633	14999
Natural gas	450275	423496	373172	417337	448481	438001
Coke-oven gas	2307	1965	1850	1495	1993	1848
Blast furnace gas	23532	24677	24109	22715	23422	22206
Fuelwood	*18479	*16311	*19448	*16302	*15390	*11535
Vegetal waste	*10068	*5344	*1245	*5245	*6229	*9622
Municipal waste	70182	70843	70793	75189	73443	70913
Others	764	3096	..	..	..	..
Total input	821918	832416	847642	865104	854906	806531
Total production	332874	332957	350680	364468	363236	347472
Estimated efficiency (% of production to input)	40	40	41	42	42	43

New Caledonia

Item	2013	2014	2015	2016	2017	2018
Production, trade and consumption	Million kilowatt-hours					
Total main activity and autoproducer	2505	3011	2903	3130	3228	3486
Combustible fuels	1992	2660	2494	2842	2794	3077
Hydro	456	289	340	232	361	317
Nuclear	..	..	..	..	..	..
Other	57	62	68	57	73	92
Main activity	2505	3011	2903	3130	3228	3486
Combustible fuels	1992	2660	2494	2842	2794	3077
Hydro	456	289	340	232	361	317
Nuclear	..	..	..	..	..	..
Other	57	62	68	57	73	92
Own use in electricity, CHP and heat plants	0	0	0	0	1	1
Net production	2505	3011	2903	3130	3228	3485
Imports	..	..	..	..	..	..
Exports	..	..	..	..	..	..
Losses	68	58	61	90	68	*64
Consumption	2437	2953	2842	3040	3161	3421
Energy industries own use	..	..	..	..	..	..
By industry and construction	1808	2324	2193	2354	2488	2739
By transport	..	..	..	..	..	..
By households and other cons.	630	630	650	686	672	*682
Net installed capacity	Thousand kilowatts					
Total main activity and autoproducer	691	683	998	1001	*1020	*1040
Combustible fuels	572	565	875	875	*875	*875
Hydro	78	78	78	78	78	78
Nuclear	..	..	..	..	..	..
Other	41	40	44	48	67	87
Main activity	630	622	937	940	*957	*972
Combustible fuels	512	505	815	815	*815	*815
Hydro	78	78	78	78	78	78
Nuclear	..	..	..	..	..	..
Other	41	40	44	46	64	79
Combustible fuel input	Terajoules					
Hard Coal	7790	10405	12389	17157	19141	*21078
Gas-diesel oil	2666	6717	3500	2700	2223	*2447
Fuel oil	13001	15320	15792	16677	14512	*14912
Other kerosene	83	293	237	311	210	*232
Bitumen	52	145	133	133	113	*117
Other liquid biofuels	*5	*5	*5	*7	*5	*5
Total input	23597	32885	32056	36986	36204	*38791
Total production	7170	9576	8979	10230	10059	11077
Estimated efficiency (% of production to input)	30	29	28	28	28	29

New Zealand

Item	2013	2014	2015	2016	2017	2018
Production, trade and consumption	Million kilowatt-hours					
Total main activity and autoproducer	43254	43538	44224	43698	44192	44380
Combustible fuels	11714	9657	9389	7466	8897	7912
Hydro	23027	24316	24528	25920	25177	26287
Nuclear	..	..	..	..	..	..
Other	8513	9565	10307	10312	10118	10181
Main activity	41830	42129	42778	42290	42735	42968
Combustible fuels	10420	8392	8106	6245	7641	6727
Hydro	23019	24312	24524	25916	25173	26283
Nuclear	..	..	..	..	..	..
Other	8391	9425	10148	10129	9921	9958
Own use in electricity, CHP and heat plants	1383	1310	1329	1216	1304	1253
Net production	41871	42228	42895	42482	42888	43127
Imports	..	..	..	..	..	..
Exports	..	..	..	..	..	..
Losses	2895	2844	2902	2955	2947	2961
Consumption	39496	39862	40422	39781	39664	39545
Energy industries own use	613	619	714	718	756	698
By industry and construction	13774	13807	13911	13806	13854	13921
By transport	62	62	62	62	62	62
By households and other cons.	25047	25374	25735	25195	24992	24864
Net installed capacity	Thousand kilowatts					
Total main activity and autoproducer	9583	9787	9448	9290	9306	9353
Combustible fuels	2757	2763	2384	2210	2209	2212
Hydro	5381	5381	5381	5381	5381	5381
Nuclear	..	..	..	..	..	..
Other	1445	1643	1683	1699	1716	1760
Main activity	9327	9518	9163	8989	8988	9015
Combustible fuels	2536	2542	2163	1989	1988	1991
Hydro	5378	5378	5378	5378	5378	5378
Nuclear	..	..	..	..	..	..
Other	1413	1598	1622	1622	1622	1646
Combustible fuel input	Terajoules					
Brown Coal	16526	13900	11331	4620	5592	9581
Biogas	2347	2625	2827	3004	2996	3012
Gas-diesel oil	43	43	0	43	43	129
Natural gas	70901	58243	56284	49048	59760	49168
Coke-oven gas	2130	2007	2119	1854	1966	1941
Blast furnace gas	5541	5482	5617	5377	5665	5314
Fuelwood	5008	5029	4860	4647	4153	3258
Total input	102496	87329	83038	68593	80175	72403
Total production	42170	34765	33800	26878	32029	28483
Estimated efficiency (% of production to input)	41	40	41	39	40	39

Nicaragua

Item	2013	2014	2015	2016	2017	2018
Production, trade and consumption	**Million kilowatt-hours**					
Total main activity and autoproducer	4165	4454	4580	4591	4525	4636
Combustible fuels	2467	2550	2740	2728	2657	2599
Hydro	456	395	295	426	468	411
Nuclear	..	..	..	..	..	..
Other	1242	1509	1545	1437	1400	1626
Main activity	3630	3909	4071	4002	3814	3901
Combustible fuels	1933	2006	2232	2140	1946	1864
Hydro	455	394	294	425	468	411
Nuclear	..	..	..	..	..	..
Other	1242	1509	1545	1437	1400	1626
Own use in electricity, CHP and heat plants	400	161	364	193	407	403
Net production	3765	4293	4216	4398	4118	4233
Imports	52	22	34	205	327	201
Exports	16	49	22	18	1	0
Losses	643	926	837	964	996	978
Consumption	3196	3325	3396	3665	3451	3594
Energy industries own use	..	..	..	..	..	..
By industry and construction	1065	1105	1128	1174	1147	1069
By transport	..	..	..	..	..	..
By households and other cons.	2131	2220	2268	2491	2304	2525
Net installed capacity	**Thousand kilowatts**					
Total main activity and autoproducer	1291	1329	1346	1396	1482	1482
Combustible fuels	869	866	866	912	985	985
Hydro	120	120	138	142	142	142
Nuclear	..	..	..	..	..	..
Other	302	342	342	342	355	355
Main activity	1157	1194	1211	1219	1305	1305
Combustible fuels	735	733	733	735	809	809
Hydro	119	119	137	142	142	142
Nuclear	..	..	..	..	..	..
Other	302	342	342	342	355	355
Combustible fuel input	**Terajoules**					
Gas-diesel oil	473	645	645	602	602	516
Fuel oil	17332	17816	20119	19473	17210	16483
Bagasse	*15255	*15695	*16735	*14221	*14226	*14277
Vegetal waste	*1943	*3007	*3044	*2528	*1927	*1934
Total input	35003	*37163	40543	36824	33965	33210
Total production	8881	9180	9864	9821	9565	9356
Estimated efficiency (% of production to input)	25	25	24	27	28	28

Niger

Item	2013	2014	2015	2016	2017	2018
Production, trade and consumption	**Million kilowatt-hours**					
Total main activity and autoproducer	516	521	522	442	566	480
Combustible fuels	508	512	511	428	552	447
Hydro	..	..	..	..	..	..
Nuclear	..	..	..	..	..	..
Other	8	10	11	13	15	33
Main activity	479	472	496	415	541	437
Combustible fuels	479	472	496	415	541	437
Hydro	..	..	..	..	..	..
Nuclear	..	..	..	..	..	..
Other	..	..	..	..	..	..
Own use in electricity, CHP and heat plants	44	44	44	68	72	38
Net production	472	478	478	374	494	442
Imports	602	727	782	779	845	1253
Exports	3	0	0	0	0	0
Losses	156	191	215	*208	*218	*238
Consumption	836	858	916	*968	*1014	*1379
Energy industries own use	..	..	..	..	..	..
By industry and construction	225	*215	218	*272	*285	*387
By transport	..	..	..	..	..	..
By households and other cons.	611	644	699	*696	*729	*992
Net installed capacity	**Thousand kilowatts**					
Total main activity and autoproducer	192	230	277	288	290	311
Combustible fuels	187	224	270	280	281	291
Hydro	..	..	..	..	..	..
Nuclear	..	..	..	..	..	..
Other	5	6	7	8	9	20
Main activity	133	170	216	226	228	238
Combustible fuels	133	170	216	226	228	238
Hydro	..	..	..	..	..	..
Nuclear	..	..	..	..	..	..
Other	..	..	..	..	..	..
Combustible fuel input	**Terajoules**					
Hard Coal	3647	4231	3535	3721	3495	4164
Gas-diesel oil	2000	1883	2253	2279	*2365	*2064
Liquefied petroleum gas	473	710	596	*449	*520	*572
Total input	6120	6824	6384	6449	6380	6800
Total production	1828	1842	1838	1542	1986	1610
Estimated efficiency (% of production to input)	30	27	29	24	31	24

Nigeria

Item	2013	2014	2015	2016	2017	2018
Production, trade and consumption	**Million kilowatt-hours**					
Total main activity and autoproducer	28927	32275	32442	33586	34445	36278
Combustible fuels	23579	26907	26697	25408	26670	29792
Hydro	5326	5346	5721	8151	7747	6458
Nuclear	..	..	..	..	..	..
Other	22	22	24	27	28	28
Main activity	23626	26247	26467	27840	28430	29608
Combustible fuels	18409	21010	20863	19856	20842	23282
Hydro	5217	5237	5604	7984	7588	6326
Nuclear	..	..	..	..	..	..
Other	..	..	..	..	..	..
Own use in electricity, CHP and heat plants	849	945	928	961	987	1039
Net production	28078	31330	31514	32625	33458	35239
Imports	..	..	..	..	..	..
Exports	..	..	..	..	..	..
Losses	4336	4838	4866	5038	5167	5442
Consumption	23689	24625	25026	25241	25912	26545
Energy industries own use	202	186	179	207	236	229
By industry and construction	3899	4057	3918	3548	3622	3684
By transport	..	..	..	..	..	..
By households and other cons.	19588	20382	20929	21486	22054	22632
Net installed capacity	**Thousand kilowatts**					
Total main activity and autoproducer	*9832	*10406	*10439	*12385	*12534	*12305
Combustible fuels	*7892	*8458	*8458	*10403	*10142	*10142
Hydro	*1930	*1938	*1970	*1970	*2380	*2151
Nuclear	..	..	..	..	..	..
Other	*10	*10	*11	*12	*12	*12
Main activity	*7690	*7356	*7388	*9071	*9302	*9073
Combustible fuels	*5800	*5458	*5458	*7141	*6962	*6962
Hydro	*1890	*1898	*1930	*1930	*2340	*2111
Nuclear	..	..	..	..	..	..
Other	..	..	..	..	..	..
Combustible fuel input	**Terajoules**					
Natural gas	235570	268850	266970	254080	266692	297913
Total input	235570	268850	266970	254080	266692	297913
Total production	84884	96865	96109	91469	96012	107251
Estimated efficiency (% of production to input)	36	36	36	36	36	36

Statistics on electricity

Niue

Item	2013	2014	2015	2016	2017	2018
Production, trade and consumption	**Million kilowatt-hours**					
Total main activity and autoproducer	3	3	3	*3	*3	*4
Combustible fuels	3	3	3	*3	*3	*3
Hydro	..	..	..	..	..	..
Nuclear	..	..	..	..	..	..
Other	0	0	0	0	0	0
Main activity	3	3	3	*3	*3	*4
Combustible fuels	3	3	3	*3	*3	*3
Hydro	..	..	..	..	..	..
Nuclear	..	..	..	..	..	..
Other	0	0	0	0	0	0
Own use in electricity, CHP and heat plants	0	0	0	0	0	0
Net production	3	3	3	*3	*3	*4
Imports	..	..	..	..	..	..
Exports	..	..	..	..	..	..
Losses	0	0	0	0	0	0
Consumption	3	3	3	*3	*3	*3
Energy industries own use	..	..	..	..	..	..
By industry and construction	1	1	1	*1	*1	*1
By transport	..	..	..	..	..	..
By households and other cons.	2	2	2	*2	*2	*3
Net installed capacity	**Thousand kilowatts**					
Total main activity and autoproducer	2	2	*2	*2	*2	*2
Combustible fuels	2	2	*2	*2	*2	*2
Hydro	..	..	..	..	..	..
Nuclear	..	..	..	..	..	..
Other	0	0	0	0	0	0
Main activity	2	2	*2	*2	*2	*2
Combustible fuels	2	2	*2	*2	*2	*2
Hydro	..	..	..	..	..	..
Nuclear	..	..	..	..	..	..
Other	0	0	0	0	0	0
Combustible fuel input	**Terajoules**					
Gas-diesel oil	31	31	34	*34	*33	34
Total input	31	31	34	*34	*33	34
Total production	12	11	12	*12	*12	*12
Estimated efficiency (% of production to input)	38	36	35	35	36	36

North Macedonia

Item	2013	2014	2015	2016	2017	2018
Production, trade and consumption	Million kilowatt-hours					
Total main activity and autoproducer	6094	5374	5646	5630	5600	5607
Combustible fuels	4501	4082	3617	3563	4304	3642
Hydro	1584	1207	1865	1897	1110	1791
Nuclear	..	..	..	..	..	..
Other	9	85	164	169	186	174
Main activity	6092	5373	5646	5630	5600	5607
Combustible fuels	4499	4081	3617	3563	4304	3642
Hydro	1584	1207	1865	1897	1110	1791
Nuclear	..	..	..	..	..	..
Other	9	85	164	169	186	174
Own use in electricity, CHP and heat plants	434	412	380	358	387	338
Net production	5660	4961	5266	5272	5213	5269
Imports	2491	3073	2656	2191	2294	2297
Exports	62	113	143	160	311	377
Losses	1152	1069	1035	1007	1004	995
Consumption	6937	6852	6743	6296	6192	6194
Energy industries own use	136	123	108	103	90	89
By industry and construction	2261	2222	1976	1653	1472	1546
By transport	17	19	17	14	14	12
By households and other cons.	4523	4489	4642	4526	4616	4548
Net installed capacity	Thousand kilowatts					
Total main activity and autoproducer	1731	1759	1790	1823	1836	1839
Combustible fuels	1107	1077	1074	1104	1104	1104
Hydro	617	630	658	660	671	674
Nuclear	..	..	..	..	..	..
Other	7	52	58	59	61	61
Main activity	1728	1756	1790	1823	1836	1839
Combustible fuels	1104	1074	1074	1104	1104	1104
Hydro	617	630	658	660	671	674
Nuclear	..	..	..	..	..	..
Other	7	52	58	59	61	61
Combustible fuel input	Terajoules					
Brown Coal	45809	43856	38046	33979	38362	32774
Biogas	..	..	75	134	191	200
Fuel oil	1246	1663	1584	1130	986	548
Natural gas	3443	1713	1481	4603	6503	5902
Total input	50498	47232	41185	39846	46041	39424
Total production	16204	14695	13023	12827	15495	13110
Estimated efficiency (% of production to input)	32	31	32	32	34	33

Northern Mariana Islands

Item	2013	2014	2015	2016	2017	2018
Production, trade and consumption	**Million kilowatt-hours**					
Total main activity and autoproducer	*415	*419	*430	*387	*380	*390
Combustible fuels	*415	*419	*430	*387	*380	*390
Hydro	..	..	..	..	..	..
Nuclear	..	..	..	..	..	..
Other	..	..	..	..	..	..
Main activity	*415	*419	*430	*387	*380	*390
Combustible fuels	*415	*419	*430	*387	*380	*390
Hydro	..	..	..	..	..	..
Nuclear	..	..	..	..	..	..
Other	..	..	..	..	..	..
Own use in electricity, CHP and heat plants	0	0	0	0	0	0
Net production	*415	*419	*430	*387	*380	*390
Imports	..	..	..	..	..	..
Exports	..	..	..	..	..	..
Losses	*92	*93	*96	*86	*85	*86
Consumption	*322	*326	*334	*301	*295	*304
Energy industries own use	..	..	..	..	..	..
By industry and construction	..	..	..	..	..	..
By transport	..	..	..	..	..	..
By households and other cons.	*322	*326	*334	*301	*295	*304
Net installed capacity	**Thousand kilowatts**					
Total main activity and autoproducer	*91	95	*95	95	*95	*95
Combustible fuels	*91	95	*95	95	*95	*95
Hydro	..	..	..	..	..	..
Nuclear	..	..	..	..	..	..
Other	..	..	..	..	..	..
Main activity	*91	95	*95	95	*95	*95
Combustible fuels	*91	95	*95	95	*95	*95
Hydro	..	..	..	..	..	..
Nuclear	..	..	..	..	..	..
Other	..	..	..	..	..	..
Combustible fuel input	**Terajoules**					
Total input	..	..	..	..	..	..
Total production	*1493	*1508	*1547	*1392	*1368	*1404
Estimated efficiency (% of production to input)	..	..	..	..	..	..

Norway

Item	2013	2014	2015	2016	2017	2018
Production, trade and consumption	Million kilowatt-hours					
Total main activity and autoproducer	134072	141970	144546	149042	149480	146889
Combustible fuels	3238	3255	3247	3201	3190	3168
Hydro	128699	136185	138450	143417	143112	139509
Nuclear	..	..	..	..	..	..
Other	2135	2530	2849	2424	3178	4212
Main activity	131393	139070	141616	146136	146635	143967
Combustible fuels	813	668	651	603	669	582
Hydro	128699	136185	138450	143417	143112	139509
Nuclear	..	..	..	..	..	..
Other	1881	2217	2515	2116	2854	3876
Own use in electricity, CHP and heat plants	587	628	642	563	717	651
Net production	133485	141342	143904	148479	148763	146238
Imports	10135	6347	7371	5740	6111	8340
Exports	15141	21932	22016	22151	21276	18489
Losses	8060	7605	7469	9170	9153	9005
Consumption	118876	116673	120255	122117	123023	126142
Energy industries own use	7877	8091	9178	8472	9327	10236
By industry and construction	43348	44446	45012	45756	46010	47004
By transport	632	654	794	866	913	1062
By households and other cons.	67019	63482	65271	67023	66773	67840
Net installed capacity	Thousand kilowatts					
Total main activity and autoproducer	33486	33697	33837	33808	34228	35348
Combustible fuels	1600	1563	1563	1073	1074	1073
Hydro	31033	31240	31372	31817	31912	32530
Nuclear	..	..	..	..	..	..
Other	853	894	902	918	1242	1745
Main activity	32898	33109	33249	33220	33654	34761
Combustible fuels	1047	1010	1010	520	535	521
Hydro	31033	31240	31372	31817	31912	32530
Nuclear	..	..	..	..	..	..
Other	818	859	867	883	1207	1710
Combustible fuel input	Terajoules					
Hard Coal	674	703	703	731	815	871
Biogas	64	193	181	130	159	130
Gas-diesel oil	258	215	172	258	172	172
Liquefied petroleum gas	0	0	0	0	0	0
Refinery gas	0	0	0	..	..	..
Natural gas	14820	15492	15345	15362	14873	15196
Blast furnace gas	845	938	1088	1006	1255	1247
Fuelwood	1269	77	94	309	1536	1549
Municipal waste	8242	9146	8670	8610	8756	8862
Other liquid biofuels	0	0	0	0	27	0
Total input	26172	26763	26252	26406	27593	28027
Total production	11657	11718	11689	11524	11484	11405
Estimated efficiency (% of production to input)	45	44	45	44	42	41

Oman

Item	2013	2014	2015	2016	2017	2018
Production, trade and consumption	**Million kilowatt-hours**					
Total main activity and autoproducer	26241	29129	32762	34232	36130	37671
Combustible fuels	26240	29128	32758	34228	36126	37667
Hydro	..	..	..	..	..	..
Nuclear	..	..	..	..	..	..
Other	1	1	4	4	4	4
Main activity	26241	29129	32762	34232	36130	37671
Combustible fuels	26240	29128	32758	34228	36126	37667
Hydro	..	..	..	..	..	..
Nuclear	..	..	..	..	..	..
Other	1	1	4	4	4	4
Own use in electricity, CHP and heat plants	580	786	680	624	457	479
Net production	25661	28343	32082	33608	35673	37192
Imports	..	..	..	..	..	..
Exports	..	..	..	..	..	..
Losses	2871	3170	3170	3249	3323	3645
Consumption	22790	25173	28912	30359	32350	33548
Energy industries own use	..	..	..	..	..	..
By industry and construction	3686	4189	4723	5153	5021	5169
By transport	..	..	..	..	..	..
By households and other cons.	19104	20984	24189	25206	27329	28379
Net installed capacity	**Thousand kilowatts**					
Total main activity and autoproducer	6599	8215	7870	8167	8236	8828
Combustible fuels	6598	8214	7868	8165	8228	8820
Hydro	..	..	..	..	..	..
Nuclear	..	..	..	..	..	..
Other	1	1	2	2	8	8
Main activity	6599	8215	7870	8167	8236	8828
Combustible fuels	6598	8214	7868	8165	8228	8820
Hydro	..	..	..	..	..	..
Nuclear	..	..	..	..	..	..
Other	1	1	2	2	8	8
Combustible fuel input	**Terajoules**					
Gas-diesel oil	7009	7697	8686	9632	8256	11524
Natural gas	285035	305274	317548	304957	314281	316552
Total input	292044	312971	326234	314589	322537	328076
Total production	94464	104861	117929	123221	130054	135601
Estimated efficiency (% of production to input)	32	34	36	39	40	41

Pakistan

Item	2013	2014	2015	2016	2017	2018
Production, trade and consumption			**Million kilowatt-hours**			
Total main activity and autoproducer	*100023	108150	110128	115502	123533	134981
Combustible fuels	*65067	70485	70556	74697	81447	93545
Hydro	30397	32210	32867	34573	32132	27729
Nuclear	4553	5090	5804	4602	6867	9849
Other	6	365	901	1630	3087	3858
Main activity	*97990	106106	107514	113189	120807	131999
Combustible fuels	*63034	68541	68382	73016	79732	91583
Hydro	30397	32210	32867	34573	32132	27729
Nuclear	4553	5090	5804	4602	6867	9849
Other	6	265	461	998	2076	2838
Own use in electricity, CHP and heat plants	3757	3984	4123	4502	3793	4310
Net production	*96266	104166	106005	111000	119740	130671
Imports	..	..	552	655	433	297
Exports	..	..	..	..	..	..
Losses	16487	16931	16941	17823	20615	23978
Consumption	83409	85818	90429	95530	103273	*107267
Energy industries own use	..	..	..	..	..	..
By industry and construction	24356	24979	25035	24010	27398	*28357
By transport	0	0	0	0	..	..
By households and other cons.	59053	60839	65394	71520	75875	*78910
Net installed capacity			**Thousand kilowatts**			
Total main activity and autoproducer	23996	24830	24699	26756	31418	34880
Combustible fuels	16315	16856	16315	17926	21684	24324
Hydro	6825	6985	7115	7115	7115	7270
Nuclear	750	750	750	750	1090	1430
Other	106	239	519	965	1529	1856
Main activity	23751	24236	24069	26063	30587	34008
Combustible fuels	16070	16395	15848	17459	21191	23831
Hydro	6825	6985	7115	7115	7115	7270
Nuclear	750	750	750	750	1090	1430
Other	106	106	356	739	1191	1477
Combustible fuel input			**Terajoules**			
Hard Coal	3949	3556	5024	20662	115611	122361
Gas-diesel oil	12470	23134	12040	11954	7955	8385
Fuel oil	299162	346010	324776	299021	*249591	264135
Natural gas	276430	286708	359108	361882	478796	520576
Bagasse	*24278	*22626	*23583	*23560	*23560	23622
Total input	616289	682033	724531	717079	875513	939079
Total production	*234241	253746	254002	268909	293209	336762
Estimated efficiency (% of production to input)	38	37	35	38	33	36

Palau

Item	2013	2014	2015	2016	2017	2018
Production, trade and consumption			**Million kilowatt-hours**			
Total main activity and autoproducer	*87	*90	*90	*95	*95	*95
Combustible fuels	*87	*90	*90	*95	*95	*95
Hydro	..	..	..	..	..	..
Nuclear	..	..	..	..	..	..
Other	..	..	..	0	0	0
Main activity	*81	*84	*84	*89	*88	*88
Combustible fuels	*81	*84	*84	*89	*88	*88
Hydro	..	..	..	..	..	..
Nuclear	..	..	..	..	..	..
Other	..	..	..	0	0	0
Own use in electricity, CHP and heat plants	*6	*6	*6	*6	*5	*6
Net production	*82	*84	*84	*89	*90	*89
Imports	..	..	..	..	..	..
Exports	..	..	..	..	..	..
Losses	*14	*14	*14	*15	*16	*16
Consumption	*65	*67	*67	*71	*74	*73
Energy industries own use	..	..	..	..	..	..
By industry and construction	*5	*5	*6	*6	*6	*6
By transport	..	..	..	..	..	..
By households and other cons.	*60	*62	*61	*65	*68	*67
Net installed capacity			**Thousand kilowatts**			
Total main activity and autoproducer	*30	30	31	40	*40	*40
Combustible fuels	*30	30	30	39	*39	*39
Hydro	..	..	..	..	..	..
Nuclear	..	..	..	..	..	..
Other	..	..	1	*1	*1	*2
Main activity	*28	28	29	38	*38	*38
Combustible fuels	*28	28	28	37	*37	*37
Hydro	..	..	..	..	..	..
Nuclear	..	..	..	..	..	..
Other	..	..	1	*1	*1	*2
Combustible fuel input			**Terajoules**			
Gas-diesel oil	*989	*1011	*1011	*1066	*1062	*1054
Total input	*989	*1011	*1011	*1066	*1062	*1054
Total production	*315	*323	*323	*341	*342	*340
Estimated efficiency (% of production to input)	32	32	32	32	32	32

Panama

Item	2013	2014	2015	2016	2017	2018
Production, trade and consumption			Million kilowatt-hours			
Total main activity and autoproducer	8962	9287	10295	10885	11054	11353
Combustible fuels	3808	4136	3604	3666	3141	2657
Hydro	5154	5034	6257	6523	7256	7858
Nuclear	..	..	..	..	..	..
Other	..	118	435	697	657	838
Main activity	8929	9256	10262	10853	11022	11192
Combustible fuels	3775	4105	3570	3634	3109	2496
Hydro	5154	5034	6257	6523	7256	7858
Nuclear	..	..	..	..	..	..
Other	..	118	435	697	657	838
Own use in electricity, CHP and heat plants	211	200	201	207	242	492
Net production	8751	9087	10095	10678	10812	10861
Imports	75	193	17	30	7	13
Exports	71	99	139	398	318	326
Losses	1220	1328	1400	1512	1448	1423
Consumption	7511	7832	8549	8761	9095	9296
Energy industries own use	..	..	..	..	..	..
By industry and construction	706	689	669	647	651	617
By transport	..	19	42	37	41	41
By households and other cons.	6805	7124	7837	8077	8403	8638
Net installed capacity			Thousand kilowatts			
Total main activity and autoproducer	2546	2829	3224	3371	3423	4055
Combustible fuels	1032	1148	1202	1235	1225	1811
Hydro	1494	1623	1726	1769	1777	1777
Nuclear	..	..	..	..	..	..
Other	20	57	296	367	421	467
Main activity	2333	2560	2992	3139	3191	3823
Combustible fuels	879	939	1030	1063	1053	1639
Hydro	1434	1563	1666	1709	1717	1717
Nuclear	..	..	..	..	..	..
Other	20	57	296	367	421	467
Combustible fuel input			Terajoules			
Hard Coal	8798	9082	9133	8075	2252	5642
Gas-diesel oil	5676	9546	2555	1935	2718	881
Fuel oil	12484	6828	19386	21312	19682	9750
Natural gas	..	..	..	..	..	6828
Bagasse	3081	2874	2900	4001	2843	4409
Total input	30038	28329	33974	35324	27495	27509
Total production	13708	14888	12974	13199	11309	9565
Estimated efficiency (% of production to input)	46	53	38	37	41	35

Papua New Guinea

Item	2013	2014	2015	2016	2017	2018
Production, trade and consumption	**Million kilowatt-hours**					
Total main activity and autoproducer	4039	4305	4560	4794	4595	*4482
Combustible fuels	2621	2863	3125	3367	3155	*3180
Hydro	996	1020	1012	1005	1018	876
Nuclear	..	..	..	..	..	..
Other	422	422	423	422	422	*426
Main activity	980	1069	1153	1274	1291	1290
Combustible fuels	335	409	491	622	622	*622
Hydro	645	660	661	650	667	667
Nuclear	..	..	..	..	..	..
Other	0	0	1	2	2	1
Own use in electricity, CHP and heat plants	75	129	236	465	259	*191
Net production	3964	4176	4324	4329	4336	*4291
Imports	..	..	..	..	..	..
Exports	..	..	..	..	..	..
Losses	454	512	442	337	*338	*340
Consumption	3513	3664	3882	3991	*3998	*3951
Energy industries own use	..	..	..	..	..	..
By industry and construction	2559	2652	2838	2931	*2935	*2901
By transport	..	..	..	..	..	..
By households and other cons.	*954	*1012	*1044	*1061	*1063	*1051
Net installed capacity	**Thousand kilowatts**					
Total main activity and autoproducer	*865	*872	*905	*971	*971	*971
Combustible fuels	*548	*566	*590	*656	*656	*656
Hydro	261	250	*258	*258	*258	*258
Nuclear	..	..	..	..	..	..
Other	56	56	57	57	57	57
Main activity	280	267	*296	*363	*369	*369
Combustible fuels	*118	116	*140	*206	*206	*206
Hydro	162	151	*155	*155	*162	*162
Nuclear	..	..	..	..	..	..
Other	0	0	1	1	1	1
Combustible fuel input	**Terajoules**					
Gas-diesel oil	5151	3896	4312	3894	4194	*4215
Fuel oil	19263	21856	22273	22693	20180	*20281
Natural gas	5150	6155	6657	8416	8709	*8796
Total input	29564	31907	33242	35003	33083	*33292
Total production	9436	10307	11250	12121	11358	*11448
Estimated efficiency (% of production to input)	32	32	34	35	34	34

Paraguay

Item	2013	2014	2015	2016	2017	2018
Production, trade and consumption			Million kilowatt-hours			
Total main activity and autoproducer	60381	55282	55744	63771	59685	59212
Combustible fuels	3	6	1	1	2	2
Hydro	60378	55276	55743	63770	59684	59211
Nuclear	..	..	..	..	..	..
Other	..	..	..	..	..	..
Main activity	60381	55282	55744	63771	59685	59212
Combustible fuels	3	6	1	1	2	2
Hydro	60378	55276	55743	63770	59684	59211
Nuclear	..	..	..	..	..	..
Other	..	..	..	..	..	..
Own use in electricity, CHP and heat plants	506	448	451	523	495	483
Net production	59875	54834	55293	63248	59190	58730
Imports	..	..	..	..	..	..
Exports	47365	41400	41127	48415	43635	42205
Losses	3492	3402	3590	3821	4000	4021
Consumption	9018	10030	10576	11012	11555	12504
Energy industries own use	..	..	..	..	..	..
By industry and construction	3567	3801	4010	4105	4452	4695
By transport	..	..	..	..	..	..
By households and other cons.	5451	6229	6567	6907	7103	7808
Net installed capacity			Thousand kilowatts			
Total main activity and autoproducer	8825	8775	8775	8761	8761	8761
Combustible fuels	15	15	15	1	1	1
Hydro	8810	8760	8760	8760	8760	8760
Nuclear	..	..	..	..	..	..
Other	..	..	..	..	..	..
Main activity	8825	8775	8775	8761	8761	8761
Combustible fuels	15	15	15	1	1	1
Hydro	8810	8760	8760	8760	8760	8760
Nuclear	..	..	..	..	..	..
Other	..	..	..	..	..	..
Combustible fuel input			Terajoules			
Gas-diesel oil	22	57	18	17	20	21
Total input	22	57	18	17	20	21
Total production	11	21	5	5	5	6
Estimated efficiency (% of production to input)	51	37	28	27	27	27

Peru

Item	2013	2014	2015	2016	2017	2018
Production, trade and consumption	**Million kilowatt-hours**					
Total main activity and autoproducer	43330	45508	48277	52720	52743	54982
Combustible fuels	20812	22882	23729	26630	22265	21946
Hydro	22320	22171	23722	24785	29075	30737
Nuclear	..	..	..	..	..	..
Other	198	455	826	1305	1403	2299
Main activity	40665	42844	45719	50465	50344	52367
Combustible fuels	18757	20778	21766	25024	20591	20125
Hydro	21709	21611	23127	24136	28393	29989
Nuclear	..	..	..	..	..	..
Other	198	455	826	1305	1360	2253
Own use in electricity, CHP and heat plants	589	800	567	1831	752	743
Net production	42741	44708	47710	50889	51991	54239
Imports	0	0	1	22	17	21
Exports	0	13	55	38	0	..
Losses	4556	5018	5324	5484	5543	5969
Consumption	38208	39719	42334	45390	46464	48293
Energy industries own use	..	..	..	..	..	..
By industry and construction	20686	21798	23446	26054	26716	27832
By transport	22	37	48	46	53	60
By households and other cons.	17499	17884	18840	19290	19695	20401
Net installed capacity	**Thousand kilowatts**					
Total main activity and autoproducer	11051	11203	12089	14517	14775	15214
Combustible fuels	7414	7302	7619	8988	9005	9154
Hydro	3556	3662	4130	5189	5246	5363
Nuclear	..	..	..	..	..	..
Other	81	239	340	340	524	697
Main activity	9635	9739	10511	13044	13239	13651
Combustible fuels	6104	5942	6145	7632	7639	7762
Hydro	3451	3558	4026	5072	5116	5232
Nuclear	..	..	..	..	..	..
Other	81	239	340	340	484	657
Combustible fuel input	**Terajoules**					
Hard Coal	13489	8095	6694	12095	9026	4743
Biogas	806	821	985	1372	391	484
Gas-diesel oil	6183	5500	8983	11425	15751	8088
Fuel oil	8633	6226	6339	7135	6327	6319
Refinery gas	1287	1485	1485	0	..	..
Natural gas	150325	175586	182405	199607	165558	168231
Bagasse	15622	21452	14363	11792	17599	13390
Biodiesel	265	236	383	489	677	346
Total input	196611	219400	221636	243915	215328	201601
Total production	74925	82375	85424	95868	80154	79006
Estimated efficiency (% of production to input)	38	38	39	39	37	39

Philippines

Item	2013	2014	2015	2016	2017	2018
Production, trade and consumption	**Million kilowatt-hours**					
Total main activity and autoproducer	75519	77476	82905	91789	95747	100123
Combustible fuels	55811	57845	62292	70519	73554	77885
Hydro	10036	9154	8682	8128	9628	9401
Nuclear	..	..	..	..	..	..
Other	9672	10477	11931	13143	12565	12837
Main activity	75266	77261	82413	90798	94371	99765
Combustible fuels	55575	57647	61818	69544	72195	77544
Hydro	10019	9137	8665	8111	9611	9384
Nuclear	..	..	..	..	..	..
Other	9672	10477	11931	13143	12565	12837
Own use in electricity, CHP and heat plants	6178	6827	7582	9314	9655	9689
Net production	69340	70649	75323	82475	86092	90434
Imports	..	..	..	..	..	..
Exports	..	..	..	..	..	..
Losses	7741	7270	7481	8286	8262	8141
Consumption	61566	63345	67808	74154	77793	82384
Energy industries own use	..	..	..	..	..	..
By industry and construction	20677	21429	22514	24119	25573	27678
By transport	112	111	98	103	112	105
By households and other cons.	40777	41805	45196	49933	52108	54601
Net installed capacity	**Thousand kilowatts**					
Total main activity and autoproducer	17452	18063	18989	21869	23341	23951
Combustible fuels	12013	12280	12864	15127	16470	16967
Hydro	3537	3559	3616	3634	3643	3717
Nuclear	..	..	..	..	..	..
Other	1902	2224	2509	3108	3228	3267
Main activity	17325	17944	18765	21425	22728	23815
Combustible fuels	11902	12177	12656	14699	15873	16847
Hydro	3521	3543	3600	3618	3627	3701
Nuclear	..	..	..	..	..	..
Other	1902	2224	2509	3108	3228	3267
Combustible fuel input	**Terajoules**					
Brown Coal	326840	344453	387713	425312	514939	575508
Gas-diesel oil	10866	14732	12711	21251	17402	16473
Fuel oil	35055	44137	47559	31666	24284	15013
Natural gas	128781	135141	127938	146239	146138	157703
Bagasse	2122	1817	4590	9867	13825	15094
Municipal waste	1499	1640	955	447	527	543
Biodiesel	191	269	233	372	307	321
Total input	505355	542188	581699	635153	717423	780654
Total production	200918	208242	224251	253867	264794	280387
Estimated efficiency (% of production to input)	40	38	39	40	37	36

Poland

Item	2013	2014	2015	2016	2017	2018
Production, trade and consumption	**Million kilowatt-hours**					
Total main activity and autoproducer	164580	159059	164944	166635	170467	170038
Combustible fuels	155467	148500	151478	151234	152297	154427
Hydro	2997	2734	2435	2622	3034	2387
Nuclear	..	..	..	..	..	..
Other	6116	7825	11031	12779	15136	13224
Main activity	155663	150178	155562	156178	158553	155192
Combustible fuels	146665	139771	142272	140971	140614	140009
Hydro	2994	2731	2432	2619	3030	2384
Nuclear	..	..	..	..	..	..
Other	6004	7676	10858	12588	14909	12799
Own use in electricity, CHP and heat plants	14501	13845	14249	14632	15598	14779
Net production	150079	145214	150695	152003	154869	155259
Imports	7801	13508	14459	14017	13271	13816
Exports	12322	11342	14793	12018	10984	8121
Losses	10247	10250	10534	9495	9996	8894
Consumption	135311	137129	139827	144507	147159	152061
Energy industries own use	11754	11783	12008	11668	11371	11590
By industry and construction	47290	47585	49482	51210	54542	56251
By transport	3156	3007	3107	3287	3327	3469
By households and other cons.	73111	74754	75230	78342	77919	80751
Net installed capacity	**Thousand kilowatts**					
Total main activity and autoproducer	35815	35989	37327	38105	42850	43046
Combustible fuels	30027	29760	29961	29783	34412	34314
Hydro	2355	2364	2370	2386	2391	2392
Nuclear	..	..	..	..	..	..
Other	3433	3865	4996	5936	6047	6340
Main activity	34009	34141	35189	36027	40077	39377
Combustible fuels	28226	27942	27934	27895	31929	31220
Hydro	2354	2363	2369	2385	2390	2391
Nuclear	..	..	..	..	..	..
Other	3429	3836	4886	5747	5758	5766
Combustible fuel input	**Terajoules**					
Hard Coal	978720	900363	912442	938903	953281	944106
Brown Coal	542388	514876	508760	485377	503718	483374
Biogas	4872	5718	6298	7231	8216	8582
Fuel oil	12726	11352	15837	16443	14867	12726
Natural gas	47363	47736	57442	68953	83638	102753
Coke-oven gas	19410	19325	22755	24895	22961	23502
Blast furnace gas	11729	13937	16242	14630	15884	16215
Fuelwood	*40601	*42549	*43633	*45096	*37123	*40861
Vegetal waste	*34017	*42121	*44425	*26528	*16529	*14163
Municipal waste	337	237	727	3959	6497	8918
Others	7887	7194	6620	5793	3933	5158
Total input	1700050	1605409	1635181	1637808	1666648	1660358
Total production	559681	534600	545321	544442	548269	555937
Estimated efficiency (% of production to input)	33	33	33	33	33	33

Portugal

Item	2013	2014	2015	2016	2017	2018
Production, trade and consumption			**Million kilowatt-hours**			
Total main activity and autoproducer	51672	52802	52420	60328	59434	59635
Combustible fuels	24110	23440	30005	29903	38346	32154
Hydro	14868	16412	9799	16909	7632	13629
Nuclear	..	..	..	..	..	..
Other	12694	12950	12616	13516	13456	13852
Main activity	42662	44367	44126	52123	50996	51311
Combustible fuels	15330	15323	22076	22104	30392	24340
Hydro	14848	16389	9784	16889	7621	13610
Nuclear	..	..	..	..	..	..
Other	12484	12655	12266	13130	12983	13361
Own use in electricity, CHP and heat plants	1260	1275	1480	1466	1765	1438
Net production	50412	51527	50940	58862	57669	58197
Imports	8100	7247	8077	4616	5506	5668
Exports	5324	6344	5811	9701	8190	8325
Losses	5455	5209	4894	4901	5101	5060
Consumption	47732	47220	48309	48880	49885	50482
Energy industries own use	2475	2025	2497	2485	3243	2522
By industry and construction	15993	15395	15481	15645	16143	16398
By transport	301	302	308	431	485	490
By households and other cons.	28963	29498	30023	30319	30014	31072
Net installed capacity			**Thousand kilowatts**			
Total main activity and autoproducer	18900	19124	19624	20613	20933	21185
Combustible fuels	8308	8113	8048	7990	7974	8080
Hydro	5661	5715	6168	6960	7226	7236
Nuclear	..	..	..	..	..	..
Other	4931	5296	5408	5663	5733	5869
Main activity	16841	17020	17575	18570	18849	18949
Combustible fuels	6409	6205	6205	6209	6205	6208
Hydro	5655	5709	6162	6954	7220	7230
Nuclear	..	..	..	..	..	..
Other	4777	5106	5208	5407	5424	5511
Combustible fuel input			**Terajoules**			
Hard Coal	110009	111645	135911	118603	135518	112406
Biogas	2736	3078	3121	2996	3224	3127
Gas-diesel oil	860	903	989	774	774	774
Fuel oil	11393	9494	9656	9938	9373	8646
Refinery gas	1188	941	644	396	446	545
Natural gas	79197	72602	97300	110638	155583	133961
Fuelwood	20169	12198	11382	15464	12423	10834
Vegetal waste	..	5824	6961	2483	5060	9280
Municipal waste	8097	6845	8155	8680	8739	8121
Black liquor	..	6552	7031	7751	9033	7093
Others	138	128	153	617	576	301
Total input	233786	230209	281301	278340	340748	295087
Total production	86796	84384	108018	107651	138046	115754
Estimated efficiency (% of production to input)	37	37	38	39	41	39

Puerto Rico

Item	2013	2014	2015	2016	2017	2018
Production, trade and consumption	**Million kilowatt-hours**					
Total main activity and autoproducer	21812	21316	21160	20887	16571	*16647
Combustible fuels	21509	20969	20771	20505	16212	*16420
Hydro	91	81	56	71	51	38
Nuclear	..	..	..	..	..	..
Other	213	266	333	311	308	189
Main activity	21562	21066	20910	20637	16361	*16427
Combustible fuels	21259	20719	20521	20255	16002	*16200
Hydro	91	81	56	71	51	38
Nuclear	..	..	..	..	..	..
Other	213	266	333	311	308	189
Own use in electricity, CHP and heat plants	553	795	602	587	461	*480
Net production	21259	20522	20558	20300	16110	*16167
Imports	..	..	..	..	..	..
Exports	..	..	..	..	..	..
Losses	*2906	*2900	*3073	*2988	*2553	*2500
Consumption	18353	17621	17485	17312	13557	*13667
Energy industries own use	..	..	..	..	..	..
By industry and construction	2579	2338	2355	2250	1741	*1750
By transport	..	..	..	..	..	..
By households and other cons.	15774	15283	15130	15062	11816	*11917
Net installed capacity	**Thousand kilowatts**					
Total main activity and autoproducer	6083	*6097	*6112	6257	*6265	*6265
Combustible fuels	5800	*5800	*5800	5900	*5900	*5900
Hydro	100	99	99	99	*99	99
Nuclear	..	..	..	..	..	..
Other	183	198	213	258	266	266
Main activity	6022	*6036	*6051	6196	*6204	*6205
Combustible fuels	5739	*5739	*5739	5839	*5839	*5840
Hydro	100	99	99	99	*99	99
Nuclear	..	..	..	..	..	..
Other	183	198	213	258	266	266
Combustible fuel input	**Terajoules**					
Hard Coal	32327	36688	34133	36352	24200	*25155
Fuel oil	111423	106688	115952	102071	90116	*92920
Natural gas	60736	60736	57717	65818	54411	*55000
Total input	204487	204112	207802	204241	168728	*173075
Total production	77431	75489	74776	73819	58362	*59112
Estimated efficiency (% of production to input)	38	37	36	36	35	34

Qatar

Item	2013	2014	2015	2016	2017	2018
Production, trade and consumption	**Million kilowatt-hours**					
Total main activity and autoproducer	34668	38692	41499	42307	45555	47913
Combustible fuels	34668	38692	41499	42307	45555	47913
Hydro	..	..	..	..	..	..
Nuclear	..	..	..	..	..	..
Other	..	..	..	..	..	..
Main activity	3090	3502	2501	2550	2742	1533
Combustible fuels	3090	3502	2501	2550	2742	1533
Hydro	..	..	..	..	..	..
Nuclear	..	..	..	..	..	..
Other	..	..	..	..	..	..
Own use in electricity, CHP and heat plants	2444	2568	2647	2642	2831	3259
Net production	32224	36124	38852	39665	42724	44654
Imports	..	..	..	..	..	..
Exports	..	..	..	..	..	..
Losses	2159	2341	2475	2532	2695	2786
Consumption	30066	33784	36378	37134	40030	*41868
Energy industries own use	..	..	..	..	..	..
By industry and construction	9944	11568	11887	12026	11262	12197
By transport	..	..	..	..	..	..
By households and other cons.	20122	22216	24491	25108	28768	*29671
Net installed capacity	**Thousand kilowatts**					
Total main activity and autoproducer	*8790	*8791	*8561	*8559	*10170	*10590
Combustible fuels	*8790	*8791	*8561	*8559	*10170	*10590
Hydro	..	..	..	..	..	..
Nuclear	..	..	..	..	..	..
Other	..	..	..	..	..	..
Main activity	*1318	*1319	*1284	*1284	*1526	*1553
Combustible fuels	*1318	*1319	*1284	*1284	*1526	*1553
Hydro	..	..	..	..	..	..
Nuclear	..	..	..	..	..	..
Other	..	..	..	..	..	..
Combustible fuel input	**Terajoules**					
Natural gas	442417	381028	399818	407605	438866	452055
Total input	442417	381028	399818	407605	438866	452055
Total production	124805	139291	149396	152305	163998	172487
Estimated efficiency (% of production to input)	28	37	37	37	37	38

Republic of Moldova

Item	2013	2014	2015	2016	2017	2018
Production, trade and consumption			Million kilowatt-hours			
Total main activity and autoproducer	905	963	939	906	896	952
Combustible fuels	859	902	885	862	839	884
Hydro	45	59	50	39	48	44
Nuclear	..	..	..	..	..	..
Other	1	2	4	5	9	24
Main activity	862	893	899	864	841	882
Combustible fuels	816	832	845	820	786	827
Hydro	45	59	50	39	48	44
Nuclear	..	..	..	..	..	..
Other	1	2	4	5	7	11
Own use in electricity, CHP and heat plants	124	126	134	136	135	130
Net production	781	837	805	770	761	822
Imports	3332	3342	3315	3325	3412	3500
Exports	..	..	..	..	..	..
Losses	431	481	393	428	429	441
Consumption	3682	3698	3727	3667	3744	3881
Energy industries own use	37	49	41	45	40	40
By industry and construction	872	906	773	751	764	771
By transport	59	47	49	62	82	72
By households and other cons.	2714	2696	2864	2809	2858	2998
Net installed capacity			Thousand kilowatts			
Total main activity and autoproducer	*1087	*1083	*1091	*1063	*1077	*1078
Combustible fuels	470	465	473	443	450	425
Hydro	16	16	16	16	16	16
Nuclear	..	..	..	..	..	..
Other	*601	*602	*602	*604	*611	*637
Main activity	*947	*948	*948	*950	*953	*958
Combustible fuels	330	330	330	330	330	330
Hydro	16	16	16	16	16	16
Nuclear	..	..	..	..	..	..
Other	*601	*602	*602	*604	*607	*612
Combustible fuel input			Terajoules			
Hard Coal	0	0	0	0	0	0
Biogas	36	178	401	361	282	313
Gas-diesel oil	0	0	0	0	0	0
Fuel oil	566	485	283	485	404	283
Other oil products	0	0	0	40	0	0
Natural gas	12061	12931	11874	11660	11511	12292
Fuelwood	0	0	0	0	0	0
Vegetal waste	0	0	0	0	0	0
Industrial waste	0	0	0	0	0	0
Total input	12663	13594	12558	12546	12197	12888
Total production	3092	3247	3186	3103	3020	3182
Estimated efficiency (% of production to input)	24	24	25	25	25	25

Romania

Item	2013	2014	2015	2016	2017	2018
Production, trade and consumption	Million kilowatt-hours					
Total main activity and autoproducer	58887	65676	66296	65103	64296	64874
Combustible fuels	27021	26903	28604	26871	28673	27307
Hydro	15308	19280	17007	18536	14853	18097
Nuclear	11618	11676	11640	11286	11509	11377
Other	4940	7817	9045	8410	9261	8093
Main activity	52368	59581	58889	57978	57282	57481
Combustible fuels	21103	21866	22215	20561	22374	20509
Hydro	15062	18953	16603	18213	14609	17859
Nuclear	11618	11676	11640	11286	11509	11377
Other	4585	7086	8431	7918	8790	7736
Own use in electricity, CHP and heat plants	4753	4977	5019	4847	4941	4699
Net production	54134	60699	61277	60256	59355	60175
Imports	2737	2811	4492	4177	4842	3697
Exports	4753	9937	11220	9194	7735	6241
Losses	7021	7097	7161	7125	6994	7056
Consumption	45408	46424	47284	47802	49328	50343
Energy industries own use	4780	4519	4254	4545	4627	4775
By industry and construction	18823	19855	20525	20817	21725	22226
By transport	1126	1062	1082	1048	1089	1056
By households and other cons.	20679	20988	21423	21392	21887	22286
Net installed capacity	Thousand kilowatts					
Total main activity and autoproducer	22948	23884	23830	23580	23572	23551
Combustible fuels	11393	11323	11233	11038	11067	11022
Hydro	6610	6613	6730	6734	6691	6700
Nuclear	1411	1411	1411	1411	1411	1411
Other	3534	4537	4456	4397	4403	4418
Main activity	19664	20441	20497	20416	20550	20566
Combustible fuels	9064	8981	8895	8887	8908	8872
Hydro	6509	6523	6619	6644	6610	6617
Nuclear	1411	1411	1411	1411	1411	1411
Other	2680	3526	3572	3474	3621	3666
Combustible fuel input	Terajoules					
Brown Coal	208366	207524	216668	190559	194600	182812
Biogas	422	597	594	472	470	465
Gas-diesel oil	344	215	129	129	0	43
Fuel oil	1535	889	1252	1656	525	970
Refinery gas	3020	2525	1881	5198	4257	4208
Petroleum coke	..	..	..	3250	3608	3510
Natural gas	102871	95207	109341	114034	121683	121155
Blast furnace gas	449	690	1265	1336	1024	1425
Fuelwood	1947	5005	5383	6034	6471	6223
Industrial waste	2	2	2	2	0	0
Others	4020	4543	4141	0	0	..
Total input	322976	317196	340656	322670	332637	320810
Total production	97276	96851	102974	96736	103223	98305
Estimated efficiency (% of production to input)	30	31	30	30	31	31

Russian Federation

Item	2013	2014	2015	2016	2017	2018
Production, trade and consumption			Million kilowatt-hours			
Total main activity and autoproducer	1059092	1064207	1067544	1090973	1094289	1115093
Combustible fuels	703481	705598	701220	706663	702882	716119
Hydro	182654	177141	169914	186640	187131	193027
Nuclear	172508	180757	195470	196614	203143	204569
Other	449	711	940	1056	1133	1378
Main activity	994597	997475	995548	1016191	1021908	1039647
Combustible fuels	640434	640412	630719	633211	631728	641826
Hydro	181206	175595	168419	185310	185904	191873
Nuclear	172508	180757	195470	196614	203143	204569
Other	449	711	940	1056	1133	1378
Own use in electricity, CHP and heat plants	64342	69547	69574	67738	70589	70556
Net production	994750	994660	997970	1023235	1023700	1044537
Imports	4706	6623	6586	3194	6410	5177
Exports	18382	14671	18244	17694	17006	17779
Losses	106994	106567	106553	107247	105261	103119
Consumption	874080	880045	879759	898111	904191	924909
Energy industries own use	129989	142215	147419	154141	143306	165327
By industry and construction	336692	333701	329000	326343	338785	340296
By transport	90559	90256	82120	82569	77587	82010
By households and other cons.	316840	313873	321219	335059	344513	337277
Net installed capacity			Thousand kilowatts			
Total main activity and autoproducer	239423	255952	257075	264730	267639	271600
Combustible fuels	163926	179397	179148	185815	187701	190215
Hydro	50104	50845	50998	51016	51241	51333
Nuclear	25304	25304	26304	27189	27952	29140
Other	89	406	625	710	746	913
Main activity	219789	230592	232223	240259	242389	245977
Combustible fuels	144744	154524	154773	161794	162912	165054
Hydro	49652	50358	50521	50566	50779	50871
Nuclear	25304	25304	26304	27189	27952	29140
Other	89	406	625	710	746	913
Combustible fuel input			Terajoules			
Hard Coal	1412388	1319217	1468222	1443157	1428813	1614200
Brown Coal	908342	857293	969909	916234	925259	924413
Peat	12098	11041	5790	7264	5112	5516
Gas-diesel oil	56373	58480	62823	50224	57375	54739
Fuel oil	82820	90658	96798	83386	57422	61414
Refinery gas	1931	2079	2129	2376	1634	*4208
Natural gas	8427679	7890479	7522764	7260211	7154601	7880830
Coke-oven gas	70600	69246	69503	68586	64978	63008
Blast furnace gas	51219	52344	56294	52739	63194	56448
Industrial waste	80246	82455	85289	90771	90703	97637
Others	1213	1152	1166	1610	1840	1950
Total input	11104908	10434444	10340686	9976558	9850931	10764363
Total production	2532532	2540153	2524392	2543987	2530374	2578027
Estimated efficiency (% of production to input)	23	24	24	25	26	24

Rwanda

Item	2013	2014	2015	2016	2017	2018
Production, trade and consumption			Million kilowatt-hours			
Total main activity and autoproducer	415	478	526	636	698	730
Combustible fuels	267	268	228	344	354	362
Hydro	148	205	284	278	328	350
Nuclear	..	..	..	..	..	..
Other	0	5	14	14	16	18
Main activity	413	476	524	634	696	728
Combustible fuels	265	266	226	342	352	360
Hydro	148	205	284	278	328	350
Nuclear	..	..	..	..	..	..
Other	0	5	14	14	16	18
Own use in electricity, CHP and heat plants	26	40	13	2	25	2
Net production	389	438	512	634	673	728
Imports	94	90	83	78	86	94
Exports	0	4	3	4	4	4
Losses	*95	*86	121	145	149	*140
Consumption	388	438	419	*560	596	668
Energy industries own use	..	..	..	..	..	..
By industry and construction	79	83	96	*150	149	182
By transport	..	..	..	..	..	..
By households and other cons.	309	355	322	*410	447	486
Net installed capacity			Thousand kilowatts			
Total main activity and autoproducer	105	142	172	193	217	217
Combustible fuels	52	52	82	99	104	102
Hydro	52	80	80	84	101	103
Nuclear	..	..	..	..	..	..
Other	0	9	9	9	12	12
Main activity	104	141	171	192	216	216
Combustible fuels	51	51	81	98	103	101
Hydro	52	80	80	84	101	103
Nuclear	..	..	..	..	..	..
Other	0	9	9	9	12	12
Combustible fuel input			Terajoules			
Peat	..	..	..	..	..	*72
Gas-diesel oil	*2623	*2580	*2081	*2064	*2967	*3010
Natural gas	*102	*161	*240	*1100	*753	*771
Bagasse	*36	*36	*36	*36	*36	*36
Total input	*2761	*2777	*2358	*3200	*3756	*3889
Total production	961	966	820	1238	1273	1303
Estimated efficiency (% of production to input)	35	35	35	39	34	33

Samoa

Item	2013	2014	2015	2016	2017	2018
Production, trade and consumption	**Million kilowatt-hours**					
Total main activity and autoproducer	121	127	134	149	154	154
Combustible fuels	86	98	93	101	108	90
Hydro	35	28	33	33	26	43
Nuclear	..	..	..	..	..	..
Other	0	1	8	16	20	21
Main activity	121	127	134	149	154	154
Combustible fuels	86	98	93	101	108	90
Hydro	35	28	33	33	26	43
Nuclear	..	..	..	..	..	..
Other	0	1	8	16	20	21
Own use in electricity, CHP and heat plants	4	4	4	4	4	4
Net production	117	123	130	145	150	149
Imports	..	..	..	..	..	..
Exports	..	..	..	..	..	..
Losses	*15	14	15	15	15	15
Consumption	102	109	115	130	*134	134
Energy industries own use	..	..	..	..	..	..
By industry and construction	7	6	8	5	5	5
By transport	..	..	..	..	..	..
By households and other cons.	95	103	107	125	*129	129
Net installed capacity	**Thousand kilowatts**					
Total main activity and autoproducer	*39	42	*44	*52	*53	*54
Combustible fuels	*27	23	*23	*23	*23	*23
Hydro	*12	12	11	*11	*12	*12
Nuclear	..	..	..	..	..	..
Other	0	7	11	18	18	*19
Main activity	*39	42	*44	*52	*53	*54
Combustible fuels	*27	23	*23	*23	*23	*23
Hydro	*12	12	11	*11	*12	*12
Nuclear	..	..	..	..	..	..
Other	0	7	11	18	18	*19
Combustible fuel input	**Terajoules**					
Gas-diesel oil	831	891	857	932	*989	*843
Total input	831	891	857	932	*989	*843
Total production	308	353	336	363	387	322
Estimated efficiency (% of production to input)	37	40	39	39	39	38

Sao Tome and Principe

Item	2013	2014	2015	2016	2017	2018
Production, trade and consumption	**Million kilowatt-hours**					
Total main activity and autoproducer	71	*78	*81	86	*91	*91
Combustible fuels	65	*70	*75	79	*83	*85
Hydro	6	8	7	*7	*7	6
Nuclear	..	..	..	..	..	..
Other	0	0	0	0	0	0
Main activity	71	*78	*81	86	*91	*91
Combustible fuels	65	*70	*75	79	*83	*85
Hydro	6	8	7	*7	*7	6
Nuclear	..	..	..	..	..	..
Other	0	0	0	0	0	0
Own use in electricity, CHP and heat plants	4	*5	*6	*6	*7	7
Net production	67	*73	*76	80	*84	*85
Imports	..	..	..	..	..	..
Exports	..	..	..	..	..	..
Losses	*16	*15	*12	12	*12	*12
Consumption	*51	*58	*64	*69	*72	*73
Energy industries own use	..	..	..	..	..	..
By industry and construction	..	..	..	..	..	..
By transport	..	..	..	..	..	..
By households and other cons.	*51	*58	*64	*69	*72	*73
Net installed capacity	**Thousand kilowatts**					
Total main activity and autoproducer	*23	*23	*26	*27	*29	*29
Combustible fuels	*21	*21	*24	*25	*26	*26
Hydro	2	2	2	2	2	2
Nuclear	..	..	..	..	..	..
Other	0	0	0	0	0	0
Main activity	*23	*23	*26	*27	*29	*29
Combustible fuels	*21	*21	*24	*25	*26	*26
Hydro	2	2	2	2	2	2
Nuclear	..	..	..	..	..	..
Other	0	0	0	0	0	0
Combustible fuel input	**Terajoules**					
Gas-diesel oil	718	*688	*710	*744	*783	*796
Total input	718	*688	*710	*744	*783	*796
Total production	234	*251	*268	286	*300	*306
Estimated efficiency (% of production to input)	33	36	38	38	38	38

Saudi Arabia

Item	2013	2014	2015	2016	2017	2018
Production, trade and consumption	**Million kilowatt-hours**					
Total main activity and autoproducer	284010	311804	338331	345104	355079	343778
Combustible fuels	284009	311803	338330	345103	355075	343773
Hydro	..	..	..	..	..	..
Nuclear	..	..	..	..	..	..
Other	1	1	1	1	4	*5
Main activity	226114	251728	263510	260614	264936	192617
Combustible fuels	226113	251727	263509	260613	264932	192612
Hydro	..	..	..	..	..	..
Nuclear	..	..	..	..	..	..
Other	1	1	1	1	4	*5
Own use in electricity, CHP and heat plants	6562	7568	7970	8010	9354	31585
Net production	277448	304236	330361	337094	345725	312193
Imports	434	466	461	343	3	2
Exports	482	515	512	1062	38	36
Losses	20017	22050	25545	26186	41201	33105
Consumption	257438	279221	285539	284405	278078	279054
Energy industries own use	9212	10981	12327	13459	13731	13402
By industry and construction	41947	48442	41429	40128	33500	44466
By transport	..	..	..	..	..	..
By households and other cons.	206279	219798	231783	230818	230847	221186
Net installed capacity	**Thousand kilowatts**					
Total main activity and autoproducer	58463	65507	69156	74703	80474	*76944
Combustible fuels	58462	65506	69155	74702	80471	*76941
Hydro	..	..	..	..	..	..
Nuclear	..	..	..	..	..	..
Other	1	1	1	1	3	*3
Main activity	50040	55340	58177	62579	65848	*57709
Combustible fuels	50039	55339	58176	62578	65845	*57706
Hydro	..	..	..	..	..	..
Nuclear	..	..	..	..	..	..
Other	1	1	1	1	3	*3
Combustible fuel input	**Terajoules**					
Crude oil	812710	952384	983602	*937537	*1029066	*749091
Gas-diesel oil	592540	541155	539779	474419	462938	*440879
Fuel oil	181234	262398	287608	315241	186365	175296
Natural gas	1751556	1801750	2194514	2322614	2435112	2338003
Total input	3338040	3557688	4005503	4049811	4113481	3703268
Total production	1022432	1122491	1217988	1242371	1278270	1237583
Estimated efficiency (% of production to input)	31	32	30	31	31	33

Senegal

Item	2013	2014	2015	2016	2017	2018
Production, trade and consumption	Million kilowatt-hours					
Total main activity and autoproducer	3253	3575	3818	4097	4418	4502
Combustible fuels	3185	3542	3779	4044	4270	4333
Hydro	..	..	..	..	..	..
Nuclear	..	..	..	..	..	..
Other	68	33	39	53	148	169
Main activity	2730	2909	3105	3239	3449	3368
Combustible fuels	2730	2909	3105	3239	3449	3368
Hydro	..	..	..	..	..	..
Nuclear	..	..	..	..	..	..
Other	..	..	..	..	..	..
Own use in electricity, CHP and heat plants	39	49	54	54	54	55
Net production	3214	3526	3764	4043	4364	4447
Imports	308	318	333	360	360	360
Exports	..	..	..	..	..	..
Losses	593	599	631	670	672	672
Consumption	3079	3245	3466	3734	3472	3998
Energy industries own use	..	..	..	..	..	..
By industry and construction	846	836	951	1073	446	1075
By transport	..	..	..	..	..	..
By households and other cons.	2233	2409	2515	2661	3026	2923
Net installed capacity	Thousand kilowatts					
Total main activity and autoproducer	*854	*875	886	*893	1016	1174
Combustible fuels	*802	*823	834	*840	884	1001
Hydro	..	..	..	..	..	..
Nuclear	..	..	..	..	..	..
Other	*52	*52	*52	*53	132	173
Main activity	*489	*489	508	*510	554	671
Combustible fuels	*489	*489	508	*510	554	671
Hydro	..	..	..	..	..	..
Nuclear	..	..	..	..	..	..
Other	..	..	..	..	..	..
Combustible fuel input	Terajoules					
Hard Coal	..	..	..	..	4665	6764
Gas-diesel oil	5891	6321	4945	2365	5805	8342
Fuel oil	21735	23715	26179	28684	28159	32118
Natural gas	1519	1466	946	878	736	461
Bagasse	*1370	*2602	*1828	*2544	*2127	*3062
Total input	30515	34104	33898	34471	41492	50747
Total production	11466	12751	13604	14558	15372	15599
Estimated efficiency (% of production to input)	38	37	40	42	37	31

Serbia

Item	2013	2014	2015	2016	2017	2018
Production, trade and consumption	**Million kilowatt-hours**					
Total main activity and autoproducer	39877	34060	38298	39342	37045	37426
Combustible fuels	29024	22437	27504	27784	27232	25870
Hydro	10853	11617	10783	11520	9752	11393
Nuclear	..	..	..	..	..	..
Other	..	6	11	38	62	163
Main activity	39675	33771	37980	38889	36519	36883
Combustible fuels	28822	22148	27186	27331	26705	25327
Hydro	10853	11617	10783	11520	9752	11393
Nuclear	..	..	..	..	..	..
Other	..	6	11	38	62	163
Own use in electricity, CHP and heat plants	2707	2161	2659	2714	2747	2642
Net production	37170	31899	35639	36628	34299	34784
Imports	4077	7008	6303	5068	6549	6400
Exports	6614	5445	7221	6990	5724	6284
Losses	5501	5163	5169	4808	4806	4532
Consumption	29132	28299	29552	29898	30317	30368
Energy industries own use	2057	2074	2363	2296	2193	2319
By industry and construction	7251	7223	7539	8001	8402	8735
By transport	478	336	351	352	375	375
By households and other cons.	19346	18666	19299	19249	19347	18939
Net installed capacity	**Thousand kilowatts**					
Total main activity and autoproducer	7163	7326	7358	7410	7416	8088
Combustible fuels	4232	4303	4327	4352	4343	4873
Hydro	2931	3017	3022	3030	3038	2936
Nuclear	..	..	..	..	..	..
Other	..	6	9	28	35	279
Main activity	7102	7249	7281	7281	7296	7948
Combustible fuels	4171	4226	4250	4223	4223	4733
Hydro	2931	3017	3022	3030	3038	2936
Nuclear	..	..	..	..	..	..
Other	..	6	9	28	35	279
Combustible fuel input	**Terajoules**					
Brown Coal	304399	233364	291528	289300	286828	268847
Lignite briquettes	667	389	705	726	717	658
Biogas	171	126	140	210	398	631
Gas-diesel oil	0	0	0	0	1	0
Fuel oil	485	323	40	81	58	2990
Liquefied petroleum gas	0	0	0	0	0	0
Natural gas	8033	7087	4997	5331	7478	8113
Blast furnace gas	1142	1841	3071	3929	4249	4760
Fuelwood	78	78	100	90	81	105
Industrial waste	12	17	15	23	20	22
Others	180	0	0	0	0	..
Total input	315167	243225	300597	299689	299831	286125
Total production	104486	80773	99014	100022	98034	93132
Estimated efficiency (% of production to input)	33	33	33	33	33	33

Seychelles

Item	2013	2014	2015	2016	2017	2018
Production, trade and consumption	**Million kilowatt-hours**					
Total main activity and autoproducer	435	445	462	496	513	518
Combustible fuels	428	438	454	487	503	507
Hydro	..	..	..	..	..	..
Nuclear	..	..	..	..	..	..
Other	7	8	8	9	10	11
Main activity	354	363	378	409	424	428
Combustible fuels	347	355	369	400	414	417
Hydro	..	..	..	..	..	..
Nuclear	..	..	..	..	..	..
Other	7	8	8	9	10	11
Own use in electricity, CHP and heat plants	*10	*10	*12	*12	*12	12
Net production	425	435	450	484	501	506
Imports	..	..	..	..	..	..
Exports	..	..	..	..	..	..
Losses	40	41	*33	*32	*30	*30
Consumption	*388	*395	*409	*452	*470	476
Energy industries own use	..	..	..	..	..	..
By industry and construction	*193	*198	*204	*226	*230	*233
By transport	..	..	..	..	..	..
By households and other cons.	*194	*197	*205	*226	*239	243
Net installed capacity	**Thousand kilowatts**					
Total main activity and autoproducer	112	114	116	*137	155	*155
Combustible fuels	106	107	110	*129	146	*146
Hydro	..	..	..	..	..	..
Nuclear	..	..	..	..	..	..
Other	6	7	7	8	10	10
Main activity	85	87	89	*108	126	*126
Combustible fuels	79	80	82	*100	116	*116
Hydro	..	..	..	..	..	..
Nuclear	..	..	..	..	..	..
Other	6	7	7	8	10	10
Combustible fuel input	**Terajoules**					
Gas-diesel oil	899	*916	*920	*942	*972	*980
Fuel oil	2705	*2868	3341	3600	3697	*3353
Total input	3604	*3784	4261	4541	4668	*4334
Total production	1541	1575	1634	1751	1812	1825
Estimated efficiency (% of production to input)	43	42	38	39	39	42

Sierra Leone

Item	2013	2014	2015	2016	2017	2018
Production, trade and consumption	**Million kilowatt-hours**					
Total main activity and autoproducer	165	181	*261	*303	*309	*164
Combustible fuels	59	63	*71	*84	*84	*80
Hydro	105	118	*189	*219	*219	*78
Nuclear	..	..	..	..	..	..
Other	1	1	1	1	6	*6
Main activity	165	181	*257	*299	*305	*160
Combustible fuels	59	63	*67	*80	*80	*76
Hydro	105	118	*189	*219	*219	*78
Nuclear	..	..	..	..	..	..
Other	1	1	1	1	6	*6
Own use in electricity, CHP and heat plants	1	3	*4	*3	*9	*7
Net production	164	178	*257	*300	*300	*156
Imports	..	..	..	..	..	..
Exports	..	..	..	..	..	..
Losses	95	78	*80	*90	*90	*72
Consumption	69	86	*177	*210	*210	*84
Energy industries own use	..	..	..	..	..	..
By industry and construction	29	35	*68	*78	*78	*31
By transport	..	..	..	..	..	..
By households and other cons.	41	52	*109	*132	*132	*53
Net installed capacity	**Thousand kilowatts**					
Total main activity and autoproducer	77	77	135	139	*142	*137
Combustible fuels	27	27	78	78	*78	*76
Hydro	50	50	56	60	*60	*57
Nuclear	..	..	..	..	..	..
Other	0	0	0	1	4	4
Main activity	77	77	133	138	*141	*136
Combustible fuels	27	27	77	77	*77	*75
Hydro	50	50	56	60	*60	*57
Nuclear	..	..	..	..	..	..
Other	0	0	0	1	4	4
Combustible fuel input	**Terajoules**					
Gas-diesel oil	*688	*731	*774	*860	*903	*817
Vegetal waste	..	..	*72	*72	*72	*72
Total input	*688	*731	*846	*932	*975	*889
Total production	212	225	*257	*301	*302	*286
Estimated efficiency (% of production to input)	31	31	30	32	31	32

Singapore

Item	2013	2014	2015	2016	2017	2018
Production, trade and consumption	**Million kilowatt-hours**					
Total main activity and autoproducer	47980	49348	50341	51733	52394	53074
Combustible fuels	47963	49310	50272	51587	52225	52905
Hydro	..	..	..	..	..	..
Nuclear	..	..	..	..	..	..
Other	17	38	69	146	169	169
Main activity	45177	46374	47100	48212	48404	48341
Combustible fuels	45160	46336	47031	48066	48235	48172
Hydro	..	..	..	..	..	..
Nuclear	..	..	..	..	..	..
Other	17	38	69	146	169	169
Own use in electricity, CHP and heat plants	17	38	70	146	169	169
Net production	47963	49310	50271	51587	52225	52905
Imports	..	..	..	..	..	..
Exports	..	..	..	..	..	..
Losses	2383	2548	2428	2431	2416	2303
Consumption	44949	46403	47514	48626	49578	50449
Energy industries own use	..	..	..	..	..	..
By industry and construction	*18843	*19753	*20088	*20418	*21451	*21451
By transport	2369	2441	2445	2640	2751	2944
By households and other cons.	23737	24209	24981	25568	25377	26055
Net installed capacity	**Thousand kilowatts**					
Total main activity and autoproducer	11258	12919	13059	13445	13612	13614
Combustible fuels	11246	12894	13013	13348	13500	13500
Hydro	..	..	..	..	..	..
Nuclear	..	..	..	..	..	..
Other	12	26	46	97	112	115
Main activity	10935	12571	12641	13027	13043	13046
Combustible fuels	10923	12545	12595	12931	12931	12931
Hydro	..	..	..	..	..	..
Nuclear	..	..	..	..	..	..
Other	12	26	46	97	112	115
Combustible fuel input	**Terajoules**					
Hard Coal	5631	9600	10714	10851	12464	12347
Gas-diesel oil	1075	86	43	1380	43	24
Fuel oil	19917	2586	1939	2424	4537	3543
Refinery gas	10841	8366	7821	3119	2822	2134
Natural gas	317941	337803	341573	350194	352198	354488
Bagasse	1130	1863	2654	2902	2851	3224
Municipal waste	26917	27063	27830	27436	26742	24819
Total input	383452	387367	392574	398305	401656	400579
Total production	172668	177515	180977	185712	188011	190457
Estimated efficiency (% of production to input)	45	46	46	47	47	48

Sint Maarten (Dutch part)

Item	2013	2014	2015	2016	2017	2018
Production, trade and consumption	**Million kilowatt-hours**					
Total main activity and autoproducer	355	*358	*369	*376	*332	*291
Combustible fuels	355	*358	*369	*376	*332	*291
Hydro	..	..	..	..	..	..
Nuclear	..	..	..	..	..	..
Other	..	..	..	..	..	..
Main activity	355	*358	*369	*376	*332	*291
Combustible fuels	355	*358	*369	*376	*332	*291
Hydro	..	..	..	..	..	..
Nuclear	..	..	..	..	..	..
Other	..	..	..	..	..	..
Own use in electricity, CHP and heat plants	0	0	0	0	0	0
Net production	355	*358	*369	*376	*332	*291
Imports	..	..	..	..	..	..
Exports	..	..	..	..	..	..
Losses	32	*32	*33	*34	*51	*56
Consumption	323	326	336	342	*282	*236
Energy industries own use	..	..	..	..	..	..
By industry and construction	58	53	58	60	*49	*41
By transport	..	..	..	..	..	..
By households and other cons.	265	272	278	283	*233	*195
Net installed capacity	**Thousand kilowatts**					
Total main activity and autoproducer	97	97	97	97	*88	*92
Combustible fuels	97	97	97	97	*88	*92
Hydro	..	..	..	..	..	..
Nuclear	..	..	..	..	..	..
Other	..	..	..	..	..	..
Main activity	97	97	97	97	*88	*92
Combustible fuels	97	97	97	97	*88	*92
Hydro	..	..	..	..	..	..
Nuclear	..	..	..	..	..	..
Other	..	..	..	..	..	..
Combustible fuel input	**Terajoules**					
Fuel oil	3167	*3248	*3361	*3470	*3297	*3066
Total input	3167	*3248	*3361	*3470	*3297	*3066
Total production	1279	*1288	*1328	*1353	*1196	*1049
Estimated efficiency (% of production to input)	40	40	40	39	36	34

Slovakia

Item	2013	2014	2015	2016	2017	2018
Production, trade and consumption	**Million kilowatt-hours**					
Total main activity and autoproducer	28832	27401	26903	27064	27738	26971
Combustible fuels	7283	6719	7008	7015	7367	7542
Hydro	5166	4462	4137	4606	4623	3879
Nuclear	15720	15499	15146	14774	15081	14843
Other	663	721	612	669	667	707
Main activity	26362	24361	23835	23980	24646	23456
Combustible fuels	5458	4402	4489	4542	4862	4650
Hydro	5060	4346	4052	4508	4523	3768
Nuclear	15720	15499	15146	14774	15081	14843
Other	124	114	148	156	180	195
Own use in electricity, CHP and heat plants	1660	2394	2145	2067	2046	2108
Net production	27172	25007	24758	24997	25692	24863
Imports	10719	12964	14999	13249	15563	12428
Exports	10628	11862	12611	10598	12535	8746
Losses	760	667	1363	1332	1263	1235
Consumption	26491	25426	25768	26300	27434	27276
Energy industries own use	1407	1269	1397	1313	1631	1341
By industry and construction	11785	12237	11605	12085	12356	12794
By transport	567	574	602	607	586	588
By households and other cons.	12732	11346	12164	12295	12861	12553
Net installed capacity	**Thousand kilowatts**					
Total main activity and autoproducer	8458	8092	7782	7742	7671	7625
Combustible fuels	3432	3068	2754	2710	2645	2651
Hydro	2523	2523	2522	2524	2523	2528
Nuclear	1940	1940	1940	1940	1940	1940
Other	563	561	566	568	563	506
Main activity	7385	6947	6658	6643	6595	6518
Combustible fuels	2847	2411	2119	2106	2012	1882
Hydro	2493	2493	2495	2493	2493	2496
Nuclear	1940	1940	1940	1940	1940	1940
Other	105	103	104	104	150	200
Combustible fuel input	**Terajoules**					
Hard Coal	17031	15816	14279	14739	17425	18353
Brown Coal	28653	27261	28042	31222	24380	22139
Biogas	2072	3857	4574	4991	5040	4977
Fuel oil	8928	6504	8201	9534	8646	2990
Natural gas	26454	19005	19379	18955	20306	21164
Coke-oven gas	887	961	1277	1077	1136	1161
Blast furnace gas	1697	1661	1438	1328	1742	1882
Fuelwood	*7809	*6809	*7284	9237	*9047	*9202
Vegetal waste	*735	*757	*2872	*802	*797	977
Black liquor	*8055	*6297	*5549	*5645	*5831	5310
Others	2485	2408	2441	2225	2942	1862
Total input	104806	91336	95336	99755	97292	90017
Total production	26219	24188	25229	25254	26521	27151
Estimated efficiency (% of production to input)	25	26	26	25	27	30

Slovenia

Item	2013	2014	2015	2016	2017	2018
Production, trade and consumption	**Million kilowatt-hours**					
Total main activity and autoproducer	16103	17437	15100	16500	16326	16330
Combustible fuels	5661	4440	5081	5730	5610	5400
Hydro	4923	6366	4091	4782	4141	4893
Nuclear	5300	6370	5648	5715	6285	5776
Other	219	261	280	273	290	261
Main activity	15481	16688	14412	15746	15596	15602
Combustible fuels	5414	4169	4813	5463	5345	5141
Hydro	4757	6138	3937	4555	3952	4672
Nuclear	5300	6370	5648	5715	6285	5776
Other	10	11	14	13	14	13
Own use in electricity, CHP and heat plants	986	951	913	954	929	883
Net production	15117	16486	14187	15546	15397	15447
Imports	7521	7254	9045	8359	9133	8930
Exports	8811	9997	9093	9535	9648	9432
Losses	848	821	864	876	893	880
Consumption	12979	12922	13275	13493	13987	14065
Energy industries own use	500	463	487	468	458	348
By industry and construction	5878	6057	6199	6234	6445	6847
By transport	154	136	152	166	233	233
By households and other cons.	6447	6266	6437	6625	6851	6637
Net installed capacity	**Thousand kilowatts**					
Total main activity and autoproducer	3434	3454	3360	3536	3619	3798
Combustible fuels	1256	1242	1133	1318	1332	1514
Hydro	1299	1296	1295	1293	1347	1344
Nuclear	688	688	688	688	688	688
Other	191	228	244	237	252	252
Main activity	3095	3070	2965	3148	3217	3395
Combustible fuels	1214	1192	1086	1272	1286	1467
Hydro	1183	1180	1179	1177	1231	1228
Nuclear	688	688	688	688	688	688
Other	10	10	12	11	12	12
Combustible fuel input	**Terajoules**					
Hard Coal	131	101	135	136	110	137
Brown Coal	53877	42032	42634	40630	45719	45508
Biogas	1357	1203	1163	1196	1024	956
Gas-diesel oil	86	344	172	86	86	129
Fuel oil	0	0	0	..	..	..
Liquefied petroleum gas	..	..	..	..	47	47
Natural gas	4824	3153	3588	3638	4299	4300
Fuelwood	*1495	*1467	*1761	*1744	*1995	1810
Industrial waste	310	321	330	357	375	409
Biodiesel	..	37	37	37	37	74
Total input	62080	48658	49819	47824	53692	53370
Total production	20380	15984	18292	20628	20196	19440
Estimated efficiency (% of production to input)	33	33	37	43	38	36

Solomon Islands

Item	2013	2014	2015	2016	2017	2018
Production, trade and consumption	**Million kilowatt-hours**					
Total main activity and autoproducer	91	94	97	105	108	110
Combustible fuels	89	92	95	102	104	106
Hydro	0	0	0	1	1	1
Nuclear	..	..	..	..	..	..
Other	1	1	2	2	3	3
Main activity	83	86	88	96	99	101
Combustible fuels	81	84	86	93	95	97
Hydro	0	0	0	1	1	1
Nuclear	..	..	..	..	..	..
Other	1	1	2	2	3	3
Own use in electricity, CHP and heat plants	*4	*2	*2	*3	*5	*3
Net production	87	92	95	102	103	107
Imports	..	..	..	..	..	..
Exports	..	..	..	..	..	..
Losses	*10	*10	*12	*12	*13	*14
Consumption	77	*82	*83	*90	90	93
Energy industries own use	..	..	..	..	..	..
By industry and construction	*30	*35	*33	*35	*37	*39
By transport	..	..	..	..	..	..
By households and other cons.	47	*47	*50	*54	53	54
Net installed capacity	**Thousand kilowatts**					
Total main activity and autoproducer	*37	*37	*37	*38	*39	*39
Combustible fuels	*36	*36	*36	*36	*36	*36
Hydro	0	0	0	0	0	0
Nuclear	..	..	..	..	..	..
Other	1	1	1	2	3	3
Main activity	*32	*32	*32	*33	*34	*34
Combustible fuels	*31	*31	*31	*31	*31	*31
Hydro	0	0	0	0	0	0
Nuclear	..	..	..	..	..	..
Other	1	1	1	2	3	3
Combustible fuel input	**Terajoules**					
Gas-diesel oil	*1148	*1165	*1075	*1011	*998	*1015
Vegetal waste	*38	*49	*55	*55	*48	*35
Total input	*1186	*1214	*1130	*1066	*1046	*1050
Total production	321	331	341	366	374	382
Estimated efficiency (% of production to input)	27	27	30	34	36	36

Somalia

Item	2013	2014	2015	2016	2017	2018
Production, trade and consumption	**Million kilowatt-hours**					
Total main activity and autoproducer	350	350	350	350	*350	*350
Combustible fuels	350	350	350	350	*350	*350
Hydro	..	..	..	..	..	..
Nuclear	..	..	..	..	..	..
Other	..	..	..	..	..	..
Main activity	350	350	350	350	*350	*350
Combustible fuels	350	350	350	350	*350	*350
Hydro	..	..	..	..	..	..
Nuclear	..	..	..	..	..	..
Other	..	..	..	..	..	..
Own use in electricity, CHP and heat plants	0	0	0	0	0	0
Net production	350	350	350	350	*350	*350
Imports	..	..	..	..	..	..
Exports	..	..	..	..	..	..
Losses	*35	*35	*35	*35	*35	0
Consumption	315	315	315	315	315	350
Energy industries own use	..	..	..	..	..	..
By industry and construction	..	..	..	..	..	..
By transport	..	..	..	..	..	..
By households and other cons.	315	315	315	315	315	350
Net installed capacity	**Thousand kilowatts**					
Total main activity and autoproducer	80	80	80	80	80	80
Combustible fuels	80	80	80	80	80	80
Hydro	..	..	..	..	..	..
Nuclear	..	..	..	..	..	..
Other	..	..	..	..	..	..
Main activity	80	80	80	80	80	80
Combustible fuels	80	80	80	80	80	80
Hydro	..	..	..	..	..	..
Nuclear	..	..	..	..	..	..
Other	..	..	..	..	..	..
Combustible fuel input	**Terajoules**					
Gas-diesel oil	*4214	*4214	*4214	*4300	*4300	*4300
Total input	*4214	*4214	*4214	*4300	*4300	*4300
Total production	1260	1260	1260	1260	*1260	*1260
Estimated efficiency (% of production to input)	30	30	30	29	29	29

South Africa

Item	2013	2014	2015	2016	2017	2018
Production, trade and consumption	**Million kilowatt-hours**					
Total main activity and autoproducer	256073	252578	249655	255208	257702	256064
Combustible fuels	237871	232516	228825	228523	227635	228082
Hydro	4040	4082	3720	3947	5323	5694
Nuclear	14106	13794	12237	15913	15743	11580
Other	56	2186	4873	6825	9001	10708
Main activity	244851	240401	233391	221756	237648	232803
Combustible fuels	226828	222649	217282	201654	216379	214919
Hydro	3917	3958	3607	3856	5183	5619
Nuclear	14106	13794	12237	15913	15743	11580
Other	..	..	265	333	343	685
Own use in electricity, CHP and heat plants	14608	14360	13938	18404	18534	13853
Net production	241465	238218	235717	236804	239168	242211
Imports	9428	11177	13059	10555	10555	9687
Exports	13929	13836	14609	16549	16549	14386
Losses	21488	20940	19895	16293	21086	22737
Consumption	212483	211678	210031	223198	222423	226730
Energy industries own use	15679	16173	16169	20457	19750	21307
By industry and construction	118203	117427	116575	107407	107107	108341
By transport	3745	3714	3463	3097	3329	3120
By households and other cons.	74856	74364	73824	92237	92237	93962
Net installed capacity	**Thousand kilowatts**					
Total main activity and autoproducer	*44148	*47643	*47109	*49930	*53028	*53487
Combustible fuels	*41559	*43238	*40581	*42581	*45497	*45497
Hydro	*728	*725	*740	*740	761	761
Nuclear	*1800	*1880	*1860	1860	1940	1940
Other	*61	*1800	*3928	*4749	*4830	5289
Main activity	*42037	*44003	*41041	*40850	*45837	*45837
Combustible fuels	*39559	*41438	*38381	*38190	*43097	*43097
Hydro	*678	*685	*700	*700	700	700
Nuclear	*1800	*1880	*1860	1860	1940	1940
Other	..	..	*100	*100	100	*100
Combustible fuel input	**Terajoules**					
Hard Coal	2938647	3083944	2827721	2944037	2916848	2756479
Gas-diesel oil	1978	1935	1892	47541	381	1892
Vegetal waste	*3730	*3730	*3730	5386	5457	5496
Total input	2944355	3089609	2833343	2996964	2922686	2763867
Total production	856336	837058	823770	822683	819486	821095
Estimated efficiency (% of production to input)	29	27	29	27	28	30

South Sudan

Item	2013	2014	2015	2016	2017	2018
Production, trade and consumption	**Million kilowatt-hours**					
Total main activity and autoproducer	472	488	578	447	542	583
Combustible fuels	470	486	576	445	539	580
Hydro	..	..	..	..	..	..
Nuclear	..	..	..	..	..	..
Other	2	2	2	2	3	3
Main activity	226	234	246	189	503	541
Combustible fuels	225	233	245	188	502	540
Hydro	..	..	..	..	..	..
Nuclear	..	..	..	..	..	..
Other	1	1	1	1	1	1
Own use in electricity, CHP and heat plants	18	19	18	14	15	12
Net production	454	469	560	433	527	571
Imports	..	..	..	..	..	..
Exports	..	..	..	..	..	..
Losses	27	28	27	21	24	19
Consumption	415	429	529	409	498	446
Energy industries own use	..	..	..	..	..	..
By industry and construction	..	..	..	..	197	157
By transport	..	..	..	..	..	..
By households and other cons.	415	429	529	409	301	289
Net installed capacity	**Thousand kilowatts**					
Total main activity and autoproducer	*81	*81	*84	*84	*131	*131
Combustible fuels	*80	*80	*80	*80	*120	*120
Hydro	..	..	3	*3	*3	*3
Nuclear	..	..	..	..	..	..
Other	*1	*1	*1	*1	*8	*8
Main activity	*40	*40	*43	*43	*90	*90
Combustible fuels	*40	*40	*40	*40	*80	*80
Hydro	..	..	3	*3	*3	*3
Nuclear	..	..	..	..	..	..
Other	0	0	0	0	*7	*7
Combustible fuel input	**Terajoules**					
Motor gasoline	..	..	177	133	89	89
Gas-diesel oil	5418	5590	7826	5934	5547	5977
Total input	5418	5590	8003	6067	5636	6066
Total production	1692	1750	2074	1602	1940	2088
Estimated efficiency (% of production to input)	31	31	26	26	34	34

Spain

Item	2013	2014	2015	2016	2017	2018
Production, trade and consumption	**Million kilowatt-hours**					
Total main activity and autoproducer	285631	278750	280911	274772	275726	274452
Combustible fuels	119111	112789	128947	113618	133002	118149
Hydro	41052	42970	31368	39865	21070	36803
Nuclear	56726	57305	57196	58633	58039	55766
Other	68742	65686	63400	62656	63615	63734
Main activity	247504	246639	247431	240730	239698	236865
Combustible fuels	81966	81783	96474	80530	97587	81760
Hydro	40109	41906	30620	39062	20593	35894
Nuclear	56726	57305	57196	58633	58039	55766
Other	68703	65645	63141	62505	63479	63445
Own use in electricity, CHP and heat plants	10232	10370	11160	10428	10808	10625
Net production	275399	268380	269751	264344	264918	263827
Imports	9887	12310	14956	21845	23762	24018
Exports	16638	15716	15089	14178	14593	12916
Losses	26694	26393	26509	26720	23823	25417
Consumption	241089	238508	243065	244640	250149	248968
Energy industries own use	11002	11611	11027	12125	11048	10503
By industry and construction	70828	71657	76055	77899	81019	78659
By transport	3819	3906	3978	3902	3987	4046
By households and other cons.	155440	151334	152005	150714	154095	155760
Net installed capacity	**Thousand kilowatts**					
Total main activity and autoproducer	113211	113638	114057	113252	111144	111093
Combustible fuels	56786	56786	56350	55454	53510	53063
Hydro	19385	19423	20253	20280	20279	20280
Nuclear	6984	7399	7399	7399	7117	7117
Other	30056	30030	30055	30119	30238	30633
Main activity	105907	106334	106753	105948	103840	103738
Combustible fuels	49786	49786	49350	48454	46510	46063
Hydro	19185	19223	20053	20080	20079	20080
Nuclear	6984	7399	7399	7399	7117	7117
Other	29952	29926	29951	30015	30134	30478
Combustible fuel input	**Terajoules**					
Hard Coal	379601	411565	481734	362042	443931	385792
Brown Coal	21620	29263	30805	18293	26263	18023
Gas-diesel oil	40377	49106	35432	32078	36077	37367
Fuel oil	66579	63913	69326	75467	76073	70862
Petroleum coke	9458	10725	37083	31103	17713	10270
Natural gas	395682	323797	384257	376162	461908	417687
Blast furnace gas	9939	12500	11345	8924	10863	10685
Fuelwood	*35692	*41082	*26243	27506	*30705	*27252
Vegetal waste	*10992	*3168	*23658	*21886	*22528	*22959
Municipal waste	16724	17098	20900	19226	21160	20926
Others	19397	19166	17614	14200	15736	19451
Total input	1006060	981383	1138397	986886	1162957	1041274
Total production	428800	406040	464209	409025	478807	425336
Estimated efficiency (% of production to input)	43	41	41	41	41	41

Sri Lanka

Item	2013	2014	2015	2016	2017	2018
Production, trade and consumption			**Million kilowatt-hours**			
Total main activity and autoproducer	12060	12862	13227	14363	15004	15985
Combustible fuels	4870	7986	6854	9721	10381	9072
Hydro	6929	4563	5969	4221	4039	6401
Nuclear	..	..	..	..	..	..
Other	261	313	404	422	583	513
Main activity	12024	12812	12046	13461	13821	14577
Combustible fuels	4870	7986	6796	9630	10296	8985
Hydro	6918	4552	4904	3482	3075	5169
Nuclear	..	..	..	..	..	..
Other	236	274	345	349	450	423
Own use in electricity, CHP and heat plants	280	438	561	633	336	612
Net production	11780	12424	12666	13730	14668	15374
Imports	..	..	..	..	..	..
Exports	..	..	..	..	..	..
Losses	1201	1426	925	997	1179	1407
Consumption	10554	10997	11741	12715	13489	14119
Energy industries own use	..	..	..	..	..	..
By industry and construction	3590	3758	3880	4149	4372	4598
By transport	..	..	..	..	..	..
By households and other cons.	6964	7239	7861	8566	9117	9521
Net installed capacity			**Thousand kilowatts**			
Total main activity and autoproducer	3301	4043	3948	4010	4094	4124
Combustible fuels	1591	2233	2108	2088	2144	2069
Hydro	1617	1664	1684	1722	1720	1793
Nuclear	..	..	..	..	..	..
Other	93	146	156	200	230	262
Main activity	3019	3723	3593	3598	3658	3642
Combustible fuels	1575	2213	2088	2064	2115	2037
Hydro	1361	1377	1377	1384	1364	1399
Nuclear	..	..	..	..	..	..
Other	83	133	128	150	179	206
Combustible fuel input			**Terajoules**			
Hard Coal	19860	39964	55099	58733	61151	58880
Gas-diesel oil	3856	12995	4240	16761	17535	7783
Fuel oil	21257	24659	12391	13227	19974	21776
Naphtha	4652	5904	6437	8010	9060	3071
Fuelwood	0	..	..	..	..	..
Bagasse	334	524	726	911	848	*1119
Total input	49959	84047	78893	97643	108568	92628
Total production	17530	28748	24673	34995	37373	32660
Estimated efficiency (% of production to input)	35	34	31	36	34	35

St. Helena and Depend.

Item	2013	2014	2015	2016	2017	2018
Production, trade and consumption	Million kilowatt-hours					
Total main activity and autoproducer	10	11	11	12	11	12
Combustible fuels	9	9	8	8	9	8
Hydro	..	..	..	..	..	..
Nuclear	..	..	..	..	..	..
Other	1	2	3	3	3	4
Main activity	10	11	11	12	11	12
Combustible fuels	9	9	8	8	9	8
Hydro	..	..	..	..	..	..
Nuclear	..	..	..	..	..	..
Other	1	2	3	3	3	4
Own use in electricity, CHP and heat plants	0	0	0	0	0	0
Net production	10	11	11	12	11	12
Imports	..	..	..	..	..	..
Exports	..	..	..	..	..	..
Losses	*2	*2	*2	*2	*2	*1
Consumption	9	9	9	9	9	11
Energy industries own use	..	..	..	..	..	..
By industry and construction	..	..	..	..	..	..
By transport	..	..	..	..	..	..
By households and other cons.	9	9	9	9	9	11
Net installed capacity	Thousand kilowatts					
Total main activity and autoproducer	8	9	10	11	11	12
Combustible fuels	8	8	8	8	8	8
Hydro	..	..	..	..	..	..
Nuclear	..	..	..	..	..	..
Other	1	1	*3	3	*3	4
Main activity	8	9	10	11	11	12
Combustible fuels	8	8	8	8	8	8
Hydro	..	..	..	..	..	..
Nuclear	..	..	..	..	..	..
Other	1	1	*3	3	*3	4
Combustible fuel input	Terajoules					
Gas-diesel oil	*99	85	72	67	*77	*69
Total input	*99	85	72	67	*77	*69
Total production	34	32	29	30	31	28
Estimated efficiency (% of production to input)	34	38	41	45	40	41

St. Kitts-Nevis

Item	2013	2014	2015	2016	2017	2018
Production, trade and consumption	**Million kilowatt-hours**					
Total main activity and autoproducer	*220	*221	*217	*228	232	*232
Combustible fuels	*211	*211	*207	*217	221	*221
Hydro	..	..	..	..	..	..
Nuclear	..	..	..	..	..	..
Other	*9	*10	*10	11	11	*11
Main activity	*219	*220	*216	*227	231	*231
Combustible fuels	*210	*210	*206	*216	220	*220
Hydro	..	..	..	..	..	..
Nuclear	..	..	..	..	..	..
Other	*9	*10	*10	11	11	*11
Own use in electricity, CHP and heat plants	*1	*2	*2	*3	5	*5
Net production	*219	*219	*215	*225	227	*227
Imports	..	..	..	..	..	..
Exports	..	..	..	..	..	..
Losses	*39	*39	*31	*36	*40	*40
Consumption	*180	*180	*184	*189	*181	*187
Energy industries own use	..	..	..	..	..	..
By industry and construction	*36	*36	*37	*38	*36	*37
By transport	..	..	..	..	..	..
By households and other cons.	*144	*144	*147	*152	*145	*150
Net installed capacity	**Thousand kilowatts**					
Total main activity and autoproducer	*62	*64	64	65	65	71
Combustible fuels	*59	*60	60	60	60	67
Hydro	..	..	..	..	..	..
Nuclear	..	..	..	..	..	..
Other	3	*4	4	*4	*4	4
Main activity	*58	*60	60	61	61	67
Combustible fuels	*55	*56	56	56	56	63
Hydro	..	..	..	..	..	..
Nuclear	..	..	..	..	..	..
Other	3	*4	4	*4	*4	4
Combustible fuel input	**Terajoules**					
Gas-diesel oil	*1982	*1978	*2051	*2107	*2077	*2090
Total input	*1982	*1978	*2051	*2107	*2077	*2090
Total production	*760	*760	*746	*781	796	*796
Estimated efficiency (% of production to input)	38	38	36	37	38	38

St. Lucia

Item	2013	2014	2015	2016	2017	2018
Production, trade and consumption			Million kilowatt-hours			
Total main activity and autoproducer	383	379	381	391	400	404
Combustible fuels	383	379	381	391	400	399
Hydro	..	..	..	..	..	..
Nuclear	..	..	..	..	..	..
Other	..	..	..	..	..	5
Main activity	383	379	381	391	400	404
Combustible fuels	383	379	381	391	400	399
Hydro	..	..	..	..	..	..
Nuclear	..	..	..	..	..	..
Other	..	..	..	..	..	5
Own use in electricity, CHP and heat plants	15	14	14	14	13	17
Net production	368	366	368	378	387	387
Imports	..	..	..	..	..	..
Exports	..	..	..	..	..	..
Losses	34	34	30	29	27	25
Consumption	334	332	338	348	360	362
Energy industries own use	..	..	..	..	..	..
By industry and construction	18	18	18	19	18	17
By transport	..	..	..	..	..	..
By households and other cons.	317	314	320	330	341	344
Net installed capacity			Thousand kilowatts			
Total main activity and autoproducer	88	88	88	88	88	91
Combustible fuels	88	88	88	88	88	88
Hydro	..	..	..	..	..	..
Nuclear	..	..	..	..	..	..
Other	..	..	..	..	..	3
Main activity	88	88	88	88	88	91
Combustible fuels	88	88	88	88	88	88
Hydro	..	..	..	..	..	..
Nuclear	..	..	..	..	..	..
Other	..	..	..	..	..	3
Combustible fuel input			Terajoules			
Gas-diesel oil	3437	3406	3422	3513	3593	3593
Total input	3437	3406	3422	3513	3593	3593
Total production	1379	1366	1373	1409	1441	1437
Estimated efficiency (% of production to input)	40	40	40	40	40	40

St. Pierre-Miquelon

Item	2013	2014	2015	2016	2017	2018
Production, trade and consumption	**Million kilowatt-hours**					
Total main activity and autoproducer	47	48	49	48	49	51
Combustible fuels	46	48	49	48	49	51
Hydro	..	..	..	..	..	..
Nuclear	..	..	..	..	..	..
Other	1	0	0	0	..	..
Main activity	47	48	49	48	49	51
Combustible fuels	46	48	49	48	49	51
Hydro	..	..	..	..	..	..
Nuclear	..	..	..	..	..	..
Other	1	0	0	0	..	..
Own use in electricity, CHP and heat plants	0	0	2	1	1	1
Net production	47	48	47	47	48	50
Imports	..	..	..	..	..	..
Exports	..	..	..	..	..	..
Losses	2	2	*3	*2	*2	*2
Consumption	45	46	*44	*45	*46	*47
Energy industries own use	..	..	..	..	..	..
By industry and construction	..	..	..	..	..	..
By transport	..	..	..	..	..	..
By households and other cons.	45	46	*44	*45	*46	*47
Net installed capacity	**Thousand kilowatts**					
Total main activity and autoproducer	28	26	25	25	25	26
Combustible fuels	27	26	25	25	25	26
Hydro	..	..	..	..	..	..
Nuclear	..	..	..	..	..	..
Other	1	0	0	0	0	0
Main activity	28	26	25	25	25	26
Combustible fuels	27	26	25	25	25	26
Hydro	..	..	..	..	..	..
Nuclear	..	..	..	..	..	..
Other	1	0	0	0	0	0
Combustible fuel input	**Terajoules**					
Gas-diesel oil	*490	*500	*500	*500	*499	*507
Total input	*490	*500	*500	*500	*499	*507
Total production	164	174	175	174	175	183
Estimated efficiency (% of production to input)	34	35	35	35	35	36

St. Vincent-Grenadines

Item	2013	2014	2015	2016	2017	2018
Production, trade and consumption	Million kilowatt-hours					
Total main activity and autoproducer	142	142	147	153	151	151
Combustible fuels	119	129	129	136	129	125
Hydro	23	12	17	16	20	24
Nuclear	..	..	..	..	..	..
Other	0	1	1	1	1	2
Main activity	142	142	146	153	150	150
Combustible fuels	119	129	129	136	129	125
Hydro	23	12	17	16	20	24
Nuclear	..	..	..	..	..	..
Other	0	0	1	1	1	1
Own use in electricity, CHP and heat plants	5	5	5	5	5	5
Net production	137	137	142	149	146	146
Imports	..	..	..	..	..	..
Exports	..	..	..	..	..	..
Losses	10	10	9	11	9	11
Consumption	128	127	133	138	137	135
Energy industries own use	..	..	..	..	..	..
By industry and construction	7	7	7	7	7	7
By transport	..	..	..	..	..	..
By households and other cons.	121	120	125	131	130	128
Net installed capacity	Thousand kilowatts					
Total main activity and autoproducer	52	*51	53	53	48	46
Combustible fuels	46	*44	46	46	41	38
Hydro	6	*6	6	6	6	6
Nuclear	..	..	..	..	..	..
Other	1	1	1	1	1	2
Main activity	52	*51	53	53	48	45
Combustible fuels	46	*44	46	46	41	38
Hydro	6	*6	6	6	6	6
Nuclear	..	..	..	..	..	..
Other	0	0	1	1	1	2
Combustible fuel input	Terajoules					
Gas-diesel oil	1137	1235	1228	1306	1227	1190
Total input	1137	1235	1228	1306	1227	1190
Total production	428	466	463	490	464	450
Estimated efficiency (% of production to input)	38	38	38	38	38	38

State of Palestine

Item	2013	2014	2015	2016	2017	2018
Production, trade and consumption	**Million kilowatt-hours**					
Total main activity and autoproducer	536	340	515	537	546	420
Combustible fuels	534	337	506	495	501	360
Hydro	..	..	..	..	..	..
Nuclear	..	..	..	..	..	..
Other	2	3	9	43	45	60
Main activity	404	268	360	360	392	284
Combustible fuels	403	266	355	339	369	254
Hydro	..	..	..	..	..	..
Nuclear	..	..	..	..	..	..
Other	1	2	5	21	23	30
Own use in electricity, CHP and heat plants	2	1	0	0	0	0
Net production	534	339	515	537	546	420
Imports	4734	4935	5413	5473	5577	5916
Exports	..	..	..	..	..	..
Losses	527	633	711	721	735	760
Consumption	4743	4642	5216	5289	5388	5576
Energy industries own use	..	..	..	..	..	..
By industry and construction	405	527	576	584	648	715
By transport	..	..	..	..	..	..
By households and other cons.	4339	4115	4640	4705	4740	4861
Net installed capacity	**Thousand kilowatts**					
Total main activity and autoproducer	161	163	172	185	190	200
Combustible fuels	160	160	160	160	160	160
Hydro	..	..	..	..	..	..
Nuclear	..	..	..	..	..	..
Other	1	3	12	25	30	40
Main activity	141	142	146	153	155	160
Combustible fuels	140	140	140	140	140	140
Hydro	..	..	..	..	..	..
Nuclear	..	..	..	..	..	..
Other	1	2	6	13	15	20
Combustible fuel input	**Terajoules**					
Motor gasoline	354	337	443	403	279	235
Gas-diesel oil	4455	2989	3939	4094	4670	3040
Total input	4809	3325	4382	4497	4949	3275
Total production	1923	1212	1820	1780	1803	1297
Estimated efficiency (% of production to input)	40	36	42	40	36	40

Sudan

Item	2013	2014	2015	2016	2017	2018
Production, trade and consumption	Million kilowatt-hours					
Total main activity and autoproducer	10423	11492	13158	14540	15659	16374
Combustible fuels	2106	2579	4738	6489	6312	6717
Hydro	8317	8913	8420	8051	9347	9657
Nuclear	..	..	..	..	..	..
Other	..	..	..	..	..	..
Main activity	10287	11376	13047	14429	15542	16256
Combustible fuels	1970	2463	4627	6378	6195	6599
Hydro	8317	8913	8420	8051	9347	9657
Nuclear	..	..	..	..	..	..
Other	..	..	..	..	..	..
Own use in electricity, CHP and heat plants	178	112	125	164	241	454
Net production	10245	11380	13033	14376	15418	15920
Imports	320	443	129	439	891	808
Exports	..	..	5	6	..	..
Losses	2365	2502	2870	3030	3140	3028
Consumption	7895	9710	10580	11799	12961	13700
Energy industries own use	..	..	..	..	..	..
By industry and construction	1279	1628	1512	1794	2003	1795
By transport	..	..	..	..	..	..
By households and other cons.	6616	8082	9068	10005	10958	11905
Net installed capacity	Thousand kilowatts					
Total main activity and autoproducer	3331	*3340	3321	3540	3770	3939
Combustible fuels	1733	*1739	1717	1935	2004	2013
Hydro	1590	1593	1593	1593	1753	1907
Nuclear	..	..	..	..	..	..
Other	8	8	11	12	13	19
Main activity	3133	3142	3120	3338	3567	3721
Combustible fuels	1543	*1549	1527	1745	1814	1814
Hydro	1590	1593	1593	1593	1753	1907
Nuclear	..	..	..	..	..	..
Other	..	..	..	..	..	..
Combustible fuel input	Terajoules					
Crude oil	..	..	*23265	*31725	*31725	31725
Gas-diesel oil	24037	29068	*30272	*31863	*39345	*39345
Bagasse	*2456	*2093	*2000	*1977	*2100	*2131
Total input	26493	31161	*55537	*65565	*73170	*73201
Total production	7582	9285	17057	23359	22722	24182
Estimated efficiency (% of production to input)	29	30	31	36	31	33

Suriname

Item	2013	2014	2015	2016	2017	2018
Production, trade and consumption	**Million kilowatt-hours**					
Total main activity and autoproducer	2035	2073	2084	2027	2117	2288
Combustible fuels	932	1276	1378	1239	1187	1284
Hydro	1103	797	702	783	926	1000
Nuclear	..	..	..	..	..	..
Other	..	..	*4	*4	*4	*4
Main activity	552	751	762	577	666	*583
Combustible fuels	552	751	757	573	662	*579
Hydro	..	..	..	..	..	..
Nuclear	..	..	..	..	..	..
Other	..	..	*4	*4	*4	*4
Own use in electricity, CHP and heat plants	85	73	70	34	93	78
Net production	1950	2000	2014	1993	2024	2210
Imports	..	..	..	..	..	..
Exports	..	..	..	..	..	..
Losses	197	190	242	217	217	426
Consumption	1737	1768	1772	1772	1773	1783
Energy industries own use	..	..	..	..	..	..
By industry and construction	741	727	716	851	852	857
By transport	..	..	..	..	..	..
By households and other cons.	996	1041	1057	921	922	927
Net installed capacity	**Thousand kilowatts**					
Total main activity and autoproducer	536	496	501	*501	*501	504
Combustible fuels	347	307	307	*307	*307	310
Hydro	189	189	189	189	189	189
Nuclear	..	..	..	..	..	..
Other	..	..	5	*5	*5	*5
Main activity	224	184	189	*189	*189	192
Combustible fuels	224	184	184	*184	*184	187
Hydro	..	..	..	..	..	..
Nuclear	..	..	..	..	..	..
Other	..	..	5	*5	*5	*5
Combustible fuel input	**Terajoules**					
Gas-diesel oil	1028	731	753	674	690	676
Fuel oil	12972	13756	13866	12420	12681	12444
Natural gas	179	149	152	136	136	195
Total input	14179	14636	14771	13230	13507	13315
Total production	3356	4595	4960	4461	4275	4621
Estimated efficiency (% of production to input)	24	31	34	34	32	35

Sweden

Item	2013	2014	2015	2016	2017	2018
Production, trade and consumption			Million kilowatt-hours			
Total main activity and autoproducer	153166	153663	162112	156010	164250	163400
Combustible fuels	15336	13632	13906	15150	15547	15571
Hydro	61496	63872	75439	62137	65168	62250
Nuclear	66457	64877	56348	63101	65696	68549
Other	9877	11282	16419	15622	17839	17030
Main activity	147312	147866	156285	150272	158035	157261
Combustible fuels	9492	7847	8090	9423	9344	9443
Hydro	61486	63860	75428	62126	65156	62239
Nuclear	66457	64877	56348	63101	65696	68549
Other	9877	11282	16419	15622	17839	17030
Own use in electricity, CHP and heat plants	3627	3706	3067	3479	3724	3723
Net production	149539	149957	159045	152531	160526	159677
Imports	12674	13852	9294	14287	11896	12202
Exports	22676	29475	31894	26022	30888	29425
Losses	10003	7335	6988	8569	9495	10537
Consumption	128075	125195	127983	130784	130495	130629
Energy industries own use	3059	3004	3124	3288	3241	3067
By industry and construction	52014	50730	50281	50289	50939	50719
By transport	2750	2615	2595	2664	2476	2573
By households and other cons.	70252	68846	71983	74543	73839	74270
Net installed capacity			Thousand kilowatts			
Total main activity and autoproducer	37915	39921	40885	41511	39798	41223
Combustible fuels	7776	9270	8945	8689	7442	8408
Hydro	16494	15996	16329	16466	16502	16431
Nuclear	9408	9507	9688	9768	8999	8656
Other	4237	5148	5923	6588	6855	7728
Main activity	36712	38718	39683	40305	38513	39775
Combustible fuels	6582	8076	7751	7495	6175	6978
Hydro	16485	15987	16321	16454	16484	16413
Nuclear	9408	9507	9688	9768	8999	8656
Other	4237	5148	5923	6588	6855	7728
Combustible fuel input			Terajoules			
Hard Coal	12813	8423	8255	5358	6493	6753
Peat	7588	5261	4441	4870	4626	7239
Gas-diesel oil	946	129	1376	1892	1075	1634
Fuel oil	3596	3232	1454	2707	1656	2060
Natural gas	14963	7695	8082	11451	4724	6769
Blast furnace gas	5122	5749	5435	5608	6833	7167
Fuelwood	*128628	*121842	*124449	*135091	*143783	*142651
Municipal waste	53494	56454	58887	61789	65148	60846
Industrial waste	1087	863	749	746	748	755
Other recovered gases	1662	1648	1542	1951	1992	1891
Others	2312	1483	1467	1646	1725	1628
Total input	*232211	*212779	*216138	*233108	*238804	*239394
Total production	55210	49075	50062	54540	55969	56056
Estimated efficiency (% of production to input)	24	23	23	23	23	23

Switzerland

Item	2013	2014	2015	2016	2017	2018
Production, trade and consumption	**Million kilowatt-hours**					
Total main activity and autoproducer	70227	71767	67720	63175	63089	69107
Combustible fuels	3679	3566	3521	3898	3864	3725
Hydro	39968	39701	39881	36689	37033	37803
Nuclear	25990	27557	23089	21146	20376	25513
Other	590	943	1229	1442	1816	2066
Main activity	63915	64902	60625	55986	55592	61146
Combustible fuels	700	457	425	681	662	596
Hydro	37135	36787	37001	34050	34421	34915
Nuclear	25990	27557	23089	21146	20376	25513
Other	90	101	110	109	133	122
Own use in electricity, CHP and heat plants	1699	1759	1565	1469	1437	1658
Net production	68528	70008	66155	61706	61652	67449
Imports	29874	28530	34033	34096	36496	31020
Exports	32270	34021	35068	30173	30946	32607
Losses	4677	4696	4577	4468	4558	4227
Consumption	61445	59812	60535	61152	62630	61632
Energy industries own use	2132	2355	2296	2922	4160	3987
By industry and construction	18767	18019	17989	17761	17896	17311
By transport	3142	3069	3136	3200	3150	3089
By households and other cons.	37404	36369	37114	37269	37424	37245
Net installed capacity	**Thousand kilowatts**					
Total main activity and autoproducer	18932	19165	19618	20839	21614	22061
Combustible fuels	1021	993	1016	961	946	940
Hydro	13817	13743	13815	14806	15354	15542
Nuclear	3278	3308	3333	3333	3333	3333
Other	816	1121	1454	1739	1981	2246
Main activity	16861	16813	16957	17736	18286	18456
Combustible fuels	291	263	260	217	257	257
Hydro	13232	13182	13304	14111	14621	14791
Nuclear	3278	3308	3333	3333	3333	3333
Other	60	60	60	75	75	75
Combustible fuel input	**Terajoules**					
Biogas	1803	1898	1990	2146	2234	2230
Gas-diesel oil	301	301	258	258	258	172
Fuel oil	0	..	..	..	..	..
Liquefied petroleum gas	47	47	47	47	47	..
Natural gas	6028	3321	4639	6679	5569	4927
Fuelwood	*6161	*6041	4944	5550	6664	6312
Municipal waste	40544	41292	42832	44564	45188	45500
Industrial waste	1920	2002	881	834	1034	1189
Total input	56804	54902	55591	60078	60994	60330
Total production	13244	12838	12676	14033	13910	13410
Estimated efficiency (% of production to input)	23	23	23	23	23	22

Syrian Arab Republic

Item	2013	2014	2015	2016	2017	2018
Production, trade and consumption	Million kilowatt-hours					
Total main activity and autoproducer	25139	21223	17982	18202	18412	18210
Combustible fuels	22139	18883	17569	17273	17658	17456
Hydro	3000	2340	413	929	754	754
Nuclear	..	..	..	..	..	..
Other	..	..	..	..	..	..
Main activity	24436	20569	17383	17556	17695	17538
Combustible fuels	21436	18229	16970	16627	16941	16784
Hydro	3000	2340	413	929	754	754
Nuclear	..	..	..	..	..	..
Other	..	..	..	..	..	..
Own use in electricity, CHP and heat plants	2872	2425	2055	2080	2104	2081
Net production	22267	18798	15927	16122	16308	16129
Imports	..	..	..	..	..	..
Exports	529	138	262	67	543	543
Losses	3510	3272	2627	2857	2415	2382
Consumption	18228	15388	13038	13198	13351	13205
Energy industries own use	..	..	..	..	..	..
By industry and construction	6130	5175	4385	4439	4490	4441
By transport	..	..	..	..	..	..
By households and other cons.	12098	10213	8653	8759	8861	8764
Net installed capacity	Thousand kilowatts					
Total main activity and autoproducer	8207	*9604	*9123	9687	*9691	10059
Combustible fuels	7356	*8109	*7550	8192	*8199	8567
Hydro	850	1494	1572	1494	1490	1490
Nuclear	..	..	..	..	..	..
Other	1	1	1	1	2	2
Main activity	7211	*8509	*8028	8775	*8779	9087
Combustible fuels	6360	*7014	*6455	7280	*7287	7595
Hydro	850	1494	1572	1494	1490	1490
Nuclear	..	..	..	..	..	..
Other	1	1	1	1	2	2
Combustible fuel input	Terajoules					
Gas-diesel oil	12556	11696	10707	11567	12814	11997
Fuel oil	64115	43874	49288	63590	69407	69407
Natural gas	163515	151174	132663	115694	114151	113534
Total input	240186	206744	192658	190851	196372	194938
Total production	79700	67979	63248	62183	63569	62842
Estimated efficiency (% of production to input)	33	33	33	33	32	32

Tajikistan

Item	2013	2014	2015	2016	2017	2018
Production, trade and consumption	**Million kilowatt-hours**					
Total main activity and autoproducer	17115	16472	17162	17232	18144	19742
Combustible fuels	44	160	302	608	1011	1348
Hydro	17071	16312	16860	16624	17133	18394
Nuclear	..	..	..	..	..	..
Other	..	..	..	..	..	..
Main activity	17115	16472	17162	17232	18144	19742
Combustible fuels	44	160	302	608	1011	1348
Hydro	17071	16312	16860	16624	17133	18394
Nuclear	..	..	..	..	..	..
Other	..	..	..	..	..	..
Own use in electricity, CHP and heat plants	90	24	25	36	229	204
Net production	17025	16448	17137	17196	17915	19538
Imports	117	13	63	103	110	559
Exports	1061	1366	1400	1427	1421	2945
Losses	2528	2804	2700	2746	*2873	*2968
Consumption	13553	12407	12511	12986	13842	13890
Energy industries own use	66	63	65	64	68	..
By industry and construction	5496	4132	4186	4758	4428	*3438
By transport	38	41	50	72	30	7
By households and other cons.	7953	8171	8210	8092	9316	10445
Net installed capacity	**Thousand kilowatts**					
Total main activity and autoproducer	6185	6280	6283	6577	*6577	*6619
Combustible fuels	318	421	422	719	*719	*719
Hydro	5867	5859	5861	5858	*5858	*5900
Nuclear	..	..	..	..	..	..
Other	..	..	..	..	..	..
Main activity	6185	6280	6283	6577	*6577	*6577
Combustible fuels	318	421	422	719	*719	*719
Hydro	5867	5859	5861	5858	*5858	*5858
Nuclear	..	..	..	..	..	..
Other	..	..	..	..	..	..
Combustible fuel input	**Terajoules**					
Hard Coal	706	2044	3047	*6075	13851	21238
Total input	706	2044	3047	*6075	13851	21238
Total production	158	576	1087	2189	3640	4853
Estimated efficiency (% of production to input)	22	28	36	36	26	23

Thailand

Item	2013	2014	2015	2016	2017	2018
Production, trade and consumption	Million kilowatt-hours					
Total main activity and autoproducer	170148	172259	176488	187554	181713	182296
Combustible fuels	163014	165028	170028	180304	171366	168552
Hydro	5748	5540	3752	3527	4694	7565
Nuclear	..	..	..	..	..	..
Other	1386	1691	2708	3723	5653	6179
Main activity	139673	139755	140715	135698	125991	118213
Combustible fuels	133459	133726	136324	131422	119651	108471
Hydro	5748	5540	3752	3527	4694	7565
Nuclear	..	..	..	..	..	..
Other	466	489	639	749	1646	2177
Own use in electricity, CHP and heat plants	6220	5931	3338	3300	3050	2822
Net production	163928	166328	173150	184254	178663	179474
Imports	12569	12289	14441	19853	24455	26665
Exports	1279	1594	2267	1385	1106	997
Losses	10340	10545	11782	12225	11920	12904
Consumption	164322	168788	174053	184960	185371	188048
Energy industries own use	..	..	..	..	..	..
By industry and construction	68606	82623	83982	88878	87774	87829
By transport	164	105	108	113	245	216
By households and other cons.	95552	86060	89963	95969	97352	100003
Net installed capacity	Thousand kilowatts					
Total main activity and autoproducer	54456	55452	58508	61032	61024	64051
Combustible fuels	47250	48238	51403	53653	53505	55251
Hydro	3436	3444	3453	3452	3452	3667
Nuclear	..	..	..	..	..	..
Other	*3770	*3770	*3652	*3926	*4066	*5132
Main activity	36482	37478	40534	43058	44075	46296
Combustible fuels	31276	32264	35429	37679	38556	39496
Hydro	3436	3444	3453	3452	3452	3667
Nuclear	..	..	..	..	..	..
Other	1770	1770	1652	*1926	*2066	*3132
Combustible fuel input	Terajoules					
Hard Coal	223334	224205	216529	220617	206690	229295
Brown Coal	204993	182557	155355	174281	168344	150121
Biogas	7395	7564	8832	8282	10987	24932
Gas-diesel oil	2537	1548	2064	1419	1634	1462
Fuel oil	12322	14665	7434	3030	1091	646
Natural gas	976868	1030723	1075488	1053538	1022823	1005520
Bagasse	*139995	*153602	*153538	*202251	*198197	*241913
Vegetal waste	..	..	..	*202357	*139385	*91490
Municipal waste	592	592	5789	1225	1521	2831
Total input	1568036	1615455	1625029	1867000	1750672	1748211
Total production	586850	594101	612101	649094	616918	606787
Estimated efficiency (% of production to input)	37	37	38	35	35	35

Timor-Leste

Item	2013	2014	2015	2016	2017	2018
Production, trade and consumption	**Million kilowatt-hours**					
Total main activity and autoproducer	297	351	353	415	430	453
Combustible fuels	295	349	350	413	427	450
Hydro	2	2	2	2	2	2
Nuclear	..	..	..	..	..	..
Other	1	1	1	1	1	1
Main activity	297	351	353	415	430	453
Combustible fuels	295	349	350	413	427	450
Hydro	2	2	2	2	2	2
Nuclear	..	..	..	..	..	..
Other	1	1	1	1	1	1
Own use in electricity, CHP and heat plants	20	23	23	22	23	27
Net production	277	328	329	393	406	425
Imports	..	..	..	..	..	..
Exports	..	..	..	..	..	..
Losses	*60	*70	*75	*80	*85	*90
Consumption	*217	*258	254	313	*321	335
Energy industries own use	..	..	..	..	..	..
By industry and construction	..	..	..	..	..	..
By transport	..	..	..	..	..	..
By households and other cons.	*217	*258	254	313	*321	335
Net installed capacity	**Thousand kilowatts**					
Total main activity and autoproducer	283	283	283	283	283	283
Combustible fuels	283	283	283	283	283	283
Hydro	0	0	0	0	0	0
Nuclear	..	..	..	..	..	..
Other	1	1	1	1	1	1
Main activity	283	283	283	283	283	283
Combustible fuels	283	283	283	283	283	283
Hydro	0	0	0	0	0	0
Nuclear	..	..	..	..	..	..
Other	1	1	1	1	1	1
Combustible fuel input	**Terajoules**					
Gas-diesel oil	*3526	*4042	*4012	*4554	*4812	*4872
Total input	*3526	*4042	*4012	*4554	*4812	*4872
Total production	1062	1256	1261	1485	1538	1622
Estimated efficiency (% of production to input)	30	31	31	33	32	33

Togo

Item	2013	2014	2015	2016	2017	2018
Production, trade and consumption	**Million kilowatt-hours**					
Total main activity and autoproducer	360	358	444	950	690	589
Combustible fuels	286	233	383	742	485	389
Hydro	74	125	61	208	205	196
Nuclear	..	..	..	..	..	..
Other	..	..	..	..	..	3
Main activity	353	347	432	937	677	582
Combustible fuels	279	222	371	729	472	385
Hydro	74	125	61	208	205	196
Nuclear	..	..	..	..	..	..
Other	..	..	..	..	..	..
Own use in electricity, CHP and heat plants	13	7	16	26	13	14
Net production	347	351	428	924	677	575
Imports	773	857	857	448	747	882
Exports	..	..	..	..	..	..
Losses	183	186	184	188	121	197
Consumption	937	1023	1138	1185	1313	1239
Energy industries own use	..	..	..	..	..	..
By industry and construction	271	309	387	413	436	604
By transport	..	..	..	..	..	..
By households and other cons.	666	714	751	772	877	635
Net installed capacity	**Thousand kilowatts**					
Total main activity and autoproducer	227	227	227	213	225	227
Combustible fuels	160	160	160	158	158	157
Hydro	67	67	67	55	67	67
Nuclear	..	..	..	..	..	..
Other	..	..	..	..	..	3
Main activity	219	219	219	205	217	216
Combustible fuels	152	152	152	150	150	149
Hydro	67	67	67	55	67	67
Nuclear	..	..	..	..	..	..
Other	..	..	..	..	..	..
Combustible fuel input	**Terajoules**					
Gas-diesel oil	645	172	559	129	258	172
Fuel oil	1382	1381	1397	5239	3621	1316
Natural gas	844	1481	1467	262	0	1767
Vegetal waste	29	..	29	29	..	..
Kerosene-type jet fuel	88	..	..	..	..	..
Total input	2988	3034	3452	5659	3879	3254
Total production	1031	839	1380	2671	1745	1401
Estimated efficiency (% of production to input)	34	28	40	47	45	43

Tonga

Item	2013	2014	2015	2016	2017	2018
Production, trade and consumption	**Million kilowatt-hours**					
Total main activity and autoproducer	53	55	55	60	62	68
Combustible fuels	51	52	52	55	58	64
Hydro	..	..	..	..	..	..
Nuclear	..	..	..	..	..	..
Other	2	2	3	5	4	4
Main activity	53	55	55	60	62	68
Combustible fuels	51	52	52	55	58	64
Hydro	..	..	..	..	..	..
Nuclear	..	..	..	..	..	..
Other	2	2	3	5	4	4
Own use in electricity, CHP and heat plants	2	2	1	2	2	2
Net production	51	53	54	58	60	66
Imports	..	..	..	..	..	..
Exports	..	..	..	..	..	..
Losses	5	5	5	5	6	6
Consumption	*46	*48	*49	*53	*55	*58
Energy industries own use	..	..	..	..	..	..
By industry and construction	..	..	..	..	..	..
By transport	..	..	..	..	..	..
By households and other cons.	*46	*48	*49	*53	*55	*58
Net installed capacity	**Thousand kilowatts**					
Total main activity and autoproducer	*15	*16	*17	20	24	24
Combustible fuels	*14	*14	*15	17	18	18
Hydro	..	..	..	..	..	..
Nuclear	..	..	..	..	..	..
Other	*1	*2	*2	2	6	6
Main activity	*15	*16	*17	20	24	24
Combustible fuels	*14	*14	*15	17	18	18
Hydro	..	..	..	..	..	..
Nuclear	..	..	..	..	..	..
Other	*1	*2	*2	2	6	6
Combustible fuel input	**Terajoules**					
Fuel oil	493	492	487	*518	*542	*594
Total input	493	492	487	*518	*542	*594
Total production	185	187	188	199	208	229
Estimated efficiency (% of production to input)	37	38	39	38	38	38

Trinidad and Tobago

Item	2013	2014	2015	2016	2017	2018
Production, trade and consumption			Million kilowatt-hours			
Total main activity and autoproducer	9505	9895	10300	10011	9933	9225
Combustible fuels	9501	9891	10296	10006	9928	9220
Hydro	..	..	..	..	..	..
Nuclear	..	..	..	..	..	..
Other	4	4	4	5	5	5
Main activity	9427	9813	10215	9929	9851	9149
Combustible fuels	9423	9809	10211	9924	9846	9144
Hydro	..	..	..	..	..	..
Nuclear	..	..	..	..	..	..
Other	4	4	4	5	5	5
Own use in electricity, CHP and heat plants	346	360	375	365	362	336
Net production	9159	9535	9925	9646	9571	8889
Imports	..	..	..	..	..	..
Exports	..	..	..	..	..	..
Losses	234	228	221	231	252	426
Consumption	8926	9306	9703	9415	9318	8463
Energy industries own use	..	..	..	..	..	..
By industry and construction	5396	5626	5866	5692	5633	5116
By transport	..	..	..	..	..	..
By households and other cons.	3530	3680	3837	3723	3685	3347
Net installed capacity			Thousand kilowatts			
Total main activity and autoproducer	2494	2499	2502	2505	2509	2156
Combustible fuels	2491	2496	2499	2502	2506	2153
Hydro	..	..	..	..	..	..
Nuclear	..	..	..	..	..	..
Other	3	3	3	3	3	3
Main activity	2405	2405	2405	2405	2405	2049
Combustible fuels	2402	2402	2402	2402	2402	2046
Hydro	..	..	..	..	..	..
Nuclear	..	..	..	..	..	..
Other	3	3	3	3	3	3
Combustible fuel input			Terajoules			
Gas-diesel oil	215	215	215	301	301	301
Other oil products	0	0	80	201	161	..
Natural gas	122343	121136	118721	109361	101417	97391
Total input	122558	121351	119016	109863	101879	97692
Total production	34204	35608	37066	36022	35741	33192
Estimated efficiency (% of production to input)	28	29	31	33	35	34

Tunisia

Item	2013	2014	2015	2016	2017	2018
Production, trade and consumption	**Million kilowatt-hours**					
Total main activity and autoproducer	18382	19024	19676	19808	20589	21012
Combustible fuels	17740	18254	18904	19002	19758	20085
Hydro	60	56	69	45	17	17
Nuclear	..	..	..	..	..	..
Other	582	714	703	761	814	910
Main activity	17637	18257	18691	18634	19402	19545
Combustible fuels	17219	17694	18174	18115	18936	19075
Hydro	60	56	69	45	17	17
Nuclear	..	..	..	..	..	..
Other	358	507	448	474	449	453
Own use in electricity, CHP and heat plants	641	653	559	492	428	457
Net production	17741	18371	19117	19316	20161	20555
Imports	177	536	403	134	450	382
Exports	233	625	500	255	483	484
Losses	2707	2842	3166	3052	3507	3584
Consumption	14970	15418	16377	16001	16542	16879
Energy industries own use	241	228	940	432	429	375
By industry and construction	5305	5445	5478	5423	5389	5737
By transport	93	93	94	96	94	99
By households and other cons.	9331	9652	9865	10050	10630	10668
Net installed capacity	**Thousand kilowatts**					
Total main activity and autoproducer	4539	5005	5447	5513	5723	5800
Combustible fuels	4270	4695	5120	5174	5372	5352
Hydro	62	62	62	62	62	62
Nuclear	..	..	..	..	..	..
Other	207	248	265	277	289	386
Main activity	4334	4792	5224	5278	5476	5456
Combustible fuels	4072	4497	4922	4976	5174	5154
Hydro	62	62	62	62	62	62
Nuclear	..	..	..	..	..	..
Other	200	233	240	240	240	240
Combustible fuel input	**Terajoules**					
Gas-diesel oil	43	43	146	86	37	32
Fuel oil	646	3394	9534	687	727	808
Natural gas	167834	174994	167766	169416	173384	176826
Total input	168523	178431	177447	170189	174149	177666
Total production	63864	65714	68054	68407	71129	72306
Estimated efficiency (% of production to input)	38	37	38	40	41	41

Turkey

Item	2013	2014	2015	2016	2017	2018
Production, trade and consumption	Million kilowatt-hours					
Total main activity and autoproducer	240154	251963	261783	274408	297277	304801
Combustible fuels	171535	200079	178871	185085	211291	208733
Hydro	59420	40645	67146	67231	58219	59938
Nuclear	..	..	..	..	..	..
Other	9199	11239	15766	22092	27767	36130
Main activity	226756	233781	243163	253746	276992	284884
Combustible fuels	159495	183126	161979	166450	193608	192399
Hydro	58344	39764	65924	66386	57252	58865
Nuclear	..	..	..	..	..	..
Other	8917	10891	15260	20910	26132	33620
Own use in electricity, CHP and heat plants	11177	12514	11883	12471	13019	14299
Net production	228977	239449	249900	261937	284258	290502
Imports	7429	7953	7136	6330	2728	2477
Exports	1227	2696	3195	1452	3304	3112
Losses	37134	37331	36528	35611	34659	31635
Consumption	198045	207375	217313	231204	249023	258232
Energy industries own use	1877	1933	2812	3034	3268	3298
By industry and construction	91384	95844	100723	105263	113215	114413
By transport	826	916	1062	1156	1248	1256
By households and other cons.	103958	108682	112716	121751	131292	139265
Net installed capacity	Thousand kilowatts					
Total main activity and autoproducer	64007	69520	73147	78497	85201	88551
Combustible fuels	38590	41730	41810	44278	46762	46712
Hydro	22289	23643	25868	26681	27273	28291
Nuclear	..	..	..	..	..	..
Other	3128	4147	5469	7538	11166	13548
Main activity	60481	65216	68694	73220	79011	82114
Combustible fuels	35671	38047	37999	40055	42345	42262
Hydro	21745	23099	25324	26131	26722	27740
Nuclear	..	..	..	..	..	..
Other	3065	4070	5371	7034	9944	12112
Combustible fuel input	Terajoules					
Hard Coal	318688	373458	423837	479342	518561	612458
Brown Coal	479314	568241	431698	518993	550750	587460
Biogas	8511	9653	11119	14721	17568	20497
Fuel oil	12605	18342	10585	10342	5010	2828
Natural gas	816124	897578	763792	684008	805751	662079
Coke-oven gas	9375	8965	9296	8328	10686	11456
Blast furnace gas	20524	23648	22876	23748	25637	21013
Fuelwood	*588	*589	*556	*986	*3288	*6269
Municipal waste	..	..	..	..	..	171
Industrial waste	184	144	1362	2067	2446	2260
Others	4773	4386	9675	7095	5074	27
Total input	1670686	1905003	1684796	1749630	1944771	1926519
Total production	617526	720284	643936	666306	760648	751439
Estimated efficiency (% of production to input)	37	38	38	38	39	39

Turkmenistan

Item	2013	2014	2015	2016	2017	2018
Production, trade and consumption	**Million kilowatt-hours**					
Total main activity and autoproducer	18870	20400	22534	22534	22534	22534
Combustible fuels	18870	20400	22534	22534	22534	22534
Hydro	..	..	..	..	..	..
Nuclear	..	..	..	..	..	..
Other	..	..	..	..	..	..
Main activity	18870	20400	22534	22534	22534	22534
Combustible fuels	18870	20400	22534	22534	22534	22534
Hydro	..	..	..	..	..	..
Nuclear	..	..	..	..	..	..
Other	..	..	..	..	..	..
Own use in electricity, CHP and heat plants	1426	1542	1703	1703	1703	1703
Net production	17444	18858	20831	20831	20831	20831
Imports	..	..	..	..	..	..
Exports	2850	3210	3201	3201	3201	3201
Losses	2385	2547	2895	2895	2895	2895
Consumption	12209	13101	14735	14735	14735	14735
Energy industries own use	1875	2012	2262	2262	2262	2262
By industry and construction	3729	4001	4500	4500	4500	4500
By transport	268	288	324	324	324	324
By households and other cons.	6337	6800	7649	7649	7649	7649
Net installed capacity	**Thousand kilowatts**					
Total main activity and autoproducer	*3800	*4000	*4400	4674	5200	5200
Combustible fuels	*3800	*4000	*4400	4674	5200	5200
Hydro	..	..	..	..	..	..
Nuclear	..	..	..	..	..	..
Other	..	..	..	..	..	..
Main activity	*3800	*4000	*4400	4674	5200	5200
Combustible fuels	*3800	*4000	*4400	4674	5200	5200
Hydro	..	..	..	..	..	..
Nuclear	..	..	..	..	..	..
Other	..	..	..	..	..	..
Combustible fuel input	**Terajoules**					
Natural gas	364393	371853	410752	410752	410752	410745
Total input	364393	371853	410752	410752	410752	410745
Total production	67932	73440	81122	81122	81122	81122
Estimated efficiency (% of production to input)	19	20	20	20	20	20

Turks and Caicos Islands

Item	2013	2014	2015	2016	2017	2018
Production, trade and consumption	**Million kilowatt-hours**					
Total main activity and autoproducer	*209	*227	*239	*250	*241	*257
Combustible fuels	*209	*227	*239	*250	*241	*257
Hydro	..	..	..	..	..	..
Nuclear	..	..	..	..	..	..
Other	..	..	..	..	..	..
Main activity	*209	*227	*239	*250	*241	*257
Combustible fuels	*209	*227	*239	*250	*241	*257
Hydro	..	..	..	..	..	..
Nuclear	..	..	..	..	..	..
Other	..	..	..	..	..	..
Own use in electricity, CHP and heat plants	*4	*5	*5	*5	*8	*8
Net production	*205	*222	*234	*245	*233	*249
Imports	..	..	..	..	..	..
Exports	..	..	..	..	..	..
Losses	*12	*13	*14	*15	*14	*13
Consumption	193	209	*220	230	219	*237
Energy industries own use	..	..	..	..	..	..
By industry and construction	..	..	..	..	..	..
By transport	..	..	..	..	..	..
By households and other cons.	193	209	*220	230	219	*237
Net installed capacity	**Thousand kilowatts**					
Total main activity and autoproducer	76	79	82	82	82	84
Combustible fuels	76	79	82	82	82	84
Hydro	..	..	..	..	..	..
Nuclear	..	..	..	..	..	..
Other	..	..	..	..	..	..
Main activity	76	79	82	82	82	84
Combustible fuels	76	79	82	82	82	84
Hydro	..	..	..	..	..	..
Nuclear	..	..	..	..	..	..
Other	..	..	..	..	..	..
Combustible fuel input	**Terajoules**					
Gas-diesel oil	*2236	*2408	*2494	*2580	*2666	*2774
Total input	*2236	*2408	*2494	*2580	*2666	*2774
Total production	*752	*817	*860	*900	*866	*925
Estimated efficiency (% of production to input)	34	34	34	35	32	33

Tuvalu

Item	2013	2014	2015	2016	2017	2018
Production, trade and consumption	**Million kilowatt-hours**					
Total main activity and autoproducer	6	6	6	7	8	*8
Combustible fuels	5	6	6	5	6	*6
Hydro	..	..	..	..	..	..
Nuclear	..	..	..	..	..	..
Other	0	0	1	2	2	2
Main activity	6	6	6	7	8	*8
Combustible fuels	5	6	6	5	6	*6
Hydro	..	..	..	..	..	..
Nuclear	..	..	..	..	..	..
Other	0	0	1	2	2	2
Own use in electricity, CHP and heat plants	0	1	1	1	1	*2
Net production	5	5	6	7	7	*7
Imports	..	..	..	..	..	..
Exports	..	..	..	..	..	..
Losses	..	..	..	..	..	..
Consumption	5	5	6	7	7	*7
Energy industries own use	..	..	..	..	..	..
By industry and construction	..	..	..	..	..	..
By transport	..	..	..	..	..	..
By households and other cons.	5	5	6	7	7	*7
Net installed capacity	**Thousand kilowatts**					
Total main activity and autoproducer	3	3	*5	*5	*5	5
Combustible fuels	3	3	*3	*3	*3	3
Hydro	..	..	..	..	..	..
Nuclear	..	..	..	..	..	..
Other	0	0	2	2	2	2
Main activity	3	3	*5	*5	*5	5
Combustible fuels	3	3	*3	*3	*3	3
Hydro	..	..	..	..	..	..
Nuclear	..	..	..	..	..	..
Other	0	0	2	2	2	2
Combustible fuel input	**Terajoules**					
Gas-diesel oil	*78	*82	*80	*78	*85	*92
Total input	*78	*82	*80	*78	*85	*92
Total production	19	21	20	20	21	*23
Estimated efficiency (% of production to input)	25	25	25	25	25	25

Uganda

Item	2013	2014	2015	2016	2017	2018
Production, trade and consumption	Million kilowatt-hours					
Total main activity and autoproducer	3416	3223	3300	3508	3854	4040
Combustible fuels	128	352	247	244	381	405
Hydro	3289	2871	3052	3261	3447	3602
Nuclear	..	..	..	..	..	..
Other	..	..	..	4	25	32
Main activity	2939	2699	2819	3037	3440	3389
Combustible fuels	2	138	73	66	231	199
Hydro	2937	2561	2745	2967	3183	3158
Nuclear	..	..	..	..	..	..
Other	..	..	..	4	25	32
Own use in electricity, CHP and heat plants	10	0	0	0	0	0
Net production	3406	3223	3300	3508	3854	4040
Imports	46	33	49	54	65	84
Exports	106	168	122	165	317	233
Losses	714	728	713	765	755	789
Consumption	2658	2289	2487	2594	2802	3067
Energy industries own use	..	..	..	..	..	..
By industry and construction	1358	1450	1581	1664	1805	2012
By transport	..	..	..	..	..	..
By households and other cons.	1300	839	906	930	997	1055
Net installed capacity	Thousand kilowatts					
Total main activity and autoproducer	828	851	861	872	913	984
Combustible fuels	136	156	166	166	178	198
Hydro	692	695	695	695	712	744
Nuclear	..	..	..	..	..	..
Other	..	..	..	11	22	42
Main activity	730	732	732	742	752	772
Combustible fuels	100	102	102	102	102	102
Hydro	630	630	630	630	630	630
Nuclear	..	..	..	..	..	..
Other	..	..	..	11	21	41
Combustible fuel input	Terajoules					
Gas-diesel oil	*22	..	43	..	..	..
Fuel oil	..	*1240	723	*1030	*3515	3015
Bagasse	*2413	*4112	*3305	*3614	*3050	*4255
Total input	*2435	*5352	*4072	*4644	*6565	*7269
Total production	459	1265	890	878	1371	1459
Estimated efficiency (% of production to input)	19	24	22	19	21	20

Ukraine

Item	2013	2014	2015	2016	2017	2018
Production, trade and consumption	**Million kilowatt-hours**					
Total main activity and autoproducer	194377	182815	163682	164573	156037	159852
Combustible fuels	95487	83549	67523	72795	58173	61115
Hydro	14472	9318	6971	9304	10520	12007
Nuclear	83209	88389	87627	80950	85576	84398
Other	1209	1559	1561	1524	1768	2332
Main activity	191177	179888	161468	158806	152061	157194
Combustible fuels	92310	80644	65328	67136	54274	58504
Hydro	14450	9299	6954	9281	10516	12005
Nuclear	83209	88389	87627	80950	85576	84398
Other	1208	1556	1559	1439	1695	2287
Own use in electricity, CHP and heat plants	15293	14385	13032	12684	11131	12755
Net production	179084	168430	150650	151889	144906	147097
Imports	39	89	2241	77	50	32
Exports	9929	8523	3591	3830	5226	6099
Losses	20714	19615	17442	16626	16787	16996
Consumption	148480	134981	126024	125257	122943	124034
Energy industries own use	10949	6594	7035	7817	5577	5377
By industry and construction	58584	54401	49963	49941	50235	51727
By transport	8690	8072	6807	6796	7044	6955
By households and other cons.	70257	65914	62219	60703	60087	59975
Net installed capacity	**Thousand kilowatts**					
Total main activity and autoproducer	55914	55843	55904	57335	52764	51508
Combustible fuels	35616	35335	35335	36475	31492	29753
Hydro	5489	5851	5883	6172	6213	6243
Nuclear	13835	13835	13835	13835	13835	13835
Other	974	822	851	853	1224	1677
Main activity	52578	52910	53145	53866	50499	49369
Combustible fuels	32290	32410	32584	33013	29265	27662
Hydro	5484	5847	5878	6167	6206	6238
Nuclear	13835	13835	13835	13835	13835	13835
Other	969	818	848	851	1193	1634
Combustible fuel input	**Terajoules**					
Hard Coal	972367	855610	691875	739606	596334	634191
Biogas	..	..	161	596	865	1565
Gas-diesel oil	301	258	215	301	430	559
Fuel oil	3192	2020	11029	24280	21210	6989
Other oil products	1769	1648	804	1005	925	4543
Natural gas	240341	204757	169205	157126	145990	178481
Coke-oven gas	26254	10037	6939	9809	14391	15911
Blast furnace gas	26079	23785	18013	25568	26744	28839
Fuelwood	..	6732	8651	0	0	4312
Peat products	0	0	127	176	195	156
Others	594	9648	9677	-35576	47	47
Total input	1270896	1114495	916695	922891	807131	875593
Total production	343753	300776	243083	262062	209423	220014
Estimated efficiency (% of production to input)	27	27	27	28	26	25

United Arab Emirates

Item	2013	2014	2015	2016	2017	2018
Production, trade and consumption			Million kilowatt-hours			
Total main activity and autoproducer	109979	116528	127366	129596	134553	135997
Combustible fuels	109926	116237	127075	129287	133761	134694
Hydro	..	..	..	..	..	..
Nuclear	..	..	..	..	..	..
Other	53	291	291	309	792	1303
Main activity	109979	116528	127366	129596	134553	135997
Combustible fuels	109926	116237	127075	129287	133761	134694
Hydro	..	..	..	..	..	..
Nuclear	..	..	..	..	..	..
Other	53	291	291	309	792	1303
Own use in electricity, CHP and heat plants	4616	4843	4429	2392	7487	4726
Net production	105363	111685	122937	127204	127066	131271
Imports	226	248	234	1141	514	488
Exports	242	276	249	506	617	517
Losses	7623	8363	9141	9697	11718	8436
Consumption	95365	101174	111076	*113929	115245	122836
Energy industries own use	..	..	..	..	..	..
By industry and construction	13564	11196	12973	*13983	15071	13850
By transport	..	..	..	..	..	..
By households and other cons.	81801	89978	98103	*99946	100174	108986
Net installed capacity			Thousand kilowatts			
Total main activity and autoproducer	27858	28829	28745	28761	30371	*30934
Combustible fuels	27735	28706	28622	28638	30048	*30349
Hydro	..	..	..	..	..	..
Nuclear	..	..	..	..	..	..
Other	123	123	123	123	323	585
Main activity	27858	28829	28745	28761	30371	*30934
Combustible fuels	27735	28706	28622	28638	30048	*30349
Hydro	..	..	..	..	..	..
Nuclear	..	..	..	..	..	..
Other	123	123	123	123	323	585
Combustible fuel input			Terajoules			
Gas-diesel oil	*28982	21887	23521	*23650	22747	24394
Fuel oil	*2141	1899	2020	*2141	*2141	*2182
Natural gas	*1271764	*1366572	*1248672	1349892	1383323	1384793
Total input	*1302887	*1390358	*1274213	1375683	1408211	1411369
Total production	395734	418453	457470	465433	481540	484898
Estimated efficiency (% of production to input)	30	30	36	34	34	34

United Kingdom

Item	2013	2014	2015	2016	2017	2018
Production, trade and consumption	**Million kilowatt-hours**					
Total main activity and autoproducer	358290	338100	339573	339899	338640	333424
Combustible fuels	249666	229566	212381	212258	198418	190601
Hydro	7605	8771	9037	8353	8774	7988
Nuclear	70607	63748	70345	71726	70336	65064
Other	30412	36015	47810	47562	61112	69771
Main activity	320575	296460	290768	287285	282740	275454
Combustible fuels	219497	198432	178115	175901	161421	152229
Hydro	6513	7518	7646	6910	7051	6325
Nuclear	70607	63748	70345	71726	70336	65064
Other	23958	26762	34662	32748	43932	51836
Own use in electricity, CHP and heat plants	17856	16483	12125	16088	15940	15957
Net production	340434	321617	327448	323811	322700	317467
Imports	17532	23244	22961	20018	18167	21332
Exports	3101	2723	1855	2273	3407	2225
Losses	26550	27448	28607	26356	26808	26599
Consumption	328251	314691	314722	315310	310654	309975
Energy industries own use	11893	11753	11137	11170	10971	10215
By industry and construction	97067	93157	93044	93424	92342	93135
By transport	4352	4505	4516	4690	4833	4983
By households and other cons.	214939	205276	206025	206026	202508	201642
Net installed capacity	**Thousand kilowatts**					
Total main activity and autoproducer	93620	96622	96395	97739	109286	108280
Combustible fuels	65034	63600	58316	55437	62767	59278
Hydro	4453	4474	4677	4736	4773	4779
Nuclear	9906	9937	9487	9497	9361	9314
Other	14227	18611	23915	28069	32385	34909
Main activity	82477	81780	78936	77571	82980	81612
Combustible fuels	59171	57085	51961	48730	50057	46055
Hydro	4221	4221	4357	4360	4361	4366
Nuclear	9906	9937	9487	9497	9361	9314
Other	9179	10537	13131	14984	19201	21877
Combustible fuel input	**Terajoules**					
Hard Coal	1276300	980129	758859	317097	229980	174294
Biogas	81642	84381	91653	98977	99758	97473
Fuel oil	7070	5575	6706	6504	4727	4686
Refinery gas	10989	11732	12128	12425	13019	9257
Natural gas	741128	784213	765476	1073072	1029713	984231
Blast furnace gas	30969	30624	26847	19347	18055	16907
Fuelwood	*68693	*92732	*113588	*120853	*120519	*142025
Vegetal waste	*12649	*19731	*24772	*17767	*30834	*24375
Municipal waste	31890	40538	53310	65750	69686	82584
Industrial waste	4583	8556	9348	16912	7732	7075
Others	13803	12445	11376	7079	7736	7319
Total input	2279715	2070655	1874062	1755783	1631759	1550226
Total production	898798	826438	764572	764129	714305	686164
Estimated efficiency (% of production to input)	39	40	41	44	44	44

United Rep. of Tanzania

Item	2013	2014	2015	2016	2017	2018
Production, trade and consumption			**Million kilowatt-hours**			
Total main activity and autoproducer	5988	6258	6772	7216	7250	7230
Combustible fuels	4257	3653	4649	4817	4861	4908
Hydro	1717	2590	2108	2366	2350	2234
Nuclear	..	..	..	..	..	..
Other	14	15	15	33	39	88
Main activity	5974	6243	6757	7183	7211	7142
Combustible fuels	4257	3653	4649	4817	4861	4908
Hydro	1717	2590	2108	2366	2350	2234
Nuclear	..	..	..	..	..	..
Other	..	..	..	..	..	..
Own use in electricity, CHP and heat plants	48	42	43	98	52	0
Net production	5940	6216	6729	7118	7198	7230
Imports	60	59	71	102	106	118
Exports	..	..	..	..	..	..
Losses	1140	1135	1120	1221	1234	1223
Consumption	4850	4991	5265	5388	5952	6460
Energy industries own use	14	15	15	18	19	88
By industry and construction	1223	1270	1362	1358	1525	1719
By transport	..	..	..	..	..	..
By households and other cons.	3613	3706	3888	4012	4408	4653
Net installed capacity			**Thousand kilowatts**			
Total main activity and autoproducer	1115	1119	1380	1394	1412	1602
Combustible fuels	*546	*546	800	808	829	1015
Hydro	562	562	567	567	562	562
Nuclear	..	..	..	..	..	..
Other	*7	11	13	18	22	25
Main activity	1088	1088	1347	1356	1358	1390
Combustible fuels	*526	*526	780	788	796	829
Hydro	562	562	567	567	562	562
Nuclear	..	..	..	..	..	..
Other	..	..	..	..	..	..
Combustible fuel input			**Terajoules**			
Gas-diesel oil	8428	5160	9804	14749	15609	15609
Fuel oil	8201	7676	9534	2262	768	283
Natural gas	31411	28623	27590	25558	23505	22181
Bagasse	1242	1152	1152	1242	1297	1297
Total input	49282	42611	48080	43811	41178	39369
Total production	15325	13151	16736	17341	17500	17669
Estimated efficiency (% of production to input)	31	31	35	40	42	45

United States

Item	2013	2014	2015	2016	2017	2018
Production, trade and consumption	**Million kilowatt-hours**					
Total main activity and autoproducer	4306371	4340371	4317159	4322038	4286423	4455439
Combustible fuels	2985891	2995556	2962870	2886040	2770050	2912042
Hydro	290113	281527	271129	292113	325114	317004
Nuclear	822004	830584	830288	839918	838861	841329
Other	208363	232704	252872	303967	352398	385064
Main activity	4128386	4166530	4139295	4141317	4100487	4262167
Combustible fuels	2822349	2835071	2802188	2725711	2608106	2746062
Hydro	286579	280195	269675	290596	323458	315587
Nuclear	822004	830584	830288	839918	838861	841329
Other	197454	220680	237144	285092	330062	359189
Own use in electricity, CHP and heat plants	212970	216819	207940	202593	200420	218511
Net production	4093401	4123552	4109219	4119445	4086003	4236928
Imports	70355	66511	75770	69601	65685	58261
Exports	11353	13298	9100	9329	9371	13804
Losses	255322	255322	255322	234807	244112	211136
Consumption	3897081	3921443	3920567	3944910	3898205	4070247
Energy industries own use	129517	132489	139731	137199	160088	169372
By industry and construction	846485	821040	806248	796896	778436	772827
By transport	7234	7605	8872	10605	11089	12283
By households and other cons.	2913845	2960309	2965716	3000210	2948592	3115765
Net installed capacity	**Thousand kilowatts**					
Total main activity and autoproducer	1065293	1074544	1072470	1086849	1100333	1119131
Combustible fuels	787297	787407	771732	764787	762765	767009
Hydro	101589	102162	102239	102692	102703	102801
Nuclear	99240	98569	98672	99565	99629	99433
Other	77167	86406	99827	119805	135236	149888
Main activity	1027776	1036351	1031496	1042991	1052995	1067931
Combustible fuels	758052	758205	742417	735654	733659	737457
Hydro	100911	101856	101933	102335	102346	102517
Nuclear	99240	98569	98672	99565	99629	99433
Other	69573	77721	88474	105437	117361	128524
Combustible fuel input	**Terajoules**					
Hard Coal	8070925	8409391	6977919	6528743	6008203	5511906
Brown Coal	8624213	8268422	7554207	6817768	6992253	6938984
Biogas	146036	162387	159616	150566	151528	148717
Gas-diesel oil	56846	84452	72455	56158	60931	106769
Fuel oil	77204	95263	92031	69044	64398	112029
Petroleum coke	135785	124475	115050	125580	106600	109883
Natural gas	9626697	9602281	11248873	11524237	10770702	12277185
Vegetal waste	*106875	*112040	*103991	*88394	*86064	*98706
Municipal waste	274962	274254	271824	280711	270065	275831
Black liquor	*127656	*133826	*124212	*105582	*102798	*117899
Others	237668	246805	234338	177102	170118	191816
Total input	27484867	27513596	26954515	25923885	24783660	25889725
Total production	10749208	10784002	10666332	10389744	9972180	10483351
Estimated efficiency (% of production to input)	39	39	40	40	40	40

United States Virgin Is.

Item	2013	2014	2015	2016	2017	2018
Production, trade and consumption	**Million kilowatt-hours**					
Total main activity and autoproducer	834	*789	*799	*797	*610	*626
Combustible fuels	820	*766	*766	*765	*589	*605
Hydro	..	..	..	..	..	..
Nuclear	..	..	..	..	..	..
Other	*14	*23	*33	*33	*21	*21
Main activity	821	*774	*779	*778	*597	*612
Combustible fuels	820	*766	*766	*765	*589	*605
Hydro	..	..	..	..	..	..
Nuclear	..	..	..	..	..	..
Other	*1	7	13	13	7	7
Own use in electricity, CHP and heat plants	93	*88	*83	*83	*61	*61
Net production	740	*701	*716	*714	*549	*565
Imports	..	..	..	..	..	..
Exports	..	..	..	..	..	..
Losses	*60	*60	*60	*65	*50	*51
Consumption	681	641	*656	*649	*499	*521
Energy industries own use	..	..	..	..	..	..
By industry and construction	309	291	*298	*273	*210	*222
By transport	..	..	..	..	..	..
By households and other cons.	371	350	*358	*376	*290	*299
Net installed capacity	**Thousand kilowatts**					
Total main activity and autoproducer	327	333	340	340	336	336
Combustible fuels	316	316	316	316	316	316
Hydro	..	..	..	..	..	..
Nuclear	..	..	..	..	..	..
Other	*11	*17	*24	*24	*20	*20
Main activity	317	321	325	325	321	321
Combustible fuels	316	316	316	316	316	316
Hydro	..	..	..	..	..	..
Nuclear	..	..	..	..	..	..
Other	*1	5	9	9	5	5
Combustible fuel input	**Terajoules**					
Total input	..	..	..	..	..	..
Total production	2952	*2759	*2758	*2752	*2122	*2178
Estimated efficiency (% of production to input)	..	..	..	..	..	..

Uruguay

Item	2013	2014	2015	2016	2017	2018
Production, trade and consumption	Million kilowatt-hours					
Total main activity and autoproducer	11657	13008	13731	13886	14364	14624
Combustible fuels	3309	2623	3351	2897	2803	2922
Hydro	8206	9649	8266	7842	7518	6557
Nuclear	..	..	..	..	..	..
Other	143	736	2114	3146	4043	5146
Main activity	10730	11728	12126	12274	12713	12857
Combustible fuels	2384	1349	1756	1295	1167	1177
Hydro	8206	9649	8266	7842	7518	6557
Nuclear	..	..	..	..	..	..
Other	140	730	2104	3137	4028	5123
Own use in electricity, CHP and heat plants	325	361	385	394	350	431
Net production	11332	12647	13345	13492	14014	14194
Imports	0	0	2	25	3	14
Exports	206	1267	1321	779	1462	1195
Losses	1281	1252	1489	1609	1694	1541
Consumption	9956	10239	10648	11229	10918	11606
Energy industries own use	106	107	111	116	44	117
By industry and construction	2625	2906	3250	3383	3392	3713
By transport	..	..	..	0	0	1
By households and other cons.	7225	7226	7287	7729	7481	7775
Net installed capacity	Thousand kilowatts					
Total main activity and autoproducer	3288	3713	3989	3913	4546	4912
Combustible fuels	1689	1690	1530	1075	1255	1615
Hydro	1538	1538	1538	1538	1538	1538
Nuclear	..	..	..	..	..	..
Other	61	485	921	1301	1753	1759
Main activity	2844	3264	3527	3447	4066	4429
Combustible fuels	1268	1268	1098	643	823	1183
Hydro	1538	1538	1538	1538	1538	1538
Nuclear	..	..	..	..	..	..
Other	38	458	891	1266	1705	1708
Combustible fuel input	Terajoules					
Gas-diesel oil	9985	2928	7534	3423	1634	2915
Fuel oil	9235	4452	1972	1220	570	1244
Natural gas	9	10	0	0	365	113
Fuelwood	478	96	236	205	64	119
Bagasse	82	100	111	86	86	88
Vegetal waste	2167	2605	2325	2496	2339	2826
Black liquor	4956	6774	9463	9670	10303	9942
Total input	26911	16965	21640	17099	15360	17247
Total production	11911	9443	12064	10430	10091	10520
Estimated efficiency (% of production to input)	44	56	56	61	66	61

Uzbekistan

Item	2013	2014	2015	2016	2017	2018
Production, trade and consumption	**Million kilowatt-hours**					
Total main activity and autoproducer	54619	55766	57414	58634	60323	62408
Combustible fuels	48914	49691	50589	51773	52393	56510
Hydro	5704	6075	6825	6860	7930	5897
Nuclear	..	..	..	..	..	..
Other	..	..	0	0	1	0
Main activity	54619	55766	57414	58634	60323	62408
Combustible fuels	48914	49691	50589	51773	52393	56510
Hydro	5704	6075	6825	6860	7930	5897
Nuclear	..	..	..	..	..	..
Other	..	..	0	0	1	0
Own use in electricity, CHP and heat plants	9172	758	780	797	820	848
Net production	45447	55008	56634	57837	59503	61560
Imports	184	6436	5520	5278	6945	2233
Exports	1293	7215	6810	6774	7585	2627
Losses	*3120	*3205	*3315	*3395	*3524	*3746
Consumption	44565	45791	47350	48503	50350	53515
Energy industries own use	..	..	..	..	..	..
By industry and construction	19670	20606	21153	21397	22623	15422
By transport	1225	1194	1166	1166	1222	1475
By households and other cons.	23669	23991	25032	25940	26504	36619
Net installed capacity	**Thousand kilowatts**					
Total main activity and autoproducer	*12614	13037	13217	14104	14377	14195
Combustible fuels	*10867	11165	11335	12222	12516	12276
Hydro	1746	1871	1880	1880	1858	1915
Nuclear	..	..	..	..	..	..
Other	1	1	1	2	3	4
Main activity	*12457	13037	13217	14104	14377	14195
Combustible fuels	*10710	11165	11335	12222	12516	12276
Hydro	1746	1871	1880	1880	1858	1915
Nuclear	..	..	..	..	..	..
Other	1	1	1	2	3	4
Combustible fuel input	**Terajoules**					
Hard Coal	..	..	..	..	..	2325
Brown Coal	65547	50395	42459	43592	45679	46161
Gas-diesel oil	0	47	41	30	39	39
Fuel oil	3353	5280	2026	3253	3681	5329
Natural gas	*596499	481504	488010	502212	484477	582301
Total input	*665400	537226	532537	549087	533875	636154
Total production	176092	178888	182121	186384	188614	203437
Estimated efficiency (% of production to input)	26	33	34	34	35	32

Vanuatu

Item	2013	2014	2015	2016	2017	2018
Production, trade and consumption	**Million kilowatt-hours**					
Total main activity and autoproducer	70	70	66	74	80	*80
Combustible fuels	57	56	51	62	63	*62
Hydro	7	7	7	5	*7	7
Nuclear	..	..	..	..	..	..
Other	6	7	9	8	9	10
Main activity	70	70	66	74	80	*80
Combustible fuels	57	56	51	62	63	*62
Hydro	7	7	7	5	*7	7
Nuclear	..	..	..	..	..	..
Other	6	7	9	8	9	10
Own use in electricity, CHP and heat plants	2	2	2	2	*7	0
Net production	68	68	64	72	73	*79
Imports	..	..	..	..	..	..
Exports	..	..	..	..	..	..
Losses	5	6	5	*4	*4	*9
Consumption	65	65	61	69	*68	*70
Energy industries own use	..	..	..	..	..	..
By industry and construction	24	24	21	23	*23	*24
By transport	..	..	..	..	..	..
By households and other cons.	41	41	40	46	*45	*46
Net installed capacity	**Thousand kilowatts**					
Total main activity and autoproducer	31	30	30	32	*33	*33
Combustible fuels	27	25	25	25	*25	*25
Hydro	1	1	1	1	1	1
Nuclear	..	..	..	..	..	..
Other	3	4	4	5	6	6
Main activity	31	30	30	32	*33	*33
Combustible fuels	27	25	25	25	*25	*25
Hydro	1	1	1	1	1	1
Nuclear	..	..	..	..	..	..
Other	3	4	4	5	6	6
Combustible fuel input	**Terajoules**					
Gas-diesel oil	421	487	426	516	617	667
Other liquid biofuels	*55	*55	*55	*27	*27	*27
Total input	476	542	481	544	645	694
Total production	206	201	183	222	228	*225
Estimated efficiency (% of production to input)	43	37	38	41	35	32

Venezuela (Bolivar. Rep.)

Item	2013	2014	2015	2016	2017	2018
Production, trade and consumption	Million kilowatt-hours					
Total main activity and autoproducer	134295	132568	128891	118206	103878	99737
Combustible fuels	52627	52009	53832	55068	43194	41510
Hydro	81499	80364	74902	62959	60507	58150
Nuclear	..	..	..	..	..	..
Other	169	195	156	180	*177	77
Main activity	132683	130959	126777	116161	101910	97844
Combustible fuels	51090	50476	51794	53099	41302	39692
Hydro	81499	80364	74902	62959	60507	58150
Nuclear	..	..	..	..	..	..
Other	94	119	80	104	*101	2
Own use in electricity, CHP and heat plants	1601	1793	1521	1566	1114	973
Net production	132694	130776	127370	116640	102764	98764
Imports	715	24	0	0	0	..
Exports	848	889	974	1107	1064	1023
Losses	25627	42699	40381	33543	32237	30982
Consumption	110022	87467	89314	82985	70154	66531
Energy industries own use	1830	1847	1634	1427	1159	945
By industry and construction	49445	25890	27283	23472	22219	20630
By transport	308	0	0	0	0	..
By households and other cons.	58439	59730	60397	58086	46776	44956
Net installed capacity	Thousand kilowatts					
Total main activity and autoproducer	31595	31771	32059	32967	32923	32923
Combustible fuels	16662	16838	16869	17777	17732	17732
Hydro	14880	14880	15137	15137	15137	15137
Nuclear	..	..	..	..	..	..
Other	53	53	53	53	54	54
Main activity	30292	30467	31049	31957	31913	31913
Combustible fuels	15359	15534	15859	16767	16722	16722
Hydro	14880	14880	15137	15137	15137	15137
Nuclear	..	..	..	..	..	..
Other	53	53	53	53	54	54
Combustible fuel input	Terajoules					
Gas-diesel oil	187652	194618	220676	199262	191522	184040
Fuel oil	36118	25654	25048	22624	21735	20887
Natural gas	254992	254371	338034	326524	313808	301586
Total input	478762	474643	583758	548410	527065	506513
Total production	189456	187233	193796	198245	155498	149436
Estimated efficiency (% of production to input)	40	39	33	36	30	30

Viet Nam

Item	2013	2014	2015	2016	2017	2018
Production, trade and consumption	**Million kilowatt-hours**					
Total main activity and autoproducer	126798	140219	163494	181653	198499	213121
Combustible fuels	68536	78439	105979	116244	109354	128576
Hydro	58170	61480	57254	65188	88875	84205
Nuclear	..	..	..	..	..	..
Other	*92	*300	*261	221	270	340
Main activity	124710	137649	159540	176739	194217	208839
Combustible fuels	66451	75951	102107	111412	105154	124376
Hydro	58169	61400	57174	65108	88795	84125
Nuclear	..	..	..	..	..	..
Other	*90	*298	*259	219	268	338
Own use in electricity, CHP and heat plants	8244	5201	5745	5269	5396	6066
Net production	118554	135018	157749	176384	193103	207055
Imports	3347	2356	2604	3313	2352	1722
Exports	2706	1650	1711	2215	1825	733
Losses	*11500	*12509	*12541	*13732	13871	14728
Consumption	115283	128627	143683	159791	174653	192701
Energy industries own use	..	..	..	..	..	..
By industry and construction	61277	69524	77189	85686	95791	106136
By transport	..	..	..	..	..	..
By households and other cons.	54006	59103	66494	74105	78862	86565
Net installed capacity	**Thousand kilowatts**					
Total main activity and autoproducer	*32458	*33761	*39133	*43416	*44334	*44815
Combustible fuels	*17700	*18269	*22779	*25783	*25953	*26125
Hydro	14721	15377	16213	17461	18161	18341
Nuclear	..	..	..	..	..	..
Other	*37	115	141	172	220	349
Main activity	*29749	*30633	*36005	*38025	*38851	*39332
Combustible fuels	*15000	*15455	*19965	*20728	*20828	*21000
Hydro	14718	15069	15905	17131	17809	17989
Nuclear	..	..	..	..	..	..
Other	*31	109	135	166	214	343
Combustible fuel input	**Terajoules**					
Hard Coal	321187	400645	529856	614098	561954	684450
Gas-diesel oil	1548	2365	1720	6751	3526	1548
Fuel oil	4404	4808	8726	8767	3798	1172
Natural gas	328579	347890	366899	366913	314848	288261
Fuelwood	658	665	1193	1173	1319	2177
Total input	656375	756373	908395	997701	885444	977607
Total production	246730	282380	381524	418478	393674	462874
Estimated efficiency (% of production to input)	38	37	42	42	44	47

Wallis and Futuna Is.

Item	2013	2014	2015	2016	2017	2018
Production, trade and consumption	**Million kilowatt-hours**					
Total main activity and autoproducer	*19	*19	*18	*20	*20	*20
Combustible fuels	*18	*18	*18	*20	*19	*20
Hydro	0	0	0	0	0	0
Nuclear	..	..	..	..	..	..
Other	0	0	0	0	0	0
Main activity	*19	*19	*18	*20	*20	*20
Combustible fuels	*18	*18	*18	*20	*19	*20
Hydro	0	0	0	0	0	0
Nuclear	..	..	..	..	..	..
Other	0	0	0	0	0	0
Own use in electricity, CHP and heat plants	*2	*2	*2	*2	*2	*2
Net production	*17	*16	*16	*18	*17	*18
Imports	..	..	..	..	..	..
Exports	..	..	..	..	..	..
Losses	*1	*1	0	*1	0	*1
Consumption	*15	*16	*16	*17	*17	*17
Energy industries own use	..	..	..	..	..	..
By industry and construction	..	..	..	..	..	..
By transport	..	..	..	..	..	..
By households and other cons.	*15	*16	*16	*17	*17	*17
Net installed capacity	**Thousand kilowatts**					
Total main activity and autoproducer	*11	*11	9	*9	*9	*9
Combustible fuels	*11	*11	9	*9	*9	*9
Hydro	0	0	0	0	0	0
Nuclear	..	..	..	..	..	..
Other	0	0	0	0	0	0
Main activity	*11	*11	9	*9	*9	*9
Combustible fuels	*11	*11	9	*9	*9	*9
Hydro	0	0	0	0	0	0
Nuclear	..	..	..	..	..	..
Other	0	0	0	0	0	0
Combustible fuel input	**Terajoules**					
Gas-diesel oil	*181	*179	*177	*187	*183	*188
Total input	*181	*179	*177	*187	*183	*188
Total production	*66	*65	*65	*71	*69	*71
Estimated efficiency (% of production to input)	37	36	37	38	38	38

Yemen

Item	2013	2014	2015	2016	2017	2018
Production, trade and consumption			**Million kilowatt-hours**			
Total main activity and autoproducer	8505	7655	6288	5105	4309	3609
Combustible fuels	8501	7646	6178	4958	4126	3151
Hydro	..	..	..	..	..	..
Nuclear	..	..	..	..	..	..
Other	4	9	110	147	183	458
Main activity	8256	7254	5851	4676	3861	2893
Combustible fuels	8256	7254	5851	4676	3861	2893
Hydro	..	..	..	..	..	..
Nuclear	..	..	..	..	..	..
Other	..	..	..	..	..	..
Own use in electricity, CHP and heat plants	1341	1178	950	759	627	470
Net production	7164	6477	5338	4346	3682	3139
Imports	..	..	..	..	..	..
Exports	..	..	..	..	..	..
Losses	2190	1924	1552	1240	1024	767
Consumption	4974	4553	2500	2371	2293	2192
Energy industries own use	..	..	..	..	..	..
By industry and construction	203	161	130	104	86	64
By transport	..	..	..	..	..	..
By households and other cons.	4771	4392	2370	2267	2207	2128
Net installed capacity			**Thousand kilowatts**			
Total main activity and autoproducer	1540	1524	1579	1769	*1769	*1769
Combustible fuels	1535	1519	1519	1519	*1519	*1519
Hydro	..	..	..	..	..	..
Nuclear	..	..	..	..	..	..
Other	*5	5	60	*250	*250	*250
Main activity	1417	1402	1402	1402	*1402	*1402
Combustible fuels	1417	1402	1402	1402	*1402	*1402
Hydro	..	..	..	..	..	..
Nuclear	..	..	..	..	..	..
Other	..	..	..	..	..	..
Combustible fuel input			**Terajoules**			
Gas-diesel oil	30874	25155	20984	18103	17028	15179
Fuel oil	30017	24280	19190	15635	13817	14948
Natural gas	34605	37478	28770	20045	24053	4009
Total input	95496	86913	68944	53783	54898	34136
Total production	30604	27526	22241	17849	14854	11344
Estimated efficiency (% of production to input)	32	32	32	33	27	33

Zambia

Item	2013	2014	2015	2016	2017	2018
Production, trade and consumption			**Million kilowatt-hours**			
Total main activity and autoproducer	13301	14455	13440	11695	14185	16191
Combustible fuels	20	413	405	670	1987	3524
Hydro	13281	14042	13035	11025	12198	12666
Nuclear	..	..	..	..	..	..
Other	..	..	..	..	..	1
Main activity	13301	14455	13440	11695	14185	16191
Combustible fuels	20	413	405	670	1987	3524
Hydro	13281	14042	13035	11025	12198	12666
Nuclear	..	..	..	..	..	..
Other	..	..	..	..	..	1
Own use in electricity, CHP and heat plants	306	331	0	325	344	408
Net production	12995	14124	13440	11370	13841	15783
Imports	73	13	785	2185	753	152
Exports	1083	1256	1176	794	1063	1226
Losses	1139	2162	1599	1903	1339	1811
Consumption	10846	10719	11450	10858	12192	12898
Energy industries own use	..	..	..	..	..	..
By industry and construction	6379	6429	6860	6455	7025	7282
By transport	28	31	33	28	32	33
By households and other cons.	4439	4259	4557	4375	5135	5583
Net installed capacity			**Thousand kilowatts**			
Total main activity and autoproducer	2038	2452	2411	2827	2897	2898
Combustible fuels	141	195	142	439	498	499
Hydro	1897	2257	2269	2388	2398	2398
Nuclear	..	..	..	..	..	..
Other	..	..	0	0	1	1
Main activity	2038	2452	2411	2827	2897	2898
Combustible fuels	141	195	142	439	498	499
Hydro	1897	2257	2269	2388	2398	2398
Nuclear	..	..	..	..	..	..
Other	..	..	0	0	1	1
Combustible fuel input			**Terajoules**			
Hard Coal	..	..	..	3928	15342	24484
Gas-diesel oil	430	430	430	430	516	*5160
Fuel oil	0	2990	3272	2747	4808	*6747
Bagasse	..	*1278	*1332	*1367	*1367	*1367
Total input	430	4698	5034	8472	22033	37757
Total production	72	1485	1459	2412	7153	12686
Estimated efficiency (% of production to input)	17	32	29	28	32	34

Zimbabwe

Item	2013	2014	2015	2016	2017	2018
Production, trade and consumption	**Million kilowatt-hours**					
Total main activity and autoproducer	9499	9812	9522	7090	7544	9418
Combustible fuels	4517	4410	4583	4175	3575	4369
Hydro	4982	5402	4939	2915	3969	5049
Nuclear	..	..	..	..	..	..
Other	..	..	..	..	..	..
Main activity	9315	9783	9468	6812	7377	9212
Combustible fuels	4333	4381	4529	3897	3408	4163
Hydro	4982	5402	4939	2915	3969	5049
Nuclear	..	..	..	..	..	..
Other	..	..	..	..	..	..
Own use in electricity, CHP and heat plants	115	184	189	35	143	175
Net production	9384	9628	9333	7055	7401	9243
Imports	1722	1127	1139	2220	2569	1177
Exports	1189	1226	1239	369	351	161
Losses	1702	1648	1654	1533	1729	1748
Consumption	8285	8238	6876	7282	7880	8506
Energy industries own use	..	..	..	..	..	..
By industry and construction	3115	3388	2524	2645	3359	3703
By transport	..	..	..	..	..	..
By households and other cons.	5170	4850	4352	4637	4521	4803
Net installed capacity	**Thousand kilowatts**					
Total main activity and autoproducer	*2112	1992	1992	2015	2015	2315
Combustible fuels	*1355	1235	1235	1265	1265	1265
Hydro	757	757	757	750	750	1050
Nuclear	..	..	..	..	..	..
Other	..	..	..	..	..	..
Main activity	*2067	1947	1947	1970	1970	2270
Combustible fuels	*1310	1190	1190	1220	1220	1220
Hydro	757	757	757	750	750	1050
Nuclear	..	..	..	..	..	..
Other	..	..	..	..	..	..
Combustible fuel input	**Terajoules**					
Hard Coal	69596	70325	74266	63954	55288	67571
Gas-diesel oil	774	731	645	559	559	688
Bagasse	2390	2074	1843	2117	2180	2687
Total input	72760	73130	76754	66630	58026	70946
Total production	16261	15874	16498	15029	12870	15728
Estimated efficiency (% of production to input)	22	22	21	23	22	22